# LEVANT FEVER

## TRUE STORIES FROM SYRIA'S UNDERGROUND

## WAJDY MUSTAFA

ISBN: 978-0-9969292-0-2

First Printing, 2015
Translated from the Arabic by
**Alisar Mustafa**

*To   the* **Levant children** *who did not stop dreaming of peace and freedom, and to* **Daniela** *who believed in this dream.*

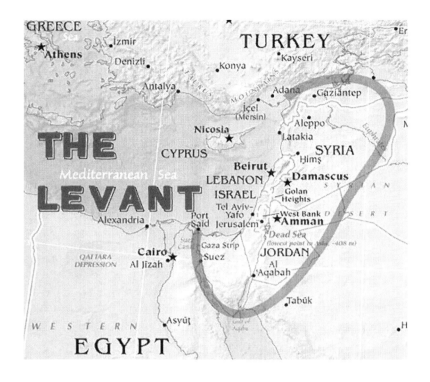

The **Levant** is an approximate historical geographical term referring to a large area in the **eastern Mediterranean**. In its widest historical sense, the Levant included all of the eastern Mediterranean with its islands, that is, it included all of the countries along the eastern Mediterranean shores, extending from **Greece** to **Cyrenaica**. The term *Levant* entered English in the late 15th century from French It derives from the Italian *levante*, meaning "rising," implying the rising of the sun in the east. As such, it is broadly equivalent to the Arabic term *Mashriq*, 'the land where the sun rises'. The western counterpart in Arabic is the **Maghreb**.

From Wikipedia, the free encyclopedia.

# CONTENTS

All events in this book are real but most of the names have been changed.

# 1 PALESTINE'S INTELLIGENCE BRANCH DAMASCUS, APRIL 1995

The iron black solitary cell door opened with its usual shriek and the jailer, Wael appeared. "Bring your luggage and follow me."

I gathered some pieces of my ripped clothes quickly and followed him through the gloom ridden corridors. On one side there were black doors lined up. Behind these doors were small solitary cells where people disappeared. During the long months I spent in one of them, I had not seen any of their faces.

I walked behind him with my head bowed down, trying to steal a look at the women's section where my wife resided in one of its solitary cells. It was an iron black door just like all the other ones, with some women hidden behind it. Sometimes, I could hear them screaming when their despair became unbearable, as nostalgia invaded their minds with memories of their families, or children.

We passed beyond the solitaries and the jailers' station at the crossing of the corridor. Ahead lay the dormitories, which I only knew about from secretly overhearing the guard's conversations.

I heard the opening movement of the big latch as my downcast eyes settled on my feet, trying to avoid being whipped for looking in front of me.

"Go in!" He commanded and gripping me hard by the shoulder, pushed me roughly inside. I shuddered, stumbling into the small room, only to fall on bodies compressed into a space of no more than 300 square feet.

The door closed and I heard the sound of the heavy latch dropping ominously into place. Then, the sound of the jailer Wael's steps, walking away.

A forest of similar bodies and eyes surrounded me. I felt as if they were smothering me with scattered looks of curiosity and indifference. I sit in the dormitories left corner. Facing the door there is a small toilet with a barely adequate cloth draped over it. I rose, struggling to find a place for my feet as I pressed myself in-between the bodies. Even though I had spent about twelve years in various jails before, this time it seemed especially cruel and painful. I didn't know what to do; despite all my experience, I looked like an idiot entering jail for the first time.

A voice rose from the abyss in-between the myriad of heads:

"What's your name newbie?"

I looked towards the voice but I couldn't see the speaker. He was invisible, hidden behind the chaos of standing and sitting bodies. Faint voices rose from here and there, conversations I couldn't comprehend.

"Come here man." One of them standing alongside, pushed me towards the voice. "This is Abu* Ahmed, the dormitory's Boss." I tried stepping towards him but all the pathways were blocked, there was no way to pass through this dense human dam.

"Make way!" Abu* Ahmed's voice called once again with a commanding tone. The human dam obeyed as a small path opened up in front of me leading to the right hand corner facing the door.

There were three men with shaved chins, wearing clean clothes and with a graceful appearance. They were gathered around a piece of cloth with plates of food and fruits, busy eating.

"What's your name?" said Abu Ahmed, smiling without looking at me.

"Six," came out of my mouth. Barely hearing it, I repeated myself, trying to raise my voice as much as I could, "Solitary Six," but the words were nothing but hissings, unfathomable even to me.

"Did you swallow your tongue?" Abu Ahmed looked at me smiling.

"Solitary Six." It took all the power I had and it still came out hissing, rattling and mumbling but it was enough for some people who were close by to hear it.

"Were you in the solitaries?"

"Yes." I answered hesitantly because we were forbidden from saying our names to anybody, we'd become merely numbers, according to the cell we resided in and I was Solitary Six, or just Six.

"What was your charge?" I hesitated a little bit, so he urged me with an obvious coastal dialect, "What are you afraid of, we're all in the same boat. I am Abu Ahmed, in the Defenses' companies and a smuggler."

"How graceful!" Abu Ali fired a loud laugh, then looked towards me speaking proudly with the same dialect. "I'm like him, a smuggler in the Defenses' companies but smuggling men are not proud."

"Politics."

3

"What?!" Abu Ahmed screamed impatiently.

"Politics," I answered with a hissing voice, as if I had just escaped from a deep cave. A sudden silence came over the dormitory. Elongated necks and eyes staring at me with curiosity.

"Politician!" Abu Ali beheld me with a mysterious look that I couldn't recognize as one of contempt or admiration.

"Please sit." Said Abu Ahmed, smiling as he patted the clean rug beside him, indicating for me to sit.

"Where are you from?" Asked Abu Ahmed.

"From Tartus." I answered hesitantly as I regained my voice, "From a village in Tartus."

The curiosity intensified in their eyes as Abu Ahmad's lineaments compressed, "How graceful, are you from the communist worker's party?"

"No, Marxist Parties, something like the Worker's party but that was 14 years ago..." I said cautiously.

"And now what?" Asked Abu Ali, suspiciously.

"I don't know, maybe now the charge is Worker's party, my wife's charge."

"Your wife is here with you?" Asked Abu Ahmed.

"Yes, in the double rooms."

"Ah! Yes!" Said Abu Ali, smiling.

They invited me for food. Some of the group's members surrounding the dorm's boss, (The Privileged Prisoners) had received a family visit and they had brought a quantity of delicious homemade food. Only the rich and privileged prisoners were welcomed to sit with Abu Ahmed in his dining group, where they enjoyed the privileges of the dormitory's Boss. These ranged from a wider sitting space to avoiding Forced Labor, such as cleaning, distributing food and serving the dormitory boss' dinning group. I hadn't eaten a homemade meal since my arrest seven months ago;

therefore, I couldn't really enjoy the food in front of me. I almost choked on some pieces of Kebba, that were filled with ground meat. So, Abu Ahmed called for a hot cup of tea, which brought back some of my hissing voice.

They didn't annoy me with any further questions after Abu Ahmed ordered them to leave me alone, so I could rest and regain my strength after the long time in solitary. I soon found myself alone, tucked between sitting or standing bodies. Some bodies were trying to catch up on their sleep while sitting, others passed their time talking or standing to relieve the stiffness from sitting. About two hours passed before a young guy patted my shoulder and urged me to stand up quickly.

The door opened and a jailer yelled: "Wajdy Mustafa!" I stood up quickly.

"Present."

For the first time in this place, someone called me by my name. It sounded unfamiliar. I was used to the name, "Six." I no longer distinguished my name. It seemed strange and maybe irritating because it reminded me of my identity, of my existence. I was a human being once again. Unreasonable! Here, there was nothing that reminded me of myself except the name that now seemed too wide for me. For a long time I had gotten used to being ashes in the remains of a human body, one that I barely acknowledged unless I was eating or defecating.

"Follow me," commanded warrant officer Abu Ramez, as he turned around, leading the way. I followed him rapidly, barefoot. It had been a very long time since I had something to put on my feet, after one of the jailers confiscated my new shoes for his own. I buried my eyes in the ground as usual and ran, trying to catch up with him, following his legs climbing the stairs to the ground floor.

"Put the Temaisha, (blind fold) on your eyes and stand by the wall," he said calmly.

I extended my arm into the big bucket of dirty water in the corner of the corridor, to pick out what he called in the language of detectives, Temaisha. The name also reminded me of a favorite children's game, Al Temaisha or Hide and Seek. The soaked Temaisha, was a rectangular piece of rubber cut from the inner tire of a car. Its ends were connected with a rubber string to ensure it stuck to the eyes, preventing vision.

I put it on, pretending to tighten it as much as I could, because if they merely suspected that I was trying to sneak a peek, the price would be several kicks and maybe some harsh slaps on my body. I had learned from experience how to put it on in such a way that looked like it was stuck tightly to my eyes, but at the same time I could see some shapes in the area around my feet. I could also recognize some of the jailers and detectives from their voices, shoes and steps.

A rough strike from behind made my forehead hit the wall. I felt a hot liquid descend down my forehead to my mouth; the taste of blood filled my lips. A swift kick to my testicles followed and I fell to the ground screaming from pain. Dimly I heard the assistant, Abu Ramez's voice yelling at him. "You asshole! Leave him! The General wants to see him!"

"Eh, I didn't do anything; he didn't want to put the Temaisha on the right way!" He replied sarcastically with a Damascus dialect. I was able to see his face; he was a young guy, perhaps not even past nineteen years old. He wore elegant black clothes as he swung a big key holder.

"Stand up straight!" Screamed Abu Ramez. So, I stood up, trying to hold myself together from the pain. He held my hand, leading me towards the bathrooms and removed the Temaisha from my eyes, trying to examine the wound on my forehead.

"It's fine; wash your face with cold water."

He gave me a piece of cloth and told me to press the wound until the bleeding stopped. He left for a little while. As soon as he came back he asked me to put the Temaisha back on my eyes and follow him. He tied my hands in front, then led me by my arm to an empty room. I recognized the room immediately. It was one of the interrogation rooms that only have torture tools like the chair, the tires and some cables thrown here and there, sometimes there was the electric chair with maybe sticks and some iron pieces.

"What is this, who did this to you?!" The General denounced with a calm but firm voice.

"Anas did this, Sir. The servant of the Branch Chief, he was passing through here…" Replied Abu Ramez.

"Take off the Temaisha." Standing in front of me was a guy in his forties, wearing an elegant black suit.

"Give him something to press on his wound." The warrant officer took a tissue from his pocket and gave it to me, so I pressed my wound and felt relieved.

For the first time I saw the face of my detective. At least now I could expect the direction of the strike. That gave me the chance to get ready to receive it with contracted muscles. If I had seen Anas' face when he kicked me, I could've protected my testicles from such a painful strike. Maybe I could've even expected his strike from the back and avoided the wound to my forehead as well.

"It's okay, don't mind us, as you see he's a dumbass, he doesn't understand," said the detective smiling. I nodded without answering. "What is the term you've spent here?"

"About seven to eight months."

"How is our hospitality? Do you like it?" he said, smiling.

"It's okay," I said with a scoffing voice.

"Look, we have to start all over. They transferred you to our department. The Parties' Department." Then he suddenly realized, looking at my confused eyes:

"They put you in the Terrorism Department," he said with a mocking smile. "You know the mistake. That happens a lot here."

He continued laughing: "I mean, what do you have to do with terrorism? I will give you a pen and a pencil. Write your story for me in detail."

I looked at him with astonishment as he gave me the papers. "Write well, no one will bother you." He shook his head, smiling and left. I realized that everything had started over. Interrogations with new people that think they are smarter than the ones before them and try to convince me that they are better.

*\*\*\**

*\*Abu:* Father and *Um:* Mother; these are the traditional Arabic terms of respect for the mature

*\*\*The Defense Companies (Saraya ad-Difa)* were a paramilitary force in Syria. They were commanded by Rifaat al-Assad the brother of the Syrian president Hafez al-Assad. In 1984 they were merged into the Syrian Arab Army.

# 2 AL HALBUNI INTELLIGENCE BRANCH DAMASCUS, MAY 1980

I was crammed in a tire; my legs were elevated upward as my hands were tied under me. He was looking down at me, smiling sarcastically:

"What's wrong? We haven't even started yet!"

My feet were burning from the cane that kept striking their soles with a vicious intensity. I could have tolerated the pain without screaming but I followed my friend's advice, "Your screams will satisfy the torturer and will ease down his brutality. Otherwise, if you are stubborn, he will get angry and increase the severity of his whips."

I don't think my torturer enjoyed what he was doing, he was a Christian from the Christian Valley. Later, I found out that he was an extreme Baathist*. He was immersed in the ideology of the

Baath and Arab Nationalism. He was born and grew up embraced by the Baath, even before Hafez al-Assad became a god superior over all the heavenly and earthly gods. Ibrahim was whipping with a smile filled with confusion, at least that's how it seemed to me. As I screamed under his whips, our eyes entwined sympathetically, as if we shared the state of pain. His strikes were soft and slow in comparison to the other torturers that came after him and I concluded that he wasn't very happy to beat me. However, he treated the other prisoners with a malice and brutality unlike any other in the Halbuni Branch. The reason behind that, I concluded, was the large number of prisoners from his home region. This created an ideological dilemma for which he struggled to find a solution. If he was fighting the reactionary from the Muslim Brothers and the Vanguards fighting for the Muslim Brothers, then why was he arresting people who were socialists like him?

"Are you a socialist, boy?" He screamed suddenly.

"Yes."

"Is the Socialist Ba'ath Party not good enough for you?" I didn't answer so he whipped me as hard as he could. I screamed in pain.

"We want democracy!"

He became furious and went on whipping my feet with his cane, becoming rougher as he accelerated.

"Democracy! Please tell me -- the system we have, isn't that democracy? Don't you like our democracy? Or do you want the American and Israeli democracy?"

I yelled in pain under his violent strikes. He stopped the whipping suddenly, just to get me out of the tire and tell me to run in the hallway. He was trying to relieve the swelling in my feet, so it didn't leave permanent scars. I ran for a couple of moments, then he put me in the tire again as he continued his boring routine task of hitting my soft soles.

"Look, let me tell you! I'm still stretching my patience. Soon the chief will come and after that remorse won't do you any good. Tell me everything now. The moral of the story is that you'll keep getting whipped until you speak."

"I'll talk, I'll talk, tell me what you want and I'll tell you."

"Look, don't be full of shit. Let me tell you, I've had to deal with people like you as many times as there are hairs on my head. Meaning, I don't want a smart mouth. You still haven't seen anything yet! Say the right thing and you'll rest and get relieved; otherwise, you'll see things you've never seen in your life."

"As you like. I'll tell you everything I know." He got me out of the tire and led me to a small room on the ground floor; across from the Branch Chief, as I came to know later. He gave me some papers and said "Write."

"Write what"?

"Your life story. Everything you know." I started writing and I indulged in writing my personal story about my childhood, my studies. I added some details about secondary issues that made me appear simple and naïve, which I hoped would help me avoid answering certain questions. I didn't know what kind of information they had on me since I was one of the first prisoners from our group. I knew they had a string of information that they'd acquired from the two spies lurking amongst us. We had decided to leave them to do their job, misleading them with fake information, so we could protect the people who were exposed and those who were about to be subject to arrest. I was one of them.

I wrote four complete pages and I was still occupied with the writing, maybe because I wanted to delay the second investigation round, when Ibrahim came back.

"Are you done?"

"No."

"Eh, are you writing a novel? Let me see!" He took the papers, tied my hands and left. Moments later he came back and led me to another room, after asking me to lower my head and close my eyes. I couldn't see anything but unclear images of the room that I was now sat in the center of.

"Oh Mr. Know-it-all, what is this beautiful writing? With all honesty, I enjoyed reading it." His voice was calm but filled with sarcasm. "Open your eyes and take a good look at me!" I opened my eyes and raised my head to find myself in a wide room. In the middle there was a big wooden table. Sitting behind it was the Branch Chief, wearing neat summer clothes. On the edge of the table sitting close to him was a young man wearing a gray summer suit with neutral features. I found out later that he was an officer from Aleppo.

"The boys seem to have had some fun with you." He commented sarcastically. "You're still new and I'm still calm. I mean, you have some hours ahead of you before we change the treatment and your form as well." Then to Ibrahim: "Take him back to the room, bring him a cup of tea and let him write in peace. He seems educated and wise." Ibrahim pushed me brutally as he led me back to the same room. He untied me and gave me more paper.

"An advice to the face of god, write correctly and save your dignity before the chief gets mad." Ibrahim's words were cold as death. I felt shivers going through my body. Tomorrow, the party would start and I didn't know when it was going to end. It was night time. I spent about an hour writing and thinking of what to write, trying to present something smart that would ease my torture without giving information that would benefit him. However, I realized I couldn't present the information all at once. I had to convince him that he was extracting the information from me by force. Ibrahim would come every now and then to ask me if I was done. I had prepared most of my information but I had to know what he already knew. I heard movement indicating that the chief had left his room, so I realized that tonight was going to be a resting night, at least until the morning.

Ibrahim came back. He looked tired. "What happened?"

"I've finished."

"Give me the papers and follow me." I went down the basement stairs in the middle of the building. He put me in a big prison cell, with a window overlooking an empty courtyard. I could see the prison cell's gate and the small hallway that they used for torture.

Al Halbuni Branch was an old Damascus home with two floors. There was a stairway in the middle that led to the second floor, which consisted of different rooms for the interrogators. The Branch Chief's office was located on the ground floor in addition to other interrogation rooms. There was also a medium sized courtyard and in one of its corners, there were small prison cells where the detainees resided during their interrogation. The only thing separating the cells from the courtyard was a closed hallway with an imposing metallic gate. In that small hallway, most of the torture rounds occurred. In the southern corner of the building there were bathrooms, or what they called in the Branch's language, "The line." I don't know why they called it 'the line.' It was a weird name for me. We would laugh trying to find the meaning behind it. One of our conclusions was because we had to stand, 'in line' to use it.

Trips to these bathrooms came three times a day, directly after each meal. I used to look forward to them as I could hear the women's and children's voices playing in a house garden, neighboring the Branch. Their happy voices came through the narrow bathroom skylight window, they made me smile.

The Branch's building was originally a home for one of the Syrian presidents during the French Mandate Era, so it was located in a residential district surrounded by peaceful families. These people now had their lives shattered by the screams of the prisoners' torture, specifically those at night. I used to feel bad for those children, forced to hear thousands of times, the howling voices of people being stripped of their humanity, turned into wild animals screeching and howling to the neighborhood skies; crying, complaining and sometimes barely catching their breaths on the floor of that ominous building.

I had barely laid down when I became aware of a rising commotion. Then the cell's door burst open and two men descended on me, hitting me and kicking me as they pushed me up the steep, stone steps inside the building. As soon as I arrived in the courtyard, they started kicking me like a soccer ball between four people. Attacking me with their fists and feet, until I fell to the ground like a wet rag with blood splattering from my mouth. The Branch Chief came out of his room, the Sheriff following him. Everyone around me froze and fell to silence. He looked at me sarcastically, brandishing the papers I wrote.

"Smartass. Very smart, Mashallah!" Then to the Sheriff he said, smiling, "They are always the same. They taught him to be a smartass."

The torturers dragged me immediately towards the torture chamber, to practice a form of sadism I had never seen in my life. They poured water down my throat whilst holding my nose and the whips danced on my feet like a whirling fan. It turned round and round on the rhythm of my gags and cries, water and whips, whips and water. I became like an idiot, lost and screaming in a dry desert. Everything turning round and round, then my mind jumps:

'You are alone in your water and fire. You are alone in your death and torture. Oh Allah! Oh Muhammad! Oh Ali! Oh Jesus! Oh Moses! Oh you, standing over there! Oh the stars and the moons! You Oh you! Oh Virgin Mary! Oh the mother of the believers! Oh Zainab! Oh to all the Prophets! Oh all my brothers!!!'

I screamed as loud as I could and passed out between every other water torture. I woke up to the water jet pounding on my head, shuddering like a tiny bird that just got wet. From water to water I didn't have the strength to even scream. The whipping fan continued dancing once again and from fire to fire and water to water, I was extinguished once again. Eternal rest did not come. The desire for death consumed me:

'Oh You! Oh Angel of Death, Oh you Grandfather, Oh Father, Oh the barefoot over the water!'

I shudder under the spray of cold water, only for my eyes to meet the Branch Chief's eyes. He was standing over me, smiling triumphantly. "And now what Mister? Is it enough or do you want more!?"

"Enough." It came out from between my teeth in gasps.

"Give him a pen and papers, let's see."

I sat in a bare corner in the room, pressed my back up against the cement wall and began. My fingers were swollen, spouting flaming fire onto the paper. I remembered all my childhood details, the school and... even my first crush on my classmate, Fedaa. At the time, I used to read all the romantic books, friendship and love magazines, just to know how to start my love story. I told of how I wrote her a love letter with the help of my friend George. My soul blossomed with love and adoration. I remembered the letter in detail and wished I could write it again now.

I think I was in the seventh or eighth grade and she was in the same class, sitting in the desk in front of me. I had just started my puberty and experienced my first sexual curiosity as I read romantic magazines about love. I remember the most important magazines at the time were Rima and Samar. They were weekly published magazines and I had just switched from the comic book stage of Super Man, Bat Man and The Flash.

I used to remember Sports Class, for she looked more mature than the rest of us. A real woman and my beard hadn't even grown yet! I don't know if I was falling in love, or if I wanted to grow up and then fall in love. I used to feel bewildered every time she would look at, or talk to me. It was the kind of bewilderment the thief has when he looks at his victim. I feared that my glances would expose me, so I lowered my eyes and fled, looking for a refuge in her smile. She had big green eyes, radiating charm and kindness; or that is what my small brain imagined back then. The school year was almost over and I was trying to find the chance to confess my love to her. Those magazines were directed towards young people over seventeen years old and maybe some of them were in college, or just finished college. Even so, I noticed that some of the letter-writers were around fourteen years old, just like me. There were a couple of pages solving lover's problems and answering their questions. Those letters were my chance to search for a solution to my problem:

How did I confess my love to her? A couple of days before the last day, I had prepared a plan with the help of my friend George, to write her a letter to be delivered the day before the end of the school year. If her answer was positive, then I would go to school on the last day but if it was a negative, I would skip school with no obligations.

I spent a couple of days writing the letter with the help of some of the sentences written in the magazine's mail. When the day before the last day ended and we left the classrooms, delivered the letter to her. I was waiting for him somewh away, anxious. I waited for a long time and he didn't cor.... As soon as I finished eating lunch I went to his house, which was an hour's walk away from my house, where he told me the dangerous news: "She said that she will tell Teacher Ali if you do it again!"

I went back crushed, defeated. I didn't sleep that night until the morning. Her picture, her smile and even her anger cornered me. I didn't know what to do. I decided to forget her since Ali the Teacher had a horrific character, with his long stick and his unforgiving slaps. I don't know what made me remember that day while I was receiving whips from the giant executioner in the torture chamber. Afterwards, whenever I remembered those moments I blamed my letter, for it must have been the reason she rejected me. If I had made a bigger effort and was more careful choosing my words without exaggerating, I wouldn't have shocked or scared her and made her threaten me.

The anxiety of seeing her again accompanied me everywhere. It happened once during that summer, when our eyes met for a while as she was walking on the street corner with her friends, heading towards the cinema. However, the bigger event was when my mother came to the school opening. I hadn't seen Fedaa in the administration office overflowing with children and their parents. Only her voice overwhelmed me from behind, like a cold waterfall drowning me suddenly.

"Hello."

I answered with disordered words as her eyes looked at me with sudden happiness. " Good, good, how are you?" I tried to escape her smile, which immersed me with its cold authority. That smile that I couldn't decode, its symbols worried me for many days. Did she really forget everything? Or is it a message for me to try again? I preferred to play safe and avoid any risk with the teacher, Ali, or another disappointment. Internally, I wished that this time she would take the initiative but nothing happened. We weren't in the same classroom that year and we were busy with other things.

"You animal, you didn't even start writing!" Ramez entered and started kicking me with his feet as I tried to protect myself with my hands. But my hands were hurting me more.

"My fingers are swollen, I can't hold the pen!" I said.

"Don't bullshit me, start writing before I start making you write with your teeth, you animal!" He kicked me as he started screaming. I put the pen in the palm of my hand, trying to tuck it in between my thumb and my index finger, which throbbed.

"What would you like me to write?"

"Write everything you know, since you were born until now." He was standing in front of me and I was sitting on the floor, pressing my back against the wall. He was a tall man and he wore cheap blue tracksuit pants with a white vest. His head was somewhat large, with an unkempt mustache. He had a Deir ez-zur** city accent, or that's what it seemed to me at the time. He was looking at me with skepticism. "Are you a Muslim Brother?"

"No, Marxist groups."

"What is this Marxism? Hah... those from Iraq." He spoke with confidence.

"No, Syrian," I answered.

"Syrian! Hah! Betraying the motherland and you call yourself Syrian!"

"We didn't do anything, a little bit of talking and writing. We didn't kill or hit or.."

"Shut up you animal, all we need is philosophy... you think we're stupid! We know everything but the Chief is still sympathizing with you and wants to help you. Write everything in order, everything you know, or I will rip out your teeth and leave you barking like a dog." He kicked me with his foot. I held the pen and I started writing, the same thing I wrote many times. Each time I would add more information, or change the structure and some details:

*I was born in Beirut, in 1960. My mother was a simple housewife, in a simple family in one of the villages in Tartus, where my family lives now. My father built our house, right beside my grandfather's house. My grandfather's family from my mother's side is a big family that lives off farming, the same as all my married aunts and uncles. My father came from Lebanon to Syria, to work for a while in construction. He then went to Saudi Arabia for some years, to earn enough money to buy a farm in the village, which he currently farms alongside doing some construction work. My grandparent's family from my father's side is small. I don't know much about them. My grandfather and my grandmother are dead, as well as my father's sister who passed away and got buried in Damascus, where she lived with her husband and children. I don't remember her name at all. My only other aunt lives with her husband and children in the village where my family currently reside. My grandfather was a priest in his village, near my mother's village.*

*I lived unstably in Beirut from the year of 1978, until my arrest. I was studying at the University in the beginning, then in hiding as a wanted person by the Security Services, until the end of 1979. We were a group of students studying Marxism.*

*I used to know one of them in Lebanon, called Sameer and he introduced me to the others. I used to meet them every now and then, we exchanged first names. I don't know if they are real or not. They are: Sa'ad; Ibrahim; Salam; Jamal and Da'ad. Most of them were students in the Lebanese Colleges. In Syria I used to know Samer. He was a Staff Sergeant in the army. I used to visit him when I came to Syria. He introduced me to Abu Ali who was a navy officer. I don't know his rank. He told me that he used to run a Military group in Latakia and I don't know anything else about him.*

*I met Samer in Beirut a couple of days ago, where he received some educational materials and political prints that we used to issue in Beirut. Since I was wanted by the police, I couldn't walk around with my personal identification card. So, I entered and exited Syria with a fake identification card that I stole and forged myself. During 1980, I got arrested on the Lebanese – Syrian borders in the Josiah Center. I was taken to the General Intelligence Department in Kafarsouseh, for interrogation. After a couple of hours I was submitted to the Halbuni Branch.*

After an hour or two, Ramez came back and I had finished writing. So, he took the papers and escorted me calmly to my prison cell. He looked really tired and maybe a little sad. I didn't look at him. I just followed him until he opened the gate to the steep stone steps, brutally shoving me towards my prison cell in the basement. I entered my wide open prison cell and he closed the door calmly and went back to climb the stairs, exiting to the courtyard. I heard the sound of the door lock, so I realized I was safe. It was only moments until I vanished into sleep on the prison cell's floor, which was covered by a dark military blanket.

I woke up in the morning for breakfast. One of the guards came to give me one boiled egg, a loaf of military bread and marmalade. I ate voraciously and soon the guard came back to take me to the bathrooms. I slept after that until noon, without anybody bothering me. At noon, before bringing lunch, they brought an Iraqi man into my prison cell. I didn't feel comfortable. He told me that he was an Iraqi fleeing Iraq and asking for political asylum in Syria. They'd arrested him and sent him to the Branch as soon as he asked for asylum. It was distrust that made me get away from him and stay silent, even though he tried to talk to me by asking me questions. His queries made me uncomfortable, so I preferred to keep to myself and pretend that I was exhausted from the interrogations. We ate lunch together, then I went back to sleep to escape his questions. They seemed innocent... but I wasn't in a position to risk it. After noon I heard a noise outside. It was the prisoners's voices as they were admitting and letting out a new group.

It was only moments before the Iraqi was called for interrogation. I looked from the corner of the small window to see a group of my friends and people I knew. Most of the day went by as they were being interrogated, so I was able to see most of them. It was clear to me now, that most of what they knew came from their spy, Samer. Along with some reports related to people I knew in my village and neighboring villages. This window was a great advantage for me. It looked like I would finish my confessions with information they actually already knew.

I began organizing my information in a logical order to ensure that all those people I saw, were in fact friends. There were no organizational links to them but maybe we had spoken politics, or discussed socialist goals together. The Iraqi came back from the interrogation and he was feeling anxious. It didn't look like they tortured him a lot... Or that's what he told me... a couple of slaps and some whips directly on his body.

At night, once again I was called for the torture round and the writing. Each time I repeated what I wrote in a different style. They took me back to my cell and I could feel a cluster of coals burning my insides. I slept immediately and didn't wake up until the next morning, to the noise of a guard knocking on the cell's door, announcing breakfast. The food was delicious, regardless of its scarcity. I ate ravenously and decided that it was time today to confess some names. Of course, they would be names they already had.

That night they led me to the detective Abu Thaer, whose room was on the second floor. He was a civil clerk, interrogating

21

me for the first time: "You're Wajdy?"

"Yes."

He started recording an official investigation report. "Your name, your father's name, his job, your mother's full name, her job, brothers and sisters, jobs, their studies, their age, dates of birth, your studies, military service etc." I was standing, tied from behind, as he sat in his office chair writing and drinking Mate Tea. He turned to the guard who was still standing at the door and said: "Tie him from the front." The guard untied me so he could tie me from the front. "You can go, you don't have to stay here, he looks like a good guy." The guard left and closed the door behind him. The clerk continued writing form some time, then he turned to me and said: "Come sit on the chair." He indicated a wooden chair beside his desk. I sat beside him as he stood to ask me:

"Tea or coffee?" I looked at him hesitantly without saying anything.

"Coffee, I love coffee for its smell." He left his office, closing the door behind him. Everything was suspicious. I was beside his desk. I could see the papers that he left exposed to me. I checked the papers in front of me. There were some names and some confessions from people I didn't expect to get arrested. They were only friends, not involved in the study groups. A couple of moments passed before I noticed the wide open window without any metal bars. I looked around me studying the area, cautiously I walked close to the window, seeking for a chance to escape. Unfortunately, the building was high and I couldn't have jumped the distance. Anyway, I would have fallen into the courtyard of the Branch.

I heard footsteps walking closer to the door, so I sat back in the chair with my head down. He opened the door and Abu Thaer appeared holding two cups of hot coffee. He put one of the cups in front of me on his desk. "Drink." I extended my arms and took the hot cup. I poured some of the coffee in my mouth. It was the most delicious coffee I've ever tasted in my life. "Professor Eyad sends his greetings." My joints froze and my chest got cold. I didn't account for this. They knew more than I expected.

"Who is Doctor Eyad, I don't know anybody by that name." He smiled as he took out a small telephone book from his pocket, he showed me the name of Professor Eyad and his phone number, saying with a faint voice: "Don't worry. No one knows anything, but the General suspects and he will surprise you with his name today. Insist on not knowing him, for he doesn't know anything important. Samer mentioned his name, just in case."

"I don't know anyone by that name," I insisted, as I got more suspicious.

"That won't do you any good. In fact it might harm you, everyone knows you know him and you have a relationship with him but that's not important. You can confess that you know him but you need to insist that it was a causal relationship, since he is from your village."

"Ah, do you mean Doctor Eyad al-Ali? He and his wife are from my village. I used to visit them sometimes."

"Great." I heard the call to prayer outside. "Do you pray?"

"No," I answered with a dim voice. He stood and said:

"I will go out for ablution and come back to pray. Finish your coffee calmly."

He left for a couple of moments. I could read more papers. When he came back he spread his prayer carpet in one of the office's corners and started praying. I watched him carefully as I drank the coffee. When he finished his prayer he came close to me and said:

"Do you need anything?"

"No."

"Be careful, just like I told you. Don't ever confess about Professor Eyad. Insist and they will be convinced. I will come by every now and then when I can." He called the guard and ordered him to take me back to my prison cell. The guard grabbed my arm and pushed me in front of him, until he put me in the cell that was now free of the Iraqi man, whom I didn't see again. Night had fallen and I could observe from the cell window that the courtyard was lit. There was a suspicious silence outside. It was long past eight o'clock and nothing was happening. However, it was only moments after that the Branch burst into life. A patrol from one of the provinces arrived with prisoners. I could see them from my cell window. There was a group of young and middle-aged men holding small bags. Their clothes were ripped. I counted fifteen of them. Two of them had beards but the rest of them were clean shaven. The Branch's Security Men were urging them to walk by cursing at them. Ibrahim kicked one of them screaming:

"What's your charge? You animal!"

"Muslim Brotherhood, but I swear I'm not involved."

"You're not involved! What is this then?" Ibrahim pulled him violently by his gray beard. The man shook a little, then continued walking silently. Everyone entered their cells and the courtyard went silent for a while.

I heard women's voices and right after, two veiled women entered the cells. I was lucky that night, they didn't put anyone with me. The night went by without anyone calling for me. I slept for the first day without torture, as well as the next day. It seemed that they were completely busy with the other group. I spent my days waiting for my turn as I listened to the daily melody of torture, of men losing their blood in howling and wailing under the infinite rain of brutality.

The Branch became active with daily work, starting at night and continuing until the next morning. It almost seemed like hearing the sounds of torture were harsher than getting tortured. It felt worse to wrap yourself like a ball in your cell, as you heard the screams of young and old men crawling on the floor like toddlers, just waiting, anticipating your next inevitable turn. You felt the cable's stings, wincing when it fell on one of them, as if you were getting stung. When you heard someone getting electrocuted you flinched as you imagined that horrific current circulating through your body.

I didn't hear the women get tortured since they were held as hostages for their husbands, though I heard one of them screaming from her cell, asking for them to stop torturing one of the prisoners. The torturer yelled at her:

"Shut up or you'll take his place!"

At that time they didn't insult the women. There was still sanctity that protected them from extreme torture. Even when they needed to torture one of them, they would give her pants that protected her body from the men's eyes. The woman quieted down after a while and disappeared into her prison cell, surrendering to this hell with:

"This is forbidden by God, show some mercy." No one answered. Only the guy's screams under the whips of the torturer, filled the silence.

Days passed before the torture eased down, then after a while, it stopped. At the time, the Branch seemed as if it was on a break for two to three days, before the torture noises of somebody else filled the sky for the whole day. The day after that came my turn. The jailer led me to the internal torture yard, in cold silence. His face was flat, expressionless, like he was from another planet. I couldn't distinguish his eye color or the size of his nose. He had no facial features, not even pores. Yellow satin face. He tied me calmly, then he pointed, silently indicating that I should cram myself into the car tire. I obeyed him, hypnotized, without resisting. He rubbed his hands calmly, then he picked a cane and started hitting me like a mechanical machine. I didn't yell in the beginning, I remained frozen like stone, looking in his dead black eyes as he attacked me with his cane, nonstop. I couldn't stand the rising pain, so I yelled as loud as I could but it was like he wasn't even there. A dead man with no soul. A corpse working in silence. A mass of bones that escaped from an abandoned grave. I screamed and he whipped, relentlessly. He stopped whipping to drink water, then started again in a monotonous rhythm. I yelled as loud as I could, begging him to stop but he wasn't there. He didn't even ask anything from me. Any confessions, any insults. I felt the fire stings increasing with each cane whip, so I screamed like I'd never screamed before, hoping he'd stop to yell at me, curse at me or to just ask something.

I screamed, "I will confess whatever you want, just stop!" He didn't look like he could hear. He stopped after about half an hour to point at me to leave the car tire and dance on the spot, so the swelling eased and my feet didn't split. I danced for about ten minutes as he was drinking a cup of tea, then he pointed at me to enter the car tire once again. I tried to resist, to beg but he held me forcefully, crammed me in the tire and continued hitting me, stopping every now and then to drink tea and make me dance. An hour or two passed and it still didn't seem like he was fulfilled. Meanwhile, I was wishing to die. I couldn't stand it anymore.

"Enough, I'll confess anything you want!" I screamed from my chest, crazily. It seemed to me that he was deaf and didn't hear, or mute and didn't speak. He continued the torture in a killing routine that defeated my dignity. I screamed, I begged, I cried like a small child, nothing stopped him. I decided to free myself from the tire with a strength I didn't think I had. He stepped away a little bit smiling, then he looked over to the metallic gate, calling: "Guys." Two guys came in to cram and kick me back into the tire again. They tied my feet to a stick. The whipping continued. The three of them took turns until night fell, then they took me to a lit, side interrogation room.

I sat down on the floor, completely collapsed, thinking of a way to die fast. I couldn't stand it anymore. Death was my way to salvation. "Do I fall?" I didn't know what to do anymore. I had lost all my senses. My memory and soul were crushed. I envied the believers for their faith, for they had something that put their mind at ease. They believe in life after death. In a god that would reward them in heaven.

Abu Thaer entered with one of the jailers to give me a couple of papers saying arrogantly:

"Write everything you know here." Secretly indicating with his eyes to reassure me that he will be with me. Everyone left while I was still collapsed on the floor, like a chewed piece of paper long passed its expiration date. I tried to write but I couldn't. My hands trembled violently. I felt my red swollen feet. A trickle of blood was running from one of them, despite the torturer's attempt to make me dance every now and then. I tried many times but as soon as I started, I would completely collapse and feel the pain multiplying. When the torturer came back, he found me still lying on the floor and my papers bright white.

He said sarcastically:

"You didn't write yet! Ha Ha... No problem, tomorrow you'll write, or after tomorrow. We don't care, we have time. Nothing to do these days."

"No, no I'll write what you want, but I can't move anything in my body, my hands are trembling. " I said stretching my trembling hands in front of me for him to see.

"Ok, I will leave you for an hour more, maybe your hands will have calmed down a little but a word of advice, write what's asked of you. " He left. I pulled myself together and picked up the papers and pen, to start writing with a trembling hand that I had no control over. Despite it all, I was still planning to tell my story like each time before but this time I added some names, like friends, using what I'd read in the detective Abu Thaer's room. I did not mention Professor Eyad. I finished almost at sunset, so they returned me to my cell. The next day they put with me two Socialist Union Party leaders from Aleppo. They were two nice educated men that gave me company and helped me to pull myself together. I wasn't called for for the next three days. On the fourth day I was called sometime late at night. The Branch Chief was waiting for me, in addition to a couple of guards and torturers.

"I'm sick of your bullshit. Today we're going to solve the issue with you, sweetheart." His face was harsh and morose. It seemed to me like they weren't convinced of what I'd said. I yelled:

"I swear to god I mentioned everything I know."

"You idiot. Tell me about Professor Eyad?"

"Professor Eyad is from my village. I used to visit him sometimes. After all, he is a Ba'athist."

He laughed:

"Hah... aren't you concentrated on the Ba'athists."

Then he left to go to his office. The torture round had lasted for almost an hour, when suddenly there was a commotion outside. Someone came over to talk to one of the torturers: "Bring him quickly and follow me." They took me to an interrogation room and left me there, tied. Meanwhile, I listened to the loud noises outside, the sounds of people running mixed with the roars of car engines and weapons fire. After a couple of hours, one of them took me back to my cell, where I learned there was an escape operation for prisoners from the armed Vanguard of the Muslim Brotherhood Militants. They'd escaped from the Kefersuseh Prison, which belongs to the Halbuni Branch. This incident halted my interrogations and tortures. A couple of days passed in the Halbuni Branch, then they transferred me to Kefersuseh Branch prison.

\*\*\*

*** The Arab Socialist Ba'ath Party:** The party who governed Iraq.*

*** Deir ez-zur:** is the largest city in the eastern part of Syria. It has a special accent close to Iraqi.*

# 3 BEIRUT
# 1975

I didn't know what was happening that evening. Truly it was a hard time. I climbed the mountain amid the shells and bullets falling around me like pouring rain. There was a battle happening in the bottom of the valley. However, the bullets reached me there in the middle of the mountain and above. I heard the sound of one as it struck the ground near my leg. Another shot passed near my ear to lodge in a tree trunk. The night closed its eyelids and some black clouds spread out as they cloaked the moonlight.

I realized that I had to run as fast as I could; climbing the mountain, not knowing when one of the bullets would pierce my body. People said that some of the bullets were explosive, poisonous or worse. Having one stuck in your body without being able to get it out, this far from help would be deadly. At that time, the mobile was not yet invented and there weren't any wireless devices since the war had just begun. So it was impossible to call for help. I ran as hard as I could, climbing the mountain between the thorns and the trees. I tried to shelter myself with the bigger tree trunks but the forest in this area was still short and not fully grown after the fire that had happened three years before.

I remembered how the fire had moved up the mountain. It set alight at the bottom, burning ferociously to the top as the wind blew. At the time, I was a twelve-year-old young boy. Feelings of fear and curiosity overcame me as I watched the fire from our house window, overlooking the mountain. Meanwhile, the firemen and the volunteers from the neighborhood, were trying to block the pathway of the raging fire by cutting the trees that were near the buildings, forming a fire break. I was watching them as I sweated from the extreme heat coming from the inferno.

Some of the residents decided to empty their houses and save what they could. While the rest did not have anywhere else to take refuge, so they decided to resist and face the danger with the firemen. My family was one of them. By midnight they were able to keep the fire danger away from the residential buildings of the neighborhood. By morning they had put the fire out completely but many pine and oak trees had turned into a mass of black charcoal. You could smell the rising smoke from the burnt wood and the firemen's tools.

A big bullet hit a branch above me and it fell. I was terrified for an instant, then I regained my confidence. I was still a teenager, no older than fifteen years and I had been given a very important mission; maybe because of my height. I exceeded 5'9" at the time, with enough muscles to give the impression that I was seventeen or eighteen years old. I'd been an athlete with a good standing in the harsh, Taekwondo sport for longer than a year and a half. The falling of the branch gave me a reason to increase my effort, to run as fast as I could. Aiming for the middle of the mountain, where it bent to embrace some rocks that I could hide behind. I was panting from exhaustion and perhaps even fear, for there was nothing to protect me from the death that followed my every step. It surrounded me from each side, nothing protected me from it but coincidence, or luck and perhaps faith. No one knows. I ran and death was behind me like a hungry wolf, almost devouring my meat. I remembered my mother at times and imagined her wailing and crying over my corpse, like I saw her wail many times over the thousands that were killed in the war. The will to live overtook me. I desired to live as hard as I could.

The air in my lungs screamed. I ran heavily, the bags of food hampering my movement. I had volunteered to deliver food to a group of young men from my neighborhood, stationed on the mountain. One of them suggested I carry with me some ammunition, just in case. I didn't agree, since it wasn't an easy mission to wander around the mountain with those heavy weights. All they owned were some light weapons from World War Two that were gathered from personal collections, some Russian-made Kalashnikov rifles and hand grenades.

I remembered the big machine gun that arrived the day before with its ammunition cache. It needed two people to operate it; the charger and the shooter. No one could stand up to shoot it. The weapon rebounded strongly and could throw you to the floor. One of the more muscular strong young men insisted that he could do it. However, he didn't get the chance to try.

The machine gun was based on the bottom of the road that overlooked another small road leading to Antelias; an area of Maronite Christians that belonged to the Lebanese Phalange Party. It had to block the gap that might be used to attack the neighborhood. The eastern region was a mix of Armenians,

Maronite and Orthodox at the time, punctuated by some concentrations of Shiites that came from the countryside. There were Syrian workers in the Ghawarneh and Mazher neighborhood, in addition to Palestinians in Al Maslakh, Karantina, Dbayeh camps and Tal Al Za'ater.

It wasn't clear to me that there was a big plan to evacuate the eastern region along the grounds of religion and nationality. All I felt was that this rightist power was trying to humiliate me because of my Syrian identity and my ancestors' Alawite sect. The Syrian was the poor worker coming from one of the Syrian villages. However, the Hourani coming from Daraa, was the porter in the harbor, the lowest rank in the hierarchy of Lebanese division of Syrians. Most of the time it was used as an insult amongst the Lebanese, as if you were cursing someone in a moment of anger "Hourani!" and it meant: backward, poor, porter. The Alawite was a symbol of poverty, backwardness and service. The rich Lebanese had female Alawite children, mostly below ten years old, as servants. I still remember my childhood in Beirut, where some children used to attack me at school. They used to come from families that supported the Rightist Christian Parties, to criticize me as a Syrian first and a Nasserist second, just as some of the Sectarians from the opposition now insulted the Alawites. We weren't poor. My dad was a hard worker in the construction field, where he had forged a good business as a small contractor. He had a number of workshops, enough to make us part of the middle class that received the respect of the Lebanese.

I arrived at the mountain's curve to shelter myself behind the rocks. The place was good. I was able to find a spot to hide me completely from the heavy bullet fire. I felt comfortable and safe, so I lay down for a while with my eyes closed. 'Am I going to be killed soon... and where? What if I was shot right now? No one will find me until the morning. If I don't die immediately, I will suffer a lot before I take my last breath, especially if my injury seriously prevents me from walking. I will suffer alone until I die.' The scene of my mother wailing over my bloody corpse worried me. Perhaps I was afraid of death for that reason. I didn't want to see her in pain. My father was home alone. I didn't think he went to work today. On days like that, he usually went back home and stayed there. My mother and four siblings went back to the village in Tartus, soon after the civil war started. I stayed with my father in Beirut, waiting for the situation to go back to normal. I felt worried about my father, home alone in an exposed area where Phalange forces were supposed to invade at any moment. I hadn't had any contact with him for a couple of days. We were in a siege and at war.

During this time, I only slept for a couple of sporadic short hours. The shooting and the bugs were enough to keep me awake despite the extreme exhaustion. For all that, here in between the safe rocks, sleep fondled my eyelids. I resisted its temptation until sleep overwhelmed me. I woke up to the absence of the sound of shooting. I felt like I was able to continue climbing the mountain, taking advantage of the relative lull in the battle. I got up quickly and started running with my head bowed down, as I climbed the bare mountain once again. For an instant, it looked safe to me and then the shooting began again from the bottom of the valley. I ran and I ran, as hard as I could, until exhaustion hit me and I collapsed to the ground.

The food bags were heavy. Once I got up, trying to run again but I got very exhausted, so I started walking, apathetic to the dangers. Suddenly, a feeling of numbness and indifference hit me. I didn't feel scared or terrified of death. Death seemed normal, just like life. Maybe, I wished it on myself in order to rest from the troubles of climbing and suffering. I wished for a mattress or a grave. There was no big difference anymore. It was a symbol for resting, sleeping in my mother's embrace. No matter how hard I tried to grow up, I remained a teenage boy trying to escape childhood. I walked up the mountain, indifferent to the bullets that fell, sometimes only ten feet, away to harmlessly pierce the soft dirt and disappear. Some of them weren't even strong enough to disappear into the dirt. They remained as a souvenir of death for the coming generations to discover, just like we used to discover the rock fossils on the same mountain. Little by little the feeling that I was stronger than death filled me. Something protected me from the bullets. I felt bulletproof and powerful, so I kept on walking, remembering the stories of giants in the ancient centuries. Recalling some of the heroes from the American Western Films, whose guns never ran out of bullets and who were immune to death.

Suddenly I heard the roar of a bullet ripping through the air, aiming to pierce somewhere near my head, or in my head... that's what I thought for a while. I felt like I died, or I was going to die. 'Do humans feel death the minute they are hit? It is seconds before falling. Those seconds were the barrier between life and death. Am I dead or alive?' The air settled, even the bugs lay quiet in the dirt. Silence fell in all places at once and I vaguely realized I couldn't feel my heart beat. 'Maybe it stopped seconds ago.' My brain only remains working for a short time as I lapsed into momentary unconsciousness.

The explosion of a nearby shell brought me back to life. My heart started beating again and all of my senses went back to work. I was safe. I felt for my head and my ear; my face, my neck. 'Haha, I'm alive!' I sprang up, I ran as fast as I could. Motivation and strength came back to me. 'I'm alive! I'm alive!'

I laughed at my stupid ideas and about my being bulletproof. I was only an idiot that almost got killed. I ran, looking for an escape as fast as I could. After a few moments of constant running, I arrived at the forest atop the mountain. The bullets from the battle in the bottom of the valley couldn't reach me here. I was safe.

I didn't know the guys exact location but I knew the place like the back of my hand, since we'd played in these trees and bushes as children. I wasn't allowed to use any source of light. I was supposed to get used to the dim light coming from the moon that disappeared sometimes, behind the clouds. This place had survived the fire. The pine trees and dense thicket of wild plants created heavy cover, especially in the pitch black night. I walked calmly towards the arranged place where four people, hidden behind a dense bush overlooking the other valley from the riverside, waited. I approached it slowly until I arrived at the place.

There was supposed to be someone yelling at me to stop and ask for the password but no one came out. The noise of insects filled the place. I walked calmly through the bushes. I stopped for a moment as my ear fluttered over a movement but no one came. I went down the slope towards the valley and now I was completely exposed. Nothing covered me but some parted tree trunks. I glimpsed a movement from afar. I walked towards it carefully. It was only a moment until I felt movements around me and the ghosts of people vanishing behind the pine tree trunks. I quickly threw myself on the ground behind an oak tree and yelled:

"Who?" I was terrified.

A ghost came out from behind the tree trunks and said, laughing:

"Take it easy Wajdy, we're just kidding!" I recognized his voice. It was Nabil, one of the members of the group.

I stood up, irritated, as the rest came out from their hiding spots, laughing and making fun of me for throwing myself to the ground.

\*\*\*

# 4 SYRIA
# 1965

My father decided to build a house for us in my mother's village, Jenin. This was so we could spend summer vacations near my grandfather's house. With the help of my maternal grandfather, my father agreed to build two houses in the village; one for us and the other for my grandfather's family, who had decided to leave their old house. I think I was about five years old when my father brought me to Syria to build the summerhouse. Crossing the borders from Lebanon to Syria was a big deal. It seemed to me as if I was crossing through a concealed curtain and behind it dawned a world of magic and secrets. For me, Syria was the small village that my mother constantly told us lively, nostalgic stories about her childhood world of longing, joy and bliss. It was a small village made of tens of small houses, mostly built out of stone and clay. Their walls were thick from the big external stones, while the internal section was stuffed with small stones, then covered with clay and hay to give a smooth finish. The ceiling was made of irregular wooden shingles made of tree trunks and thick branches cut from the nearby oak forest, while the roof was covered with a thick layer of clay and hay. At that time, only a few lucky ones were able to build a house out of firm cement that protected them from the winter cold and the summer heat.

My grandfather was one of those lucky ones. In fact, I have witnessed lots of controversial conversations from the villagers, arguing about their preference for the old clay house over the concrete house. The ones who favored the clay house, argued that it is the ideal house for their life, where they felt warmth in the winter and a breeze in the summer. They claimed this was not the case in the modern concrete house, where the cold leaks in from its thin concrete walls in winter, and then in the summer, it turns into an oven that is uninhabitable. On the other hand, people who favored the concrete house argued that it is clean and firm. Its roof doesn't need constant care. In addition, it protected them from the small animals, rodents and bugs.

I didn't understand those conversations so much but I liked the old clay house with its warmth, its columns that supported the ceiling that had many things hung from it. I recall a small mirror with my grandfather's shaving tools, old pictures in black and white of some of my family members and my grandmother's sewing kit. I used to love that house and the fig tree, growing right in the middle. I loved its delicious fruits. However, what fascinated me the most was that small part of the tree trunk where a small pebble was lodged. It was said that when my grandfather was furious at one of them, he threw that pebble with such force, that it hit the tree trunk and got stuck there. Everyone would joke about that pebble. It caused my grandfather to be surrounded with an aura of admiration from the village's young men. The inside of the house, however, was small. It consisted of two rooms only. One of them was big and had a ground stove in the center used for heating the house and preparing food. We would add small pieces of firewood whenever it was needed. The remnants of images remain playing in my mind, of the many times I'd spent around that stove, both in laughter and quiet meditation.

The house's floor was made of bunged clay, the same material the stove was made of. During the winter, the floor was carpeted with cheap, handmade rugs. I don't remember seeing any beds. There were only rugs and some wool mattresses that were spread out to sleep on soon after the sun had set. My aunt would tell me scary, Jinni stories under the dim cresset light.

The mountain car crossed the Syrian borders. "We are now in Syria," my father said, staring into the plains that stretched before us. I looked into the distance, keeping watch for the almighty giant, or the blond Genie. Then I would look into the plains ahead of me, hoping the magical gardens that my father used to creatively describe through his daily stories, would save me. He had fed my imagination with the most beautiful gardens and beautiful creatures that loved children and protected them. There was none of this though, only green plains and farmers hustling under the sun's rays. I wasn't shocked, for they looked like magicians or dwarfs. I was able to imagine things the way I wanted. Even when we started traveling through the mountains coated with olive trees, I was still looking for magical creatures that might jump out here or there. Especially when we delved deep into the huge dense oak forests, for it seemed to me that I watched one of the giants disappear into the forest and somewhere there, in the depth of the forest in a big oak tree trunk, was the seven elves' house.

Suddenly the car stopped in the middle of the village, breaking my reverie. It was only moments until the villagers gathered around the car, together with my grandmother and some of my uncles and aunts, who hugged me as my uncle carried me to the house. They competed to spoil me, for I was the son of their maiden daughter and none of the others were married yet. I try to capture some of those moments in my mind but most escape me. They are pictures filled with happiness and comfort, for I was a child coming from the roaring, loud Beirut, to a village that slept with the sunset and woke with the sunrise. I felt tranquility and the deep white light that lives inside me. Was that in the year of 1965, or 1966? I assert it was the year of 1965, which was a little while before I entered school at the age of five years old.

My father decided to put me in the village school as a listener, because they did not accept me officially due to my young age, while he was building our house in the village. My father had mastered the art of construction and that is why he decided to build our house by himself, with the help of the villagers to assist him with hard work that needed cooperation to finish. With the harvest, grinding the wheat and building the house, the villagers with their young men and women were cooperative, which made my dad's mission comfortable. I would usually watch someone, or a group of people, helping him in construction. I also had the honor to join in the building of the house by moving some of the bricks, until one of them fell on my hand and I was forbidden that great honor.

I don't remember the first day I entered the elementary school but I do remember that it consisted of two rooms. Each room had three classes, supervised by two teachers. They were both Christian, while the majority of the villagers were Alawites. The teacher had to teach three classes together in the same room. He would move from the first grade group, to the second grade, then to the third and he had to maintain his coordination between them without any confusion. It wasn't a hard task for the teacher, who knew the students one by one with every detail of their life. This was just part of his daily life in that small village.

The school had a small terrace overlooking a small courtyard, where the students gathered daily to salute the flag and receive the distributed milk ration, which would be heated in large quantities before class started. One of my school needs was a plastic cup that my dad bought me. It was made out of cheap material and most students had one in different colors. However, my father added a bag of cakes that I would take a piece of every day to school, to eat with the milk. When the cold intensified and there was a need for heating, the students were required to bring one piece of firewood with them each week, to add to the huge fireplace that was located beside the teacher's desk. At the time it seemed like it was there especially for the teacher, since we did not get enough of its heat to protect us from the harsh cold. So the smart thing to do was to always wear heavy clothes.

We used to go each week and sometimes every other day, to cut wood in the nearby forest, where we had to search for a piece of thick dry wood. That was our ticket to enter the school. There was no chance for anyone to enter without a piece of firewood, even me, the little child who was an exception to the school. The trip to find firewood wasn't something irritating for me; it was something I enjoyed, something filled with adventure and suspense. The forest was calm, full of magic, especially during winter days where everything was wet and the refreshing humidity poured down from the ripe green branches. The pungent scent rose from the musky soil, to remind me of the warmth of the earth and the fragrance of love.

Finding a dry piece of wood in this rainy winter was hard to do. We would spend hours sometimes, trying to find one. My uncle, who was four years older than me, was my companion and guide during these trips. Actually, he was the one who would find me that piece of wood. His mission wasn't easy because he had to find two pieces, one for me and another for himself. The teacher examined the piece of wood and turned it over in his hands saying: " Fine, I will accept it because of your young age, but next time you have to bring a bigger one just like the others."

Of course he didn't forgive the rest. They would have to go back to the forest to find a bigger piece, or they couldn't enter the school and might get exposed to physical punishment from the teacher and maybe even their father, who wasn't usually any less harsh than the teacher. Al Falaqa, (foot whipping) was the teacher's favorite form of punishment for those who needed to be severely admonished. For small punishments however, he had a long harsh ruler that he would hit the open palms with. The Falaqa punishment was very common at the school. I still remember Fares, the tall kid, or that's how it seemed to me at the time, his feet tied and raised on a stick that two students held from each side, as the teacher whipped the soles of his feet with a stick. He screamed and cried from the pain.

The Jenin village was located on a small plateau, surrounded by high mountains. On the top of the hill there was a small forest, providing the village with firewood and sometimes even construction wood. This forest later diminished when oil became a fuel replacement for fire wood and the cement houses took over from the old clay ones. On the bottom writhed a deep green valley, pervaded by a river made from the main village spring and other springs that exploded in the rainy seasons. The cave that opened on the bottom of Al Bat-haa mountain, or the Mashta mountain according to the people of Mashta al Helu, the town that overlooked that mountain from the other side, carried a massive waterfall that exploded from the big cave's mouth. It poured forth like a colossal monster spewing copious water and forming a small river that could sometimes overflow, covering the small stone bridge built by one of the expatriate villagers.

The towering Al Bat-haa Mountain embraces the valley like a giant with his head touching the clouds. An extinct volcano, its black stones are scattered on its slopes like catapult shells from the Middle Ages. On the other side of the village, there was another valley with the villagers fields stretched out on each side. It was the summer valley, where some of the village families would move to their simple houses in the orchards of apple and other fruit trees, to take care of them and harvest their fruits. At the top of the forest it opens up to pastures where my mother was raising her small number of sheep and cattle, alongside terraces, planted with wheat and hummus. My mother would always tell us about her farmer father, the poor shoe cobbler that refused to send his daughters to serve the Lebanese houses, like the poor Alawite villagers did at the time to fight poverty. My grandfather preferred to work as a shoe cobbler, fixing shoes for some wheat, eggs or whatever was available, in addition to planting the small piece of land that he owned from the feudal mortgage, after he paid its worth many times.

My mother would always brag about him proudly as she told me about her strong father, who didn't accept work from the feudal lord. His small land that he inherited from his father remained his. However, to help his brother travel to America when hunger and poverty struck the country during the Ottoman era, he mortgaged this land to the feudal lord and in return received a certain amount of money. With his hard work and determination, as well as the help of his family, especially his eldest daughter, (my mother) and by cutting down on spending, he was able to regain it from the feudal lord.

*

He stood with his giant figure and seized my neck, like a great jinni that just left his bottle. "What are you doing boy?!" I couldn't move. My tongue was paralyzed and my vocal cords were cut. "Who's your father?" I remained silent, frozen from horror. He bowed down a little as he put his face near mine. His mustache was thick and his face was like a wolf. His beard grew blue fur. He smiled a little as he asked me, "What's your name?"

"Wajdy" It came out from my chest.

"Wajdy! Who's your father?!"

"Kamel"

"And who's Kamel? Where are you from?" I didn't know what to say so I remained silent. "Who? Kamel Abbas?"

"No, Kamel Mustafa." He loosened his grip, saying,

"What are you doing here?"

"I'm eating figs." He smiled as he laughed.

"Naima's son, right?"

"Yes." He laughed as his face brightened.

"Good appetite, I'm your mother's uncle, your grandfather, love. Eat what you like, but don't ruin anything."

"Yes," I said as the blood in my veins froze, not out of fear this time but out of admiration. My grandfather, Habib, my mother's uncle fought the French and defeated them in many battles. He was a legendary character and my mother had been telling me about his heroism, strength, legendary courage and how he was able to escape the French gendarmes and mock them, many times. His deeds were part of my mother's daily bedtime stories, ones which made us rush to bed before sleeping. All of my mother's stories had to do with our village, which was her only world for twenty two years. She left it, escaping with my father to Lebanon, after a four-year- long relationship, since my mother's parents refused to let her marry my father. As soon as my mother started talking about her village and her life, the world turned into a world filled with dancing, Al Dabkeh*, cattle raising, harvest and love stories; a strange mixture of a semi-wild life where everything consisted of nature's melodies. She adored Al Dabkeh, the harvest nights and the local folk songs, which mostly spoke of love and adoration.

I woke up that day to the sound of movement in my grandfather's old house. Everyone was getting ready to leave, to watch the magical appearance of Ali Bin Abi Taleb Zu Al Faqar's sword, in the depths of the sky. My aunt told me as she put on her shoes in a hurry.

"C'mon, hurry up before it disappears."

I think it was before dawn when the villagers gathered in an empty space near the church, fascinated by this celestial sword inlaid with heavenly jewels. "This is Zu Al Faqar no doubt!" One of them said in amazement, and then continued, "Look, the forks are obvious."

"Oh, God bless your name, a sword made of light!"

Maybe I was more amazed than anybody by this scene. The remembrance accompanied me for many years after, eventually I was able to disassemble its symbols when I started reading about orbs, comets and meteors. There were shrines and graves resembling the prophets and the intercessors scattered over the mountains tops. You could distinguish the summits that had shrines, by recognizing a dense evergreen forest with old trees. Cutting the trees around the shrines was forbidden and its punishment was extreme, set by the shrine that protected it. Some of them were built with a high dome containing a large stone grave. Its upper part was covered with a green robe and some small censers were distributed around it, to light incense. Our village's shrines consisted of graves for unidentified people. It was thought that they belonged to some Turkmen from the Janissary army. Their shrines were located in the valley, in the middle of the road that led to the Sheger, which contained the villages' fruit and especially apple orchards. In the middle of their orchards, was the spring with the cement irrigation channels, which were built by the French to water the nearby fields. At the top of the spring, there were the waterfalls descending rapidly downstream, to where there was a magic cave. On the side of the river near the graves, there was a stone grave surrounded by a wall made out of stones that was about three feet high. You could only enter it through a gateway, made from a large flat stone located in a small opening in the wall. That way, the only way you could enter the shrine was by squatting down and crawling. When you left the shrine you had to face the grave, as you are not allowed to turn your back on it, then reverse crawl.

The other shrines and graves used to daunt and scare me when I passed by them, along with the forests of ancient oak trees which shaded them. It was the only pathway to the village's fields and it surrounded you suddenly with its silence and dense shadows, like entering a deep tunnel.

It wasn't long until my father decided to go back to Lebanon, where my mother and younger siblings were, after a disagreement emerged with my mother's parents. The house wasn't finished, only some columns and walls with no roof.

***

---

*Dabke* is a modern Levantine Arab folk circle dance of possible Canaanite or Phoenician origin.

# 5 THE HIDING

## 1979

This was months before my arrest. I don't know exactly when but it was definitely before the Artillery School Massacre*, in Aleppo. The political situation was tense and alert, filled with blood and counter blood. The Fighting Vanguard movement had stepped up its military activity through sectarian assassinations against Alawites. Particularly in those areas it considered that the Alawites controlled the regime. I belonged to the Alawite sect by birth. I was just like any other Syrian citizen, governed by a group of officers from the Ba'ath Party with an Alawite officer ruling over them.

My mother's village, which had become my village by residency and property ownership, was a mix of Alawites and Christians who showed solidarity over poverty and forgiveness. Both groups believed in heavenly messages and reincarnation. They had similar traditions and religious holidays. So, for the new generations it had become more of a social sect, rather than a religious one. For the villagers, centuries of massacres, wars, fear and escape had isolated them. For them, this isolation was a long history of oppression that began with Ali Bin Abi Taleb**, his kids and his successors. Their isolation had crushed many traditional, Islamic customs. In their place came a new social ethos that blended Islamic and Western Christian cultures, together with some global, philosophical influences. This is the culture that embraced us; us, the afflicted, émigré family from Beirut who had fled from the civil, sectarian war that had erupted there.

I was nineteen years old. A ripe young man but confident of the future that, to me at the time, looked like a democratic change was on its way. One that would bring a big change towards true socialism and renounce the dictatorship pursued by the socialist bloc, led by the Soviet Union. I was, just like many other young men, a leftist at the time and I dreamt of a socialist democratic homeland. One, which would bring justice to the poor class that I belonged to. This was at a time when the Ba'athist regime, despite its professed socialist ideology, was oppressing the poor. We used to view the regime as a regression of the real principles of the Ba'ath Party. Instead, we sympathized with the February 23rd Movement, which had branched off the official Baath Party and supported a new solution. Later, it was called the Democratic Arabic Ba'ath Party. Their Marxists ideals were attractive to us, the young men that aspired for change. Therefore, we started creating study groups of young men to investigate them. The discussion evolved to considering issues related to its political outcomes, then to participation in actual political actions. The romanticized enthusiasm of these young and sometimes more mature men, rested on the activity and political thoughts of that time. Back then, working secretly was the only way forward for those who wished to participate in political actions, or any form of protest. It was a Security State, where all competencies and loyalties were harnessed to serve and secure the homeland. Which really meant that it was for the security of, "The father beloved leader, Havez al-Assad," who quickly arose to the rank of divinity.

My village was part of the landscape that fell under the influence of this state, its party and its security forces. In addition, the village was subject to its civil and peoples' administrations, mixed with some myths and naïve concepts that belonged to farmers. It was controlled by illusions of freedom from the defeated minorities' history, by its class and sectarian standards.

The upcoming educated youth, started playing with all these concepts and looked forward to a future broader than that isolation. The youth started feeling their Arabism and their possibility for prosperity, within the bloc they called the great Arab homeland. Through which they saw their affiliation and expansion of the original history of Arabism. Their dreams were bigger than the remnants of the history that was destroyed; leaving only the small groups of people that languished under the rule of the Ottomans, or the French. The dream of recovering their lost kingdom seemed possible to this educated youth. However, differing views emerged on how this could be achieved. These ideas coalesced into ideologies held by two major opposing groups.

Initially, the Arab Nationalists formed a revolution based on the entirety of the old history, which involved the socialist countries and the Soviet Union. With their help, it seemed possible to recover the role of small countries that had been oppressed throughout history. In the context of that national tendency, socialism was the system of justice that anticipated the heavenly justice in the future paradise that was both deferred and invisible.

My generation was the remnants of the Arab Nationalists' shipwreck. We turned to Marxism to form a revolutionary criticism of the Formal Arabic Communist Parties and Soviet Union's experiment. It was attractive in a rural environment which leans towards a simplistic charm, shaded by idealism. I was one of those who chose this path, this group.

On the other side, the refraction of the pan-Arab dream was a rebound towards the Salafi religion. This second group believed in the dream of an Islamic Caliphate, one of jihad, one that leans towards the heavenly paradise.

We would all run away from our reality, towards a fast salvation from this earthly crisis, towards the unknown.

However, their escape was a bloody, scary and desperate one rushing headlong into the past, laden with promises of heavenly paradises. Whilst ours was a peaceful, optimistic escape to the future and of earthly paradises.

We were active in relative secrecy and peace, believing that the Security Services weren't keeping an eye on us. We created the study groups in a desire to investigate Marxism, which matured in our minds as the kingdom of justice on Earth brought about by the fight of the workers, peasants and the educated class that led it. We were that educated class which were supposed to lead. Perhaps, we thought that with our naïve calling we weren't an organization, or a party. That we were only study groups that discussed Marxism, ones that the Security Services had no need to keep an eye on. Especially since we were leftists, just like the ruling Baath Party. At that time, the Baath Party and its Progressive National Frontage, was leading a monstrous war against the Muslim Brotherhood and their Fighting Vanguard. We used to believe that the solution was in democracy and the ballot box, not force of arms.

It seemed as if the Fighting Vanguard were winning their war with the regime, through a series of sectarian assassinations that targeted literary and scientific figures of Alawite origins. This created a sectarian backlash from the Alawite sect. Thus restoring a long history of Arabic Sunni, Ottoman and feudal persecutions. Alongside those of the urban bourgeoisie, which came mostly from the years that the Alawites were denigrated as poor farmers.

Poverty and the lack of livelihood in the Alawite regions pushed many of the young men to join the military and Security Services. Many of the Christian and Alawite villagers belonged to the Baath Party and organizations that believed the Baath Party slogans of unity, freedom and socialism.

\*

I was visiting my uncle's house in the village, when my younger brother came to tell me that the Security Men were all over the village, searching for me. I immediately jumped out through the window in the backroom, overlooking the ripe olive field. I hid behind a few rocks, catching my breath. My uncle closed the window and let the blinds down, as I watched my younger brother leaving along the dirt track.

I watched the place carefully and I didn't see any suspicious movement on the road ahead of me. The place I hid was convenient for watching the roads leading to my uncles' house. I started running upwards, to the plateau, where the shady oak forest was. However, I risked that someone from the village would see me and I didn't trust many of them that belonged to the Ba'ath Party, or worked for the military and security. I decided to stay hidden in some rocks, until it was dark.

The brisk cold started creeping into my body. I had forgotten my jacket at home. I was only wearing a light shirt that didn't protect me from the cold wind that blows from the east. This eastern wind was extremely strong and cold, since it blew from the tall mountain covered with snow. This wind was part of the village's life, its houses and balconies overlooked the west to avoid this wind, so you could sit on your balcony without its iciness stinging you. Even if it was sunny and you were wearing summer clothes, when you tried to leave the balcony and move towards the exposed area, it would give you chills. You would soon rush to wear heavy clothes and a muffler to protect your head and face.

I tried to hide from the wind behind the rocks but because I had to watch the road and the areas ahead of me, I kept being exposed to it. I started shivering from the cold. I raised part of my shirt every now and then, trying to protect my face. An hour passed before I observed a masked ghost, leaving from behind my uncle's house and disappear behind the olive trees, coming towards me.

The blood in my veins froze. From where I was I only had a partial view to study this ghost. I couldn't recognize him, so I poised ready to escape, as I held onto a big rock beside me. I scanned the area, trying to estimate the distance between my position and the forest. It looked a long way. I would have to cross about half a mile to get there and the ghost looked like he was only a few feet away. He would catch me before I could reach the forest.

I gathered a group of rocks beside me and grabbed a big one, getting ready to fight back, 'He doesn't know where I'm hiding exactly, so I will be able to surprise him with a hit and run.'

Suddenly, I hear my uncle's voice:

"Where are you?"

Quickly I remembered his clothes, figure and voice. He is no doubt my uncle. I answered whispering:

"I'm here."

My uncle approached me holding a small basket in addition to my jacket.

"What are you thinking of doing? They are waiting for you."

"I will stay here until nightfall. They might catch me if I tried going into the forest in daylight."

"Take your jacket and some food, take care of yourself."

"Give me the scarf." I said, pointing to his red and white wind stopper mask.

He took it off his head and gave it to me. I wrapped my head and my face with it and pulled on my jacket. I found lots of food in the basket. It looked like it was enough for weeks. I ate some pieces of dried figs with some bread and recovered some body heat, as well as a good deal of courage. I felt like I was able to confront them and run. I resolved not to let them capture me. If I couldn't avoid capture, then I would make it very hard for them to do so.

I had to warn my friends in case I got caught. Perhaps, I could to find a way to warn them while I was still free, though nothing remained a secret in this small village. Some of my friends will know in minutes. I knew I would have to withstand the torture for at least two days, before I could mention the names we agreed on. The torture would be harsh during the first couple of days. They would try to get the information quickly, before the people I knew could hide.

No one in the village moved because of the eastern wind that had been blowing for a couple of days. Some of the villagers would leave their houses to finish an urgent task, then they would disappear quickly back inside their warm homes, where they spent their days playing cards, drinking Mate tea and watching television.

The village was on a plateau that stretched upward towards the east, surrounded by mountains and valleys on both sides. A valley opens up in front of the village. On its bottom, little springs gather to form a small river, whose winding pathway moves towards the Mediterranean. The valley was a dense tangled forest, difficult to pass through. While on the distant horizon, the towering Akkar Mountain was crowned with snow.

I admired that valley from my hiding place, remembering the times we tried walking by the small river, crossing the dense thickets that surrounded it, to end up at a small waterfall, where a wide pond was formed at the bottom. We swam in it, along with lots of the young men, women and teenagers that came to it from nearby villages.

Suddenly, I became aware of a security car climbing the road leading to the forest. I watched it carefully from my hiding place as it stopped directly above me. It was five hundred yards away, near the colonel's house. He was the most important character in the village. On the top of the village, he'd built a large house with a big field surrounding it. He'd seized part of the forest and what surrounded it, invoking his authority to private ownership. This authority allowed him to break all the laws on public property. He used to brag that he built that large house without paying a penny. He'd used the army warehouse machines and devices, in addition to the soldiers that he used as expert laborers. He didn't even pay anything to the children of his village, including his relatives, who worked in his house and farm. In return he just made sure they wouldn't have to attend the military posts. The poor and Ba'athist villagers would praise the officer strongly for his betrayal. My mother would praise the colonel constantly, stressing that he was her uncle. She would often say: "That's what my colonel uncle did." Sometimes she would shortcut it, referring to him simply as, "my uncle." Being my mother's uncle meant he was like a grandfather to me; the grandfather I only saw from afar, amongst his guards and soldiers.

Two Security Men got out of the car to go into the house, or perhaps to just stand outside of the house. I couldn't see the entrance. They disappeared for a couple of minutes, then they returned to the car and headed back to the village, towards our house.

I had spent a couple of hours in my hiding place, spending my time with my uncle's basket, eating some of the fruits and sometimes, some of the other food. Soon, I wasn't thinking about my need for food any more, since twilight was upon me, so now I could take shelter in the dark forest.

As the darkness fell, I commenced studying the terrain and buildings around me in great detail, fearing that there could be an ambush on my route. There was a brutal wind blowing. When it was completely dark, I traversed the plateau through the small fields, avoiding the small roads and pathways. Climbing steadily I made it to the extremely dark oak forest without incident. The violent movement of the wind, swishing noisily through the oak leaves and branches, was indistinguishable from those of the small and big animals, sprinting quickly around me, running away from both me and the wind. I wasn't afraid of the forest. It was something familiar and nice, something that warmed my fear and protected me. I felt comfort and strength. The forest and its creatures seemed like they were welcoming me into their magical kingdom. Whilst hiding, I had thought a lot and drawn many plans of what I was going to do after arriving in the forest, only for them to evaporate once I got there. I went deeper into the small forest, drifting, unaware of what I would do next.

'And now what?! I don't know! Where am I going to sleep?' I can't go back to my house. I can't sleep at one of my friends' houses either. Not even at places of people I know in other villages, since they might already have heard the news. At the very least, their fear would force them to kick me out, even if they didn't surrender me to the police.

Fighting the authority now, at this time period, when they were fighting the enemies of Arabism and Socialism, was considered the utmost form of betrayal. Some would even take it to the extent of considering it as supporting The Muslim Brotherhood. In other words, some people used to think that Hafez al-Assad and his brother Rafat, in addition to some Alawite officers like Ali Duba, were fighting to protect the Alawites from the Sunni persecution through the Muslim Brotherhood. Members who announced out loud that they were fighting the Alawites, who returned to the time of Ibn Taymlyyah, believing that since they are infidels, avowed to kill every Alawite.

I kept walking, adrift unable to think. There was no answer for that urgent question, 'what now?!'

The wind didn't bother me anymore. The dense trees protected me. Rather, I thanked that wind for it hindered the Security Men and their people, in trying to catch me.

I go deep into the forest, 'Where are you going man?' I stop in front of a small glade in the middle of the forest. There there was a small rock overlooking a cave's mouth. The villagers called it, "Al Jeb" for it looked like a pit. A small mouth, about six feet in diameter and from that mouth, you could see the bottom of the deep cave. At the bottom lay the belongings of the Mukhtar's twenty years old daughter, (the mayor's daughter) who died from cancer. Her simple parents threw her belongings down into "Al Jeb," through fear of infection, or apprehensions of the malignant disease, whose name should not be mentioned, may claim other souls.

I knew that girl very well. She visited us in Beirut with her father, to get examined by one of the famous doctors in the American University, who diagnosed the illness as an incurable cancer. I remember when her father came back that day and his face was glowing red. His tears welled up as he told my mother the painful news, with a wounding lump in his throat.

"There is no hope, the disease has spread."

I was nine years old, listening to the conversation from behind one of the sofas where no one could see me. She was a beautiful, twenty years old girl. Not even once did I think that she could die, her face was so healthy and alive with vitality. She lived in our house for more than two weeks. Sometimes, she would get weak but tried to hide it by laughing, while teaching me various types of games and tricks that she knew. Perhaps, most of what remained in my memory were the paper designs she so imaginatively created, to decorate our rooms as if it were Christmas holiday.

When I visited "Al Jeb" for the first time, it was with a group of young men who bragged about being able to descend its gaping maw, with a ladder made of thick ropes they'd made specifically for that reason. They told me that the belongings were from Mukhtar's daughter and another girl, who had committed suicide with poison.

I looked through the mouth of "Al Jeb" but I couldn't see anything. "Al Jeb" was enormous, bulged in the middle and was filled with stalactites and stalagmites. You could hardly see them settling in its stomach. On the bottom of "Al Jeb" there was an opening on the right, leading to a cave the young men weren't able to reach the end of. To the left, another opening led to yet another cave. I thought that if I could get down "Al Jeb," it would be a great hiding place. I could hide in it until the Security Men got desperate and left.

There was another cave in between the rocks that I knew of, but I believed it was filled with water at this time and so, hard to enter. The opening of its mouth was only wide enough for a skinny man. Caves can afford you shelter but are also dangerous. They can be a shelter for some dangerous wild animals that would find you an easy meal. What scared me the most, was the hyena. I always heard it. I watched it once but it ran away, escaping since there was more than one person with a rifle. One of the hunters tried shooting at it but he couldn't hit it.

I didn't have any weapons to defend myself with, in case I had to face the hyena. The many stories about the hyena and the farmers fighting it, confirmed that the hyena follows you, lurking for the moment of your weakness, to prey on you. That's why you shouldn't show it your weakness and try to hit it with rocks and make fire. 'Oh God!' I touched my small lighter in my pocket and took out a cigarette and lit it. I'd only smoked two cigarettes that day. I hadn't wanted cigarettes that day, perhaps because I was worried, or maybe because of the high wind. I was able to light my cigarette after a huge struggle. I was afraid that my lighter's gasoline was going to run out.

I sat on a rock beside the mouth of "Al Jeb," smoking my cigarette. I thought 'It's not a good thing to light fire in the forest. If someone was following me they will find me easily.' Ah, but the joy of smoking that cigarette defeated my caution. I enjoyed my cigarette, "Al Hamra," nationally made. I wanted to smoke another cigarette but I resisted my temptation, trying to ration what I had left. I lay on the green grass meditating the stars. Trying to organize my thoughts and put together a plan that would get me out of this chase, safely. I thought that if I started walking now, I would arrive to the Lebanese borders at daylight, where I could sneak into Lebanon. My friends there could deal with the situation regarding my official papers. I couldn't use my normal identification card anymore, or any official papers. I was wanted and my name would be all over the security checkpoints that spread everywhere, due to the events with the Muslim Brothers.

I noticed that beside me was the food basket that I'd forgotten about. Hunger stalked me and I started eating its contents, voraciously. The taste was delicious. Today was coincidentally one of the many Alawite holidays, though I don't remember what it's called anymore. During these holidays, the religious ones would cook food and distribute it amongst the relatives and neighbors, to draw closer to God and his righteous heirs. Originally, serving food was to help the poor but since there were no poor people anymore, meaning that they have enough food, they replaced them with the relatives and neighbors of the village. Many of the villagers were able to contribute towards the feast and cooked large quantities of groats, (hulled kernels of various cereal grains,) with the chicken that was Halal slaughtered, by the village's Sheikh. I remember the table full of food in our kitchen on that day. It was crowded with large quantities of plates and pots, filled with all kind of groats and chicken meat. My share on that holiday would be a groats' plate with a large piece of meat.

Suddenly, I heard a movement in the trees around me. Following it there was a flash of light moving north and right, exploring the area. I jumped immediately. Holding my food basket, I began to hide by crawling under an oak tree with dense foliage. The flash of light kept walking towards the gap where "Al Jeb" was located. I wasn't able to recognize the face of the torch bearer, because the flash-light in his hand was lighting the area in front of him and blinding my eyes. He couldn't see me because of the dense foliage that almost reached the red dirt and covered me completely. He studied the place for several minutes then started turning away, to leave. I saw his face then.

"Salem!" I whispered, still hiding under the tree.

Salem was searching for me. I got out by crawling, dragging my basket behind me.

He said jokingly:

"This is the end of you, strong man"

"You terrified me man. I thought they came to look for me."

"Yes, the Security Men are in the Mayor's house and there are some Ba'athists helping them find you."

"Did they request anyone else?"

"They don't seem like they're looking for anyone else. I took my precautions in the beginning but after a while, it was clear that they didn't know anything about me. I think someone confessed about you in Damascus."

"No, I don't think they arrested anybody anywhere. I think it's a informer from here."

"Well then, what are you intending to do now?"

"I don't know exactly," I said hesitantly, then I continued a little disordered. "Perhaps I should travel to Lebanon, or Damascus."

"And how? Are you going to walk to Damascus? All the roads are watched." He said mockingly. "You know that the Ba'athist comrades are establishing security checkpoints and ambushes on all the roads?"

The security checkpoints and ambushes of the Ba'athist Party were in almost every village, to help the Security Branches protect the Alawite and Christian villages from the vengeful Muslim Brotherhood operations. They were in addition to the static and mobile security checkpoints, on the public roads and junctions. The Alawites mainly and the Christians after them, felt targeted for their existence. This made them see the Secular Ba'ath Party, as a savior for their historical right to life and development. At that time they did not fear the mightiness of the Ba'athists, not until after the authorities defeated the Muslim Brotherhood Revolution that ended with the Massacre of the City of Hama.

"Maybe I have to hide while the situation calms and the roads are safe."

"Great, do you know the small cave?"

"No!"

"It is very close to here. No one knows its location besides me and some young men from Damascus, who discovered it with me. Come with me."

We walked through the forest using the beam of the flash-light, until we reached a rocky, volcanic area.

"Here it is." He said pointing to the group of rocks.

I approached the rocks, studying them.

"Where? I don't see anything!"

He approached the rocks, smiling as he pointed towards a tiny gap that looked like a small animal's burrow.

I smiled at his joke.

"Yes, this is why you marvel. Not even the jinni would think of hiding here." He said as he squeezed himself, struggling to crawl inside it.

"Follow me."

I put my foot inside, searching for something to stand on as I slipped within. Not until I had descended about ten feet, did the gap widen up a little and my legs hit the ground where Salem was waiting for me, with his flash-light. There we kept on crawling for a couple of feet, until we reached an edge. Hidden behind it was a small rocky room, with a relatively high ceiling that you could sit comfortably in. We sat in one of the corners with our backs against the smooth rocky wall.

"What do you think?" He said smiling.

I looked around me, studying the place. It consisted of small rocks and a half rocky, half dirt, floor. In another corner there was there was a small hole that no human could fit through. Perhaps it led to another cave? There was some humidity but it was tolerable.

"Fine, but how am I going to sleep? I will need something warm. A blanket, a mattress, anything I could sleep on."

"Don't worry." He thought for a little then said, "I will bring you two blankets from my room."

"I need candles, cigarettes and a lighter."

"Of course, of course, food as well." He said as he moved crawling towards the outside:

"Wait for me here, I will come back shortly."

Complete darkness fell in the place after he left with his flash-light. I thought momentarily to call him back and ask him to give me the torch but I stopped myself, reckoning that he would need it more than me.

It was pitch black. I couldn't see anything at all, complete loss of sight. I took my lighter out and lit it, illuminating the place briefly before it became too hot on my thumb and I had to turn it off. It was a cheap plastic lighter. I waited until I got a little cold, then I lit it again for a while. Thoughts of poisonous bugs assailed me, so I started searching with the help of the lighter but I didn't find anything. I touched the humid dirt; I started to dig deep with my fingers to find that the dirt was just a light cover for the solid rocky floor.

What really worried me was that little hole. It was big enough to hide in its depths some of the smaller wild animals, snakes, scorpions or maybe even wolves. So, I kept routinely lighting up my lighter, while I would listen closely to any noise or light hissing sound, that would emerge when the lighter wasn't lit.

I remembered my cigarettes, so I lit one and started smoking it calmly, enjoying that glowing red light that appeared at its end, especially when I took a drag. The glowing ember seemed like a divine energy raging in the grim darkness, revealing and resisting the unknown that surrounded it. I started getting used to the place, without entirely feeling comfortable. Once my cigarette was extinguished I went back to lighting my lighter, every now and then. I worried that it would run out of gas all too soon. So, I thought and then decided to use only the flint strike, since it produced a sufficient spark to observe any danger.

I couldn't concentrate, flitting from one thought to another, with no order. All I cared about was enduring this time period in this scary burrow. My fear of the Security Men was stronger than the snakebite, or any wild animal. I thought of my parents and the situation they were in right now. I thought of my beautiful girlfriend in Beirut, of my friends in Tartous, Lattakia and Damascus. My friends in Lebanon were my favorite. I'd spent the most beautiful and dangerous moments with them. I pulled myself together and the ghost of fear was leaving me. I had an intense belief in the future of human justice. My strength was the sacrifice and endurance, for the good of humanity as a whole. Luckily, I was wearing a watch with phosphorous symbols that glowed in the darkness, to help me know the time. It was the only thing lighting up the place. It was colored in gold. My father gave it to me when he came back from Saudi Arabia, where he used to work.

I looked at my watch every now and then, as I awaited Salem. Two hours had passed and he hadn't returned yet. I estimated the distance to his house and back. It didn't take more than forty minutes. I was worried but I resisted, trying to find an excuse for him. Perhaps, fear prevented him from coming back. Perhaps, he was waiting for the right time. I couldn't resist my concern, so I decided to leave, sensing my way out with the help of the light from the lighter.

'What if he worked for them?!' The thought jumped into my

head frantically. 'Is that possible?!' My concern increased. 'Yes, everything is possible. Didn't Saad surrender his brother? Didn't our friends in Lattakia discover that Guevara, the young man that was most educated and the de facto leader of the groups, had fallen into the clutches of the Security Men and hadn't they turned him into an informer?!'

I crawled quickly and my concern had doubled. Thoughts attacked me. 'What if he came back with the Security Men? Ha, ha! I would be an easy meal for them. They will take me out of my hole with their proud smiles and stinging mockery. Am I that naïve to fall for this trap like a lamb?!'

I climbed the last section, reaching up towards space, panting. I breathed a huge sigh of relief when I reached outside. It was a nice feeling to breathe in the pure air. I walked away, to a convenient distance from the cave opening, hiding in between the trees. I estimated that it was a safe place just in case I was betrayed.

It was only moments until Salem came back, with a big bundle and some bags. He went into the cave, while I stayed in my place watching the area carefully. Perhaps I exaggerated my caution. I waited for him to come out of the cave, looking for me. When he did, I approached him with a smile as my worries had vanished.

He apologized for being late, explaining that he feared being watched because it wasn't easy to find cigarettes, lighters and candles because the village's shops had shut down early. He helped me organize the place with some worn-out blankets, explaining that he'd chosen old ones so we wouldn't have to return them. He told me that he would discover the most appropriate way for me to escape. When he was assured that everything was fine, he would come back to me. He insisted that I shouldn't leave the cave, until his return. We talked for a while in the light of the candle, then he left, crawling.

I laid down, trying to sleep but my thoughts and concerns didn't escape me. I sat down with my back against the rocky wall and my desire to smoke was intense. Salem had brought me plenty of tobacco packets and despite the fact that it was the cheap, "Sharq" brand that I didn't relish, it was excellent for times like these. At least I could continue smoking during these hard times. I was used to the "Hamra" brand. I preferred national smokes at the time. However, in Lebanon my favorite brand was, "Jitan" with no filter, just like all the rest of the youth at the time, especially the leftist youth.

I lit my last "Hamra" cigarette and started smoking it, thinking about how I was going to spend my days here. The light from the candle was dim, yet enough to keep me warm. I would watch its flame and imagine the fireplace in my uncle's house. I noticed that the smoke from the cigarette saturated the air in the small cave, condensing with each puff of smoke. I liked the scene that I was unable to see before because of the darkness. Now, with the light of the candle, which in turn contributed to produce smoke, it looked like a tangled cloud settling in front of me. Soon, I felt shortness of breath and realized that the smoke was not a good idea. Oxygen was scarce in the cave, in the first place.

I extinguished my almost finished cigarette and started crawling outside. I breathed a sigh of relief as I received that refreshing cold night air. I realized that it wasn't possible to smoke in the cave since I needed to save the scarce oxygen, so I wouldn't suffocate. I decided to stay outside until I felt sleepy. So, I chose a nearby place, behind one of the bushes that overlooked the other side of the plateau. There I could see some remote lights in the distant villages. I enjoyed those lights in the dark; they gave me back the feeling of life.

The forest wasn't strange to me. I would always go there to

read, or even write sometimes. Its sunny spring days were wonderful, alive with the colors and textures of many beautiful types of grass and wild flowers. I would go to a specific place and never go anywhere else; that magical place used to hide me from the eyes of the intrusive. Actually, I wasn't the one that discovered it. My beautiful girlfriend discovered it and used to go there to study and meditate, far away from the eyes of the watchers. This place was where we had our first love date. I didn't know exactly why but I didn't feel like going to that place to spend some time in it. I guess I didn't want to profane that pure place with fear and politics.

I smoked a couple of "Sharq" cigarettes, in a speed I wasn't used to. 'Do I really love her?' It seemed to me that I loved her. Something in my chest moved, fluttering, when I remembered her. I felt thirsty. Salem, brought everything but forgot water. Even I didn't remember that. 'I'm such an idiot, how could I forget the water?' I thought about how I could get some water. The village's spring was on the bottom of the valley but it was right beside the main road. However, there was a pump house to elevate the water to the tank on top of the plateau, supervised by an employee from the village. Maybe, he even slept there sometimes? So I discounted this, I decided to be careful and not go near the spring. Maybe I could find some water on the bottom of the valley, on the edge of the forest, since it had rained intensely only a few days ago. Surely, there must be some rocks that stored some water.

I thought of a container to keep the water in, I didn't have a big enough container. Only some boxes filled with food. I went inside the cave, crawling into my burrow. I searched through the basket and the bundle Salem brought me. I couldn't find anything but a plastic box of Halva filled with groats and a piece of boiled chicken meat. I was hungry, so I decided to eat the food and use the box to fill with water. I left after that, to look for water in the nearby valley, carefully crossing the dense thickets and the rocky grassroots. On the bottom of the valley I found some still water that remained in rocky pools. The water didn't taste good but it was enough to slake my thirst. I cleaned the plastic container from the food, unable to remove the remainders of fat and margarine completely. So, when I filled it with water, some globs of margarine floated on the surface and I removed them with my hands. I drank as much as I could from the rocky pool, until the water ran out. Then I went back to hiding in the woods. I decided to spend the night outside and hide at sunlight, so I would be tired enough to sleep in that dark cave.

I spent the night sitting. I would smoke sometimes and other times I would walk here and there, drawing up my escape plans. In the morning I entered the cave once again, to lie down on the old blankets, trying to sleep.

Three days passed before Salem returned and informed me that the road was safe. Now I could walk at night, towards the city of Safita, where I could board a bus to Al Dabosya. From there I could sneak through the Lebanese borders.

I left after midnight, crossing the mountains and thickets on foot, for almost twelve miles. The cold was spiteful, especially during the early morning. Fear of the unknown, that awaited me at each crossroad and behind each tree, especially when I would get near residential houses, kept pushing me towards stopping and hiding. I listened continuously for any noise, or indication of someone tracking me and resisted the temptation.

I arrived at the outskirts of Safita at daybreak but I decided to hide in the nearby thickets, waiting for the city to come to life. Later, I made my way towards the terminus where there were buses that took travelers to Al Dabosya. I boarded one of the pickup trucks, which had been converted into a bus to take passengers. Whilst we waited for the bus to fill with passengers, I overheard a conversation between the drivers, talking about the security checkpoints along the road, which hampered their smuggling missions. One of them complained about the greed of the security checkpoint's officer that shared their profit.

I sneaked out of the bus and started walking towards the street leading to the castle, thinking of a solution for crossing the checkpoint. I knew the area. It was exposed and I couldn't risk crossing the checkpoint on foot. Even if I decided to change my way to Damascus, I still had to cross the fixed checkpoints, not to mention the surprise security patrols. Suddenly, I remembered my cousin's identification card he gave me, so I could register him in one of the Lebanese Institutes. I resisted a moral struggle for a couple of moments, then I decided to use the identification card, to save myself.

I needed a picture, an iron, baby powder and some water. This was a technique I had learnt once from a person I met in Baalbek, on my way to Beirut. I had stopped in one of the cheap hotels for a day, after the road to Beirut was cut off due to the battles on the Beirut-Damascus road.

I bought the powder in one of the nearby markets and headed towards the valley far from sight, where I soaked the small picture in a small mortar I found, filled with water. I peeled the layers of the picture, until there was only the exterior layer that contained the picture itself. I lit a fire and I put a piece of smooth iron over it. I put my picture over the original picture on the identification card, then I sprinkled it with a layer of baby powder. I covered the picture with my undershirt and pressed the heated piece of iron on the shirt. I weighed it down with heavy rocks, until the embossed seal imprinted on my picture. I taped my picture in the place of the original picture, happy with what I'd achieved. I looked at it for a while, studying it. To me, the stamped seal looked identical to the original one and no one would notice the wilts in the corners. The only thing left was a small problem that I felt sure I could solve. This was the normal ink seal. Abu Mehdi did not teach me that, I don't know why, maybe I forgot to ask. I had watched a movie that talked about a prisoner escaping his prison cell, after he copied a seal off of his visitor's arm with a peeled hot egg. So, I decided to buy a hot egg to copy the seal to my picture.

The restaurant's worker looked at me strangely when I asked for a piece of bread and two eggs. I assured him, smiling, that I liked to eat the eggs with the bread, without it being wrapped. He smiled and gave me the two hot eggs. I sat in a nearby corner that protected me from his view and started trying to copy the seal by rolling the hot egg on the original picture. I failed, so all I could do was eat the white egg in desperate revenge.

I looked again at my identification card and it seemed good enough and maybe they wouldn't notice the normal ink seal. I couldn't do anything but take a risk. I boarded the bus heading towards Tartous, hoping that there would be no security checkpoints in that direction. A good while before reaching Tartous, we were stopped. There was a long line of vehicles waiting to be inspected at the checkpoint. I looked outside, searching for a way to sneak out but that didn't seem possible, for there was an armed Security Man watching the vehicles. Also, I would have aroused the suspicion of the passengers and the driver; there was no guarantee they weren't Security Men, or Ba'athists who would hamper my escape.

I was sitting in a single seat and had a local newspaper, which I was using to pretend that I was solving its crossword puzzle. I took my new identification card out, studying it, trying to memorize the information in case they asked me. My anxiety intensified as I studied the picture lacking the rest of the seal. Suddenly, I looked at the pen that I was using to solve the crossword puzzle and decided to take a risk. I started drawing the incomplete, simple part on my picture. I looked at what I've done and felt some comfort, tinged with concern.

The Security Man came up asking everyone to get their identification card out but I had my card ready. When he came close, I pretended that I was still solving the crossword puzzle, while I ate some sunflower seeds, indifferently. He studied my face then he gave it back to me, moving to the neighboring seat. I felt like I'd just gotten my life back and the bus moved away.

I continued to Damascus, now trusting my identification card. Then, directly onwards toward Beirut. I crossed the borders and all the security checkpoints easily and with confidence, reaching Beirut with no further obstacles.

***

---

*The **Aleppo Artillery School massacre** was a massacre of Syrian Army cadets by members of the Muslim Brotherhood, which was part of the Islamist uprising in Syria, 1976-1982.*

# 6 KAFARSOUSEH BRANCH

## MAY 1980

My name was called and I was asked to pack my belongings and follow the guard immediately. I gathered some personal items and put them in a small plastic bag, then followed the guard. In the yard in front of the State Security Branch building, (Al Halbuni) they tied us from behind and led us into the small prison car, where they packed us in the back. We were moved to Kafarsouseh, where the modern building for Al Halbuni prison was located in the main State Security Department Complex. There, we were distributed into small dormitories and I was put in dormitory number four.

Dormitory number four was a small room of about 350 square feet. The prisoners had dark military blankets that barely fit their bodies spread on the floor. They were folded in either three or four folds, depending on the number of prisoners. The ones that have been there for a while found a place in the corners to sit but the ones that hadn't been there for as long settled around the room, relaxing their backs against the wall. The most recent comers had to stay in the middle where there were no walls to relax against. I was placed there. I didn't know any of the faces that hovered around me, asking about my charge:

"Study groups," I said, without hesitating.

"Where are you from?" A deep voice from behind the faces asked.

"From Tartus," I answered.

"Christian?"

"Alawite."

They looked melancholy.

"An Alawite in prison!"

I would have to explain this fact thousands of times for those that would come through this dormitory on their way to Palmyra, or release.

"Do you think that all those who were born in the Alawite sect support the regime?" they asked.

"Many of them belong to parties that oppose the regime and their fate is prison, just like you."

A look of distrust hovered in their eyes, so I kept my peace, realizing that my origins had blinded them with hatred; a hatred that was based on prejudice. They were thinking back to the old grudges between Sunnis and Shiites, mixed with the symbols of the monstrous Alawite suppression. They were the Fighting Vanguard for the Muslim Brotherhood.

The people around me adjourned to engage themselves in whatever they were doing before I entered; praying, playing chess or cooking. There were about fifteen people in the place.

In the far corner of the room, a thin man in his forties with a large beard caught my attention. He was a Lebanese man from the

Popular Front for the Liberation of Palestine; the Haddad collectives who planned and joined missions to steal airplanes.

He was sitting in the corner of the room, semi-secluded from the rest, practicing yoga and meditation on a clean white sheet that concealed his military blanket. Another sheet drooped from the iron shelf over him, so he could seclude himself from the rest whenever he pleased.

You didn't need to know much about him to realize that he was one of the ones that had resided here the longest and that he was treated with respect. It wasn't the yoga or his age that gave him respect; it was the frequency of the visits and materials he received from Beirut, which he generously shared with others.

A couple of hours passed until another group, including my brother and some of my friends, entered. My younger brother was no more than fifteen years old. I didn't know the reason why they put him in jail at such a young age. He had nothing to do with our study groups, and he didn't know anything about what had happened. He informed me, that my seventeen-year-old sister was in jail as well. They released everybody but my brother and sister. I thought only days would pass before they released them but the days turned into years; without any reasonable explanation for their imprisonment, except perhaps, revenge. We were distributed amongst different groups. Each person told his story or would become curious and ask others questions.

In the corner of the interior room there was a door that led to the bathroom area. First, there was a small room, a lobby, roughly ten square feet. Along one of its walls there were urinals and on the opposite side there were two toilets. Each one of these was about twenty-five square feet. One of them was used as a room for supplies, since there were iron shelves hung on the walls right under the heavy iron windows. These windows were covered with a solid iron grille in addition to black iron rods. You could barely see through it because of the accumulation of dirt and dust.

We were asked to bathe and change our dirty clothes to clean ones. Those who didn't have a change of clothes, which was most of us, had to wash their clothes and wear something to cover themselves. The blanket, in some cases, was the only cover for those who couldn't find a change while their clothes dried. We put them on a string under the shelves and they practically covered the heads of those that sat under them. Some found a change of clothes with the help of some friends or comrades, especially the Muslim Brotherhood members and the Fighting Vanguards who were there before us.

The dormitory wasn't crowded when we first came. However, the large amount of supplies and materials indicated that there were lots of people living here before. Only the Lebanese man looked like he was well off. Most of the others were recently arrested, other than two or three from the Fighting Vanguards of Muslim Brotherhood. The food, imported canned goods, and fruits and vegetables filled the shelves in the supply room and some of the dormitory's shelves. Thus, our lunch was diverse and delicious, especially for those of us who had come from the interrogation Branches, where the food was scarce and of low quality. At night, some people who didn't desire to sleep, gathered in the urinal lobby and the supply room to smoke, drink tea and converse. I was one of them, as sleep eluded me.

Sleep time was ten o'clock at night, when one of the guards would come to inspect the dormitory through a small window on the top of the thick iron door. Everybody would pretend to sleep and cover their faces with the military blanket. Whoever didn't desire to sleep, would get up after that to enter the urinal lobby quietly. Together, we gathered, sitting upon small iron milk crates, or the edge of the toilet that was turned into the supply room and entertained each other.

It was forbidden to turn the lights off in the dormitory, but the jailers would take it easy on us after the inspection. Two of the prisoners would get up; one of them would stand on the other's shoulders to turn off the four lights on the ceiling by loosening the light bulbs from their bases. There was no light switch in the dormitory.

I only had few moments to talk to my brother and my friends the first day. We were cautious of informers, so we would talk quickly, asking some questions about the interrogations, what had happened to us and what we expected. Our first day was filled with expectations. Kafarsouseh belonged to the Al Halbuni Intelligence Branch; or rather it was the new building that belonged to the Al Halbuni Branch, which belonged to the State Security Department. Therefore, whoever they finished interrogating would come here to wait in this station for his transfer to a new prison, usually Palmyra. We used to live with these expectations floating around in the dormitory, listening to every movement in the exterior corridor. Hoping for some resolution each time the locks thudded open, only to bring in one of the prisoners, or call another. We didn't know where they were taken in the beginning. In time we started to recognize their destination based on the prisoner's body language, the extent of its severity and the charge against the prisoner: Palmyra, the Internal Branch or release. The new prisoners would come from all parts of Syria.

I couldn't sleep that night, so I entered the urinal lobby after I was invited by one of the curious prisoners who didn't like the idea of me being a leftist. I didn't know how he was going to take the news of me being a Marxist and an Alawite in the opposition. He was a man in his forties, dark skinned and strongly built, with a thick black mustache.

"Come here brother, sit down." He spoke with what I thought was an Aleppo dialect; one with a tone full of potency, imitating the strong men of the neighborhood but with the kindness of a farmer.

He gave me a milk crate to sit on. I sat down, trying to balance myself in between three men. I knew later that they were from the countryside of Aleppo, practiced magic, Skewer Piercing and believed in their Great Sheikh and his miracles.

"Where are you from?"

"From Tartus, Safita."

"Safita itself?"

"No, from a small village near Safita."

"Yes I know it, a paradise. Are you from our Christian brothers?"

"Are you Muslim?" another interjected, skeptically.

"Yes," I replied. "I am personally not religious but I come from a religious family."

"Alawite?"

"Yes, exactly."

"God bless," said my questioner, smiling maliciously.

Our conversation lasted until the early morning. They were very happy with the rest of the abundant food left in the dormitory by prisoners who had run away, or left to Palmyra. They did not stop eating and they insisted I join them.

I was informed that a few days before there was an escape from prison. Some of the Vanguard's leading members, with the help of some jailers in the Branch, escaped. The day I arrived, many of the prisoners were transferred to Palmyra. The situation was tense in Kafarsouseh that day and there were many new measures the prison governor enforced, so we had to be careful.

In the morning we woke up to the movement of the jailers bringing food. It was a big container of halva and some boiled eggs, with a big pot of tea. There was a huge demand for the toilet because there was only one working, with one sink, to service the needs of the thirty prisoners in the dormitory. My turn came up after an hour. Soon after I finished washing my hands and face, some of the prisoners had already finished their breakfast. Some finished their food and gathered in the corners to talk, their voices lost amidst the sounds made by the other prisoners' morning activities. All you could hear was a loud roar of unharmonious noise.

My brother and some friends were waiting for me to eat breakfast. They laid out a big piece of halva, a boiled egg for each person and some loaves of harsh military bread, over a large sheet of the government's daily newspapers. We had to empty the bread loaves of the half-baked, inner doughy section to be able to eat it with the eggs, halva and tea. I was able to talk to my brother alone for a while. He told me about his friends and his arrest in school at night. Also, he spoke about the arrest of some girls from our village, as well as from neighboring villages. They led them all to Tartus Prison, before transferring them to the Al Halbuni Branch. From there he had been transferred to Kafarsouseh.

His smile did not leave his face as he explained to me how he played soccer with his friends, using some clothes wrapped in the shape of a ball. My brother became preoccupied with helping one of the others organize his place, so I had the chance to study some of the faces of the people there. Some of them were bearded with mustaches and others had their beard grown due to not shaving. We understood later that the prison governor had stopped the weekly shaving, so the prisoners would grow beards and he could distinguish them from the guards, in case they tried to escape.

Two sets of iron shelves stretched across the dormitory's walls. In the depths of the room across from the iron door, along the wall, there was a window with an iron net and crossed iron bars. The windows overlooked the front courtyard, which belonged to the State Security Management, a big building that looked like an inverted pyramid. The dormitory window directly overlooked the Department of State Security director's office.

The building of Kafarsouseh Branch consisted of two sections, south and east. The southern section consisted of three floors. The first floor contained the offices of the Branch director, the vice director and the court. The second floor and the basement were for the dormitories. We were in the ground floor, where there were four rooms (dormitories). The third, fourth, fifth and sixth were separated by a corridor leading to an iron gate that led to the jailer's room at the bottom of the stairway.

In the basement there were two dormitories. The first and the second were called the double rooms, consisting of small rooms, theoretically made to fit two people. While the solitaries sat across from them. In between, there was a small corridor leading to an iron door that opened to a yard with high walls about 600 square feet. It was the breathing yard, where we were supposed to go for about 45 minutes every day to breathe in the fresh air and enjoy the sun.

Part of the extreme measures enforced by the Branch Governor was to forbid us from going outside to the breathing yard. Therefore, we didn't get out like we were supposed to. This was what the older inmates told us.

In one corner of the dormitory lay Abu Saaed by himself. He was covered partly by his clean white sheet. He smiled at me while he sat up a little, as if he was inviting me to sit with him. I didn't hesitate. I responded to his smile with a similar one, then I approached him to say hello. He invited me to sit, making room for me beside him.

I sat down with my back against the wall near him, to introduce myself and converse. He had spent about one year in the Kafarsouseh Branch, which was strange. He was a thin, calm, tall man that practiced yoga and read most of the time. He was a member of the Popular Front of the Liberation of Palestine (Wadih Haddad's wing). He had great experience with armed combat, especially in Europe. The authorities arrested him with his friend, who now resided in the basement in the double rooms section, where the situation was better. I later got to meet his friend through the double room windows that overlooked the breathing yard.

Abu Saeed warned me about the informers recruited by the security. They were told to hunt for anything that would confirm their loyalty and in return they would get released from prison. He observed that we would probably stay in this prison and they wouldn't take us to Palmyra, or Mezze prison. Which they'd started doing with the Muslim Brotherhood members, after failing to negotiate with them.

He cautiously talked about escaping, without satisfying my curiosity. I preferred not to press him and be patient. Most of the Fighting Vanguards who'd escaped had resided with him for months before it was decided they should go to Palmyra prison. That was his reason for accelerating his escape mission. They interrogated him; therefore, he decided not to talk lengthily about the subject because he didn't want to cause himself any problems. Also, he was hoping to be released very soon, maybe in a deal with the Popular Front.

Only a few days had passed before some of the communists from the Communist Action League, the Communist Party (The

Political Office) and two from the Aleppo Socialist Union, (Nasserist) joined us. They were released again a few days after. The dormitory would become tight during the day as it got crowded with the newcomers and then would become spacious by dawn, when groups of Muslim Brotherhood members got transferred. Most of them were from the Fighting Vanguards, arrested by the intelligence Branches in other provinces. Kafarsouseh was a collection center before deportation to Palmyra Military Prison.

In the middle of the dormitory one of the bearded men caught my attention. He was talking to a group of men, smiling with signs of satisfaction on his face. Soon he started preaching, inviting everybody to pray. A big group aligned, standing behind the bearded man, while two of the prayers remained seated due to injuries in their legs from torture. I had never seen a live prayer before. The scene was strange. They bowed down in humility, mumbling, while their Imam recited from the Quran.

I was never religious and never received a deep Islamic education. I was born in Beirut among residents that were mostly Christian, except the few poor Shiites who'd emigrated from their villages to make a living, just like most of the other Syrians. Christianity was the religion I was taught in school, because there was no class for the few. However, I do remember in one of the classes in elementary school, a young Sheikh came to us to teach us Islam and we were only a couple of kids, mostly Syrian. Not many of the verses from the Quran that the Sheikh tried to make us memorize, stuck in my head.

As soon as the prayer was over, the bearded man approached me with a smile. He greeted me with formal language.

"Al Salam Alaykom."

"Wa Alaykom al Salam" I answered, stammering just like

in the history films.

"I think you're from Tartus, right?"

"Yes."

"God bless. From our Christian brothers?"

"No, from your Nusayris brothers," I said, jokingly.

"Yes, gracefully."

We laughed together, then continued talking about what was happening, as he was curious about politics and religion. He was an educated man, a civil engineer from Aleppo in his thirties, muscular, tall and handsome in nature. He got released a few months afterward, on the occasion of negotiations with the Muslim Brotherhood but when the negotiations failed, he was arrested again.

Soon, trust and kindness, motivated by an extreme desire to convince me of the Islamic religion and Prophetic Sunnah grew between us. However, as time passed these feelings turned into mutual respect, after long sessions discussing philosophy, history and of course, politics. During one long night after the Morning Prayer, we sat down for him to tell me the story of his seventeen friends who escaped from Kafarsouseh Prison. How he'd stayed behind, awaiting his approaching fate, which was the death sentence. Abu Anas looked at me, smiling as he shifted his position on the metal milk crate:

"The Alawite is an apostate that must be killed. There are jurisprudences to accept his repentance and his return to Islam, after subjecting him to a plight," he said. He had a clear Aleppo dialect, despite the fact that he liked to speak in the classical language, like the educated Salafists of Muslims usually did.

"We do not accept his repentance," he corrected.

It seemed to me to be a joke from the end of the twelfth century. I'd never heard such phrases before. It seemed as if I was living in a different century.

"Do you want to hear the prison break story?" He continued.

We were four newcomers, from various backgrounds but I was the only secular, leftist Alawite; who, according to the Jihadists, had to be slain twice. We hovered around Abu Anas after midnight, sitting on the empty metal milk crates, our necks stretched and our focus on him, curious to hear the story. For me, the escape incident was more than a story that could happen anywhere, it was what had saved me from the clutches of the interrogators during my last torture episode. They'd become preoccupied with what was more dangerous and important, the escape.

"The sergeant, Taher, was distinctive and influential in this Intelligence Branch, because he is the nephew of the Branch Chief." Abu Anas said, batting his eyelids as his facial features changed a little. "His uncle called for him to serve the military in the Branch. Taher is religious, committed to the Sunnah of Allah and his Messenger. However, he wasn't convinced of Jihad yet, until he met with the Brothers in this prison and the truth was revealed. He became one of the Mujahedeen, for the purpose of restoring the rule of God and his laws to this blessed land and to free it from the polytheists." He looked at me, smiling, as if he was apologizing for an inevitable ruling.

"I got to know Taher quite well. He was my jailer for the two periods I spent in that jail. I was jailed for a couple of months before, then they released me for a couple more months before arresting me again, because the negotiations had failed between the authority and the Brothers in the Muslim Brotherhood. Taher was a pious, religious young man seeking to please God in everything. He was not pleased with the injustice committed against his Muslim nation. He felt extreme contradiction in his position as their jailor, until God inspired him to help his brothers in prison. He used to help us in everything. He would bring us what we needed and he was our connection to the outside world."

"But he used to torture the other prisoners, especially the leftists," Asaad, the communist young man, commented.

Abu Anas looked at him, smiling, then joked:

"Of course, you know people are different. In the end, you are infidels and your fate is beheading. Whipping is too merciful for you."

Everyone smiled as he continued:

"The plan was to wait a little while, until they got a clear chance to escape from Kafarsouseh prison. But the stepping up of prisoner transfers to the Field Court in Palmyra Prison, made them accelerate the escape plan. It would be almost impossible to escape from Palmyra Prison. The situation here though was very convenient, especially with Taher being a powerful trusted sergeant, nephew of the Branch Chief himself. Is there anything better than that?"

"The escape plan was based on circumstances special to the Branch. They knew that the administration of Al-Halbuni Branch would move here soon and there would be no separate administration, or prison in this case. At present, when there is a serious medical situation that needs an emergency response; they send a special car from the Al-Halbuni Branch, to take the prisoner to the State Security Department Clinic, or to al-Mazza Military Hospital. This was the procedure the plan was built upon."

"That night, when the Patrol leader left as usual to sneak back to his house and family, Taher put sleeping pills in the Milo drink he offered his guard friends inside the prison, to celebrate his engagement. In no time, the guards felt sleepy, so they went to the sleeping room on the upper floor, reassured by Taher's presence and convinced he would wake them up, in case of an emergency."

"As soon as Taher was assured they were asleep, he informed the brothers in the dormitories that everything was ready. After they seized the weapons from the sleeping Security Men, some of the brothers shaved their beards and wore their civilian clothes. Meanwhile, Taher called the Halbuni Branch, requesting an ambulance to move a prisoner that was in a state of emergency."

"The military ambulance entered the Branch's courtyard, where Taher led the patrol members into the prison, to help him move the supposed immobile patient to the ambulance. The brothers, who were awaiting them, gathered in the corridor pretending to be curious to help their friend. Two Security Men started screaming at them to go back to their dormitory but the brothers were able to turn around and control them, by injecting them with drugs."

"The brothers boarded the military car, which fit seventeen prisoners in addition to sergeant Taher. Leaving the prison gate and then crossing the Security State gate wasn't difficult. One of the brothers drove the car, while sergeant Taher sat beside him. The guards didn't suspect anything because the car was expected to leave as usual, especially with the presence of the sergeant Taher, who was known to them. Some of the other prisoners started happily chanting Allah-o Akbar, as they were crossing the Branch gate without the guard's interference. They were immediately silenced, because the plan was that the car would return to move another group of the prisoners. Usually, the car with the prisoners was supposed to return to Kafarsouseh, then to leave for the al-Halbuni Branch. Therefore, I stayed behind, waiting for their phone call, which we'd agreed upon with sergeant Taher, in the jailers' room. I remained on alert and glued to the prison phone to ensure that they hadn't been caught and the situation was safe to come back. But it seemed that caution and fear controlled them, as they didn't dare to return. I waited for about two hours, pointlessly, even though they were supposed to call minutes, or at most half an hour after they left. Nothing happened, no contact. So, we went back to sleep, believing in God and His will."

"After a couple more hours the warrant officer, Abu Ahmad, called the prison to check on the patrol that hadn't returned yet. Since no one answered, they called the exterior gate guards, who found the Security Men handcuffed and drugged. They went crazy and entered the prison to interrogate us but without success. The brothers were free and they would never find a trace of them."

Abu Anas smiled proudly as he finished his story.

***

# 7 MY GRANDFATHER

The last image I remember of my grandfather was of him living in our house in Beirut; despite the illness his lungs suffered due to his severe smoking, he was a tall, broad-shouldered and strong man. He would wear a Turkish Shirwal with an Arabic head wrap, while his big pipe hung from his mouth. I find it hard to remember whether he had a mustache but a distant memory always returns with an image of a man with a long mustache, or maybe that is how I wanted to see him. His illness had become more severe. He would cough all night long, spitting something black from his mouth. All of my father's attempts to stop him from smoking had failed, despite the doctor's warning that if he continued smoking, he would die soon. His lungs were completely damaged, yet he would smile, surrendering to his fate unconvinced of the doctor's prediction. He was at least seventy years old, or even a little older but certainly wasn't over eighty, since he'd traveled to Argentina before World War I.

I was eight, or nine years old when my father assigned me to watch my grandfather and inform him if he was smoking in secret. My father had imposed an absolute prohibition on smoking after their last visit to the doctor, who had informed him that my grandfather was in a critical state. I would watch him sneakily and didn't succeed in catching him for days because my father had confiscated his big pipe. Therefore, he'd lost his tool to smoke, or that is what my father thought. However, he began to disappear for hours each day. Curious, I followed him stealthily to find out where he went. To my surprise, I found him sitting in the shoemakers shop, exchanging conversations and smoking cigarettes while the shoemaker was busy with his work.

My grandfather glimpsed me staring at him, so he called me to give me ten piasters as he teased me. I bought some candy then, went home. Was that a bribe to remain silent? I don't know, he didn't ask for anything in return and he didn't seem to be nervous about his lit cigarette that he kept smoking, indifferently. Perhaps, it didn't cross his mind that I am the young police officer that was assigned to watch him. Anyway, I accepted the bribe and didn't tell my father. I thought that I will delay it to the next day, or perhaps, I didn't dare to do so. My grandfather had an eeriness I could not cross, for he was an old Sheikh. A man that the old and young bow down to and kiss his hand obediently, so how could I, his young grandchild dare to think of snitching on him? Even my father didn't ask me about anything, in truth, it was a request born of fear and worry for his father and maybe, he didn't mean it in a literal sense. However, as a child I took his request with all seriousness, trying to protect my grandfather from death.

In the following days, I would purposely ensure my grandfather saw me walk in front of the shoemakers' shop, greedy for more piasters and so, he would give me some, occasionally. When we started sharing together the secret of his life in the shoemaker shop, something bigger happened to our relationship. Friendship and sympathy grew with his enjoyment of smoking and his surrender to his fate. I forgave him for his intervention and refusal to allow me to keep the dove that I was taking care of in a small cage on our house balcony; as well as his constant annoyance with the noise we caused from playing, which had reduced our playtime to only a few hours.

My grandfather wasn't exceptional. His father had sent him to the village teacher, (al-khatib) just like most of the children at the time, to learn writing, reading and memorizing the Quran. In the following years, when he reached adulthood and understood his religion, he also learned the oral history transferred from grandfather to father. A history full of fear, hunger and death:

"At a time before the monotheistic religions appeared, the mountains used to be a refuge for all those fleeing from oppression and injustice. Mountains and valleys coated with the forests and inhabited by wild animals, which were always more merciful than the humans. An animal attacks a human for food, or self-defense, while a human being attacks another human out of greed, revenge, or malice and all the other vocabularies the animals don't know. To these mountains: the Phoenicians took refuge, escaping from the successive attacks of the kingdoms and great empires; the Jews took refuge there, escaping from the oppression of the other nations; then the early Christians, searching for safety and peace from the Roman oppression. In successive centuries they also became a place of refuge to the Alawites escaping from the oppression of their religious enemies. The new refugees integrated with the old refugees and their culture to form a new culture, crowned by the dream of escaping reality towards worlds of imagination, mingled with the legends of the past. The races blended and mixed together with the blood of the invaders from each corner of the world, to become a wondrous race mixture that extended from the dark brown Arabic color to the Northern European blond. Poverty was what brought the coastal mountain inhabitants together; the cultural structure was liberal and contained elements from many cultures and civilizations."

My family belonged to the khayateen, (tailors') clan. It is said that it was one of the first Alawite clans to inhabit the mountains and its origins dated back to the Ghassani tribes,the original inhabitants of the region. Some of them converted to Islam. Many of the tribe members were busy with religious philosophy and from it, modernist religious men emerged. These men played a role in maintaining the teachings of the Alawite doctrine, during the long isolation that extended for many centuries.

My great grandfather was one of the religious men who immigrated from one of the nearby villages, with their family, to perform a religious role in a shrine of the Prophet Jonah. Guardianship of this shrine was then conferred to his sons, after him. Meanwhile, a piece of land was allocated for him which he farmed, living from its produce in addition to some of the scarce alms fund, which believers would leave in the shrine's box. When my grandfather turned seventeen he decided, together with his brother and many Alawite, or Christian young men who resided in those mountains, to travel to the Argentine as an escape from hunger and the oppression of the Ottomans. The First World War hadn't started yet and the big ship was waiting to transfer them to Argentina, the land of labor and wealth.

It was a long, strenuous trip. They gathered in the ship's hold's, eating what was available from food they'd packed. Once there, they worked in building the railway and other strenuous labors, until my grandfather ended up working as a train driver and I could swear that once I saw a Brazilian driver's license. Maybe he used to work on a train between Brazil and Argentine, or he worked for a while in Brazil, as well. He spent fifteen years there. He returned afterwards to inherit the Chiefdom from his father and take care of their land. The money he saved was enough to marry one of the village's girls, who gave birth to a boy and two girls but died from a snake-bite whilst they were still babies.

His brother remained in Argentina where he started a new life for himself. He got married there and had children. My grandfather didn't know much about them besides one of the children studied engineering. He knew nothing about his sister. Soon, he completely lost contact with them and they faded into another civilization.

As for their third brother, he died under torture at the hands of the men working for the Clan Chief. His wife had complained to the feudal lord that her husband didn't treat her well and that he hit her sometimes. Jaber al-Abbas, the feudal lord, was a cousin of my ancestors and represented the government. So, he had sent his men to 'arrest' my grandfather's brother, to bring him to answer his wife's complaints. He sentenced him to flogging for his crimes. However, he didn't survive under the whips and thick sticks, so he died and his wife became a widow with her children.

I didn't know if my grandfather was actually happy with his return from America. At the time he had spent half of his life there, however, I assert that it was his choice. After all, he would have been able to stay there and start a family, like his brother. Maybe nostalgia, or culture brought him back to his small village. He was fluent in Spanish and Arabic languages, which enhanced his ability to find information about the secrets of his religion and philosophy. He devoted himself to the service of the shrine. He protected his believers, answering to their pleading in every illness and pandemic; for he was the healer and the savior to whom they appealed, to help mediate for them between god and his angels

\*\*\*

# 8 KAFARSOUSEH PRISON

## 1982

Our days became routine, spent in reading and living our daily life, from making food to occasionally listening to the story of one of the new prisoners. The seemingly endless train of new prisoners brought updates from the outside world. They were like a daily live news show. We kept in touch with the outside and its hot bloody events, through the people involved in it. Kafarsouseh's Branch was a gathering center for all the other intelligence branches from the provinces. New prisoners stayed with us for a couple of days, or weeks before being transferred. We often never saw them again. Some of them would get executed, or just disappear. A few of them would return from Palmyra Prison, after confessions by new prisoners required them to be re-interrogated. It was very unlikely that someone would be returned for release.

As I recall, it was March when, after four months of continuous reading, I finished *The Story of Civilization*, in eleven volumes by Will and Ari Durant, It was at this time when a young boy who didn't look over thirteen, or fourteen years old, entered our dormitory. He had a small physique and childish, delicate face. That wasn't a strange occurrence at the time, we were used to some situations where kids were brought in as hostages, then held in the prison until their parents turned themselves in. However, he looked like he was younger than usual. He came in with some of the new arrivals, confused, not knowing what to do and he looked extremely exhausted. He immediately sat in the middle, silently.

There was a bad smell coming from him, so someone suggested he take a shower, as he gathered a change of clothes for him. The child looked at him with confused eyes and said hesitantly:

"My pants are stuck and I can't take them off."

He was wearing jeans that were filled with mud mixed with coagulated blood. Nabil, the Christian medical student who hadn't graduated yet, got closer to him, trying to ask him some questions about his legs. Then, with the help of others he started to pull the pants from his sides. The young man screamed from pain, so they stopped after Nabil asked them to. He brought a piece of metal shaped like a knife to rip the sides of his pants, until the fabric ripped his skin off. In reality there was no skin, since the skin of his rotten legs was glued to his coagulated blood. Meat appeared, and some of it bled. Nabil cleaned the deep wounds from the rot and coagulated blood with soap and clean water. Some others helped the boy take off the rest of his clothes and cleaned him with a piece of wet cloth.

It wasn't long, only a few days, until the color returned to his face and his eyes brightened. When he was comfortable with us and we were comfortable with him, he told us his story

He was from Hama, a city known to us from our radio for its rebellions and fights. We had a small radio with tiny earphones. The radio remained after the seventeen prisoners had escaped

Kafarsouseh Prison. Someone told us that it was one that Taher, had smuggled to the prisoners at that time. We used to hide it in the toilet, (after putting it in a plastic bag to protect it from the filthy water) when there were inspections. There were only a few trusted people that knew about it. It stayed with one of us, who would listen to the news from the few stations available at the time, then report it. A few trusted people then spread the word, whispering. This is how we knew about the Hama events, after only a few days.

He sat against the wall as we gathered around him in a semi-circle, silently, then he began his story..

*\*\**

# 9 HAMAH

## 1982

My name is Ameen, Mohamed Ameen. A composed name, as the people of my city used to do to bless the prophet, 'God's peace be upon him.' I am the only boy among six sisters. My dad was extremely happy when I was born. God honored him with me, a boy to carry on his name. He celebrated me, thanking god for his generosity, praying for me in secret and in public. My dad was a very religious man, who never skipped a prayer. He fasted the month of Ramadan and Al Senna but he wasn't able to go to Al Hajj. He used to dream of Al Hajj, delaying it from one year to another, until he was able to save enough money. God did not allow it, as he died soon after celebrating my Circumcision. That's what my mother and grandmother later told me.

My father's family worked in the sheep and wool trade for generations but my father lost his trade, due to a disease that infected the sheep. He spent his last years desperately trying to pay off the many loans the business had accrued. Some of his brothers helped him in the beginning but he went to heaven, before he could recover his former status. My mother became a widow at twenty eight years of age. She was left with me, her baby son, of only a few months and six daughters, the eldest of them being just twelve years old. We all lived with my paternal grandmother. My father didn't leave us much to live on, so my mother decided to open a workshop, making paper bags at the house. Everybody worked in the workshop, including my grandmother and me when I grew up, despite their objections and insistence that I should spend my time studying.

Everybody worked hard to spoil me, meeting my demands without complaining for I was the man of the house, even though I was young. My oldest sister, Noor was the one that spoiled me the most, giving in to almost all my desires. She, like the rest of my sisters and at the request of my only uncle, left education at the age of twelve, after graduating elementary school.

Nobody at the house liked my fat uncle, who worked in the sheep market. He was thick-headed, coarse and always smelled like livestock. However, we had to obey him even though he didn't give us any help. He hadn't even helped my father in his distress. My grandmother always complained about the son that would only appear when he wanted to scream demands.

After a long struggle, my mother died of cancer. I was only twelve years old. However, my grandmother, despite being over seventy years old, took charge. She would manage the work with the help of my oldest sister Noor, who took on the role of my mother, until my uncle married her to a man that was twenty years older than her. No one asked for my approval since I was young but if I had been old enough, I would have disapproved of this marriage. Yes, women were supposed to get married but he was a thickheaded, violent man that would often hit her and forbid her from visiting us.

I was always small, thin and looked three or four years younger than my actual age. I remember when my mother took me to the mosque to meet the Imam, begging him to accept me into his gathering, to memorize the Quran. I still recall how the Sheikh refused, thinking that I was four or five years old, when I was actually over eight years of age. I was a hardworking student, memorizing the Holy Quran, so I could mutter it in a speed my Sheikh praised. On occasion, he started taking me into prayers, asking me to recite the Quran in the voice that everybody loved.

My mother was very proud of me. She would assure me that my learning would have made my father happy, so I worked even harder just to please him. I often visited his grave to recite what I had memorized from the Holy Quran. I maintained my attendance at the mosque and listened to the speeches of the Imam, even after the death of my mother. I would rarely miss an order from al-Sheikh. I was studious in chanting for the pleasure of Allah and His Messenger and I still do, thank God.

In the ninth grade, my sister Mona got married with the blessing of my grandmother and the reluctant approval of my uncle, because the groom was a poor Palestinian from the camp. However, he finally gave in to my grandmother's stubbornness. I was the only one who was extremely sad for her departure because she had taken over from Noor, as a mother figure to me. For a long time, she had persisted in telling me bedtime stories. I would miss her dearly.

Two years later, my uncle disappeared. It was said that he got arrested because of an altercation that occurred between him and soldiers trying to search his house. We haven't heard anything about him since then. My grandmother tried reaching the Intelligence Branches, to ask about him but with no luck. Nobody had heard of his name, except for one person who told my grandmother that they took him to Damascus and from there, they transferred him to Palmyra Prison.

Despite this situation, my old grandmother and remaining sisters, struggled to manage our house, our workshop and to help all of us. I would try and help them sometimes but they would force me to go to my room, to study. I was superior in school, never missing Al Sheikh Friday Prayers. Al-Sheikh used to pity me and call me, Ameen the Believer. I liked him for that, it encouraged me to study and be more diligent.

Before the actions in Hama started, the situation was tense. There were daily house searches. Every day, we would hear about someone getting arrested, on the charge of being part of the Muslim Brotherhood Vanguards. It wasn't strange to hear gunshots here and there, especially in the evening but this time it was even more than usual. We heard it from inside the mosque. The Sheikh stopped reciting his lessons and listened carefully. Soon, someone quietly informed him of something and he immediately rushed from the mosque, ordering us to go back to our houses.

"That night, following the gunshots, we woke up to the sound of explosions,. My sister, Halmia woke me up in horror, telling me to rush to the ground floor, where we all gathered. My room was on the upper floor, next to my grandmother's bedroom. She slept alongside my paralyzed sister, Amal who had suffered polio when she was very young. The rest of my sisters resided on the lower floor. Horror controlled everybody but as soon as the gunshots calmed down, we decided to sleep in the guest room, until we understood what was going on. I could only sleep fitfully, just like the rest of us. We were on spring break and I was in the eleventh grade, therefore, I didn't have to wake up early that morning.

We woke up to the sound of the announcer at the mosque

calling:

'Allah-o Akbar (God is great)... Allah-o Akbar... Long live al-Jihad... Long live al-Jihad.'

I immediately tried to leave to explore the situation but my grandmother and scared sisters, prevented me. They insisted I stay as they listened to the Jihad calls and the chants of Allah-o Akbar getting louder outside, along with profuse gunshots. The calling for Jihad and my natural curiosity, were pulling and pushing me to get out but the horror of my grandmother and sisters, forced me to submit and wait a while.

It was only moments later when the exterior doorbell rang. It was our neighbor, Um Muhamed, my grandmother's friend. She entered, her face filled with fear and panic as she talked quickly and loudly. She told us how she had watched the first two martyrs fall, because of a shell at the edge of the neighborhood. Then she started talking about what happened. The rebels had seized the armory of the People's Army and were distributing weapons among some Mujahedeen, in our neighborhood. The Mujahedeen had blocked all the roads leading to the neighborhood, as they were fighting the Security Men and the Army. It was revolution against the infidels and Alawites. 'Hama has always striven completely for the establishment of God's law.' They'd arrested many of the Security Men and informers. They'd killed many of them but they said they would apply the Sharia, (Islamic Law) to the remainder. She was talking quickly, as if she was cursed by the devil. The gunshots and explosions got louder everywhere. I decided to go out to the mosque, regardless. I didn't answer to my grandmother's persistence, or my sisters' pleading. I had to meet my Sheikh and my colleagues, to discover what was truly happening.

The street in front of my house was packed with men, women and children. All running in search of shelter, or searching for their children, to take them home. Some carried luggage and food, walking towards their shelter. I entered the nearby mosque's door, to find my Sheikh among some of the brothers. They were urging some students and neighborhood men, to the Jihad. Enthusiasm filled some of them, so they left immediately towards the barricades, armed with what was available to them. Some were still arguing with the Sheikh, not convinced, insisting that it was not the time. That we shouldn't drag ourselves behind the Muslim Brotherhood members, maybe towards our death. They felt there was no chance for them to fight and win against the vast armies and the Security Men; all of whom were extremely well armed with both light and heavy weapons. They thought that they would destroy the neighborhood and its inhabitants. The Sheikh insisted, with a certain smile, that the rest of the cities would follow in our footsteps. That most of the army's members were Sunnis, who would desert and join the revolution for the triumph of Islam.

Some went back home, preferring to stay in their houses and protect their families; while the Sheikh continued explaining the importance of al-Jihad and sacrifice, in the name of God. I became very excited, so I raised my hand, requesting they give me a weapon, so I could fight on the barricades but the Sheikh looked at me smiling:

"God bless your father Ameen, for he would be proud of you but you are still young son and you won't be helpful in the fighting. We need those who have finished compulsory military service and are trained to take up arms. But you can help in supplies and medical emergencies."

He indicated to one of the Brothers, who took me by my hand, smiling as he said:

"Al-Jihad isn't only in fighting. There are similar things to fighting, which will help the fighters to victory. We will do that.

Come with me."

He led me to one of the nearby houses, where there was a group of young men and women constantly on the move, as they came in and out with boxes and pots. Everyone was working with incomparable enthusiasm. From the interior room I heard the sounds of a woman crying, mixed with voices of condolences:

"God accepts him, God rest his soul and he is a martyr, if God is willing."

I stood in the corner of the room, watching, without any tasks assigned to me. No one seemed to care. I was left alone, while the young man that brought me there, disappeared into one of the interior rooms of that big house. He came back after a while, accompanied by a woman covered by a heavy head-scarf and wearing medical glasses:

"Welcome, come with me," she said.

I followed her down a long hallway to a type of room I hadn't seen before. It was a medical clinic. It had another door leading to a separate room, where a young man lay on the bed. A bullet had penetrated his shoulder.

"Bring me a box of band aids from there."

My friend pointed towards one of the metal boxes on a nearby shelf. He didn't give me a chance to ask, or hesitate. He was firm and didn't have any time to waste in preparing me for this job. He was preoccupied with treating the injury quickly, while I heard some moaning in the other room.

By the evening, there was no room left for the wounded. Many young men and women came to help. They were treating patients quickly, to transfer them to other houses. I felt exhausted, since I hadn't eaten anything the entire day, nor had a chance to rest. Soon, the woman came and led me to the clinic. Later I got to know that she was the doctor's wife and she was also a doctor. She prepared sandwiches, which we ate quickly while one of the injured, who had lost most of his leg, writhed in pain on the bed. The sheets were quickly growing red from his blood.

In the evening, I was shown how to clean and dress wounds and started helping the doctor more effectively. Then he let me tend some light wounds without his help. Suddenly, I remembered my grandmother and sisters. I had told them that I was going to explore the situation and come back quickly. Concerns attacked me rapidly. 'Oh my god! what has happened in my absence? No doubt they are extremely worried about me!' I had found myself in the middle of this madness and completely forgotten about them. I asked permission from the doctor to leave for an hour, to tell my family about my whereabouts. He agreed hesitantly, asking another to take my place.

The night had already fallen and darkness draped outside. I ran towards the house as fast as I could, while hearing the gunshots and missile strikes from all over Hama, or at least that's what I though at the time. I knocked on the door but no one answered. I knocked harder, screaming:

"Open the door, it's Ameen."

No one answered and the door didn't open. I climbed the tree and jumped over the fence, like I did when I was a kid, sneaking off to play in the neighborhood with the other kids. I entered the dark house and couldn't find anybody. I searched all the rooms, including the supply room but I couldn't find anyone.

I left quickly, fear and anxiety overwhelming me. My eyes searched for them in each doorway and street. All the houses looked empty, deserted and dark. I checked our neighbors' doors but it didn't look like there was anyone there. No one opened the door and I didn't hear any sounds. I leaned my back against one of our neighbor's fences, desperate, almost collapsing from fatigue and fear. Suddenly, a woman's shadow appeared, then quickly turned into a side street.

I called to her, so she stopped and turned around as she recognized my voice:

"Who, Ameen?" It was our neighbor Um Muhammed.

"Yes! I can't find my grandmother and my sisters at our house. Do you know where they are?"

"Everyone is in Abu Muhammad's house. In the basement, it is the safest shelter."

I ran to Abu Muhammad's house, to find half of our neighborhood crowded into the basement, as they read the Quran and yelled Allah-o Akbar, (God is Great) with each explosion.

My sisters and grandmother welcomed me, crying. They were worried, despite the fact that they knew where I was. After I had left that morning, my grandmother went to the mosque, where al-Sheikh informed her about where I'd gone. I spent some time with them, telling them about what had happened. Time passed quickly. It was past midnight and my sisters begged me to sleep a little, before going back to the clinic. Truthfully, I was exhausted, especially since I hadn't slept the night before. I lay in the section designated for men, to rest for a little while, thinking to leave without my sisters and grandmother noticing me but I didn't wake up until the Morning Prayer. I prayed and left quickly, without any of my family seeing me.

The street was empty except for some men coming back from the battle, having handed over their weapons to those who took their place on the front line. I passed by the mosque and couldn't find al-Sheikh. I started walking towards the clinic, where I found a group of the neighborhood's young men, pushing another man violently in front of them. He had a blood-spattered face and one side of it was dripping red. It looked like he had received a deep knife wound in his left cheek. One of the men pushed him violently, so he collapsed to the ground, trembling.

"Take him to the mosque." The voice of al-Sheikh came from the nearby house. So, one of them helped him stand up and pushed him violently forward. I was told that he was an informer they'd caught from the neighborhood.

I entered the clinic. It was filled with the wounded, who were moaning from pain. The doctor and his wife were working as hard as they could to treat them, while blood ran everywhere. Some of the brothers and sisters were helping them. The doctor didn't notice my presence, so I stood waiting for his orders to help.

"We don't have any more cotton dressings. We need dressings and bandages, quickly!" Screamed one of the helpers.

The doctor's wife turned to me and said, "Do you know Abu Latif's house?"

"Yes," I answered quickly.

"Run there and bring us some dressings and bandages."

I left swiftly. I started running down the alleyways, towards the house at the edge of the neighborhood. The battle started to intensify, reaching areas near to me, forcing me to stop and hide at times. It looked to me like I was directly amidst the battle. I had almost arrived at the house, when one of the neighborhood men stopped me. He was armed with a small gun and a big kitchen knife. I informed him of my mission. He told me that the house was located near an ambush and that it was a very dangerous area. I insisted on reaching it and bringing the requested items. He pointed to a side door at the edge of the alley, telling me to approach it carefully, to be wary of the sudden missiles and bullets.

I approached it, shielding myself in doorways. No missiles fell or bullets passed close by. The battle was happening just behind that house. It had a wide-open metal door leading directly towards the inside. I yelled at the door, warning of my entrance, so his Harem could hide.

"Yallah, yallah," his voice yelled form inside. "Come in, there's no Harem, what do you want?"

His voice mixed with the sound of gunfire as some shots were fired from the upper floor of his house. I told him what I needed and he gave me a big bag. I took it and left quickly, weighed down from carrying it.

"Tell them this is the last bag we have." His voice followed me outside.

I ran down the long alley, until I fell to the ground from the impact of a nearby missile. I felt as if the earth quaked around me and the dust scattered everywhere. More missile strikes followed, so I started running as hard as I could, carrying that heavy bag on my shoulder. I fell once again, as a missile exploded behind me in a nearby house. I felt my nose begin to bleed and an extreme headache instantly erupted. Two men ran to carry me into a basement, in a nearby house. There, they treated me quickly, since my injuries were minor, just some bruises. They didn't let me leave because the bombing had become more ferocious everywhere. When the bombing calmed down they let me leave, giving me some advice about how to walk around and to hide.

I arrived at the clinic around noon, where I delivered the bag and prayed. I relaxed a little, before joining the doctor in the clinic. The work was hard and painful when I saw the sons of my neighborhood, injured or dead. We couldn't rescue many of the severely wounded. We could only treat some of the minor wounds. For those with fatal injuries, all we could do, which was some consolation, was to relieve their pain with injections or pills.

A couple of days passed and we were still in a siege. Only a few of the residents were able to escape to other, safer neighborhoods, while the defenders' willpower started running out. It was obvious that the army followed the Scorched Earth Strategy. The house that shot bullets got destroyed. The Brotherhood decided that the only chance they had, was to withdraw. Some withdrew to some nearby neighborhoods to join the opposition there, while some sneaked to the al-Hader district, where the resistance was more severe and effective.

I decided to go with them, as the Brotherhood advised. For there would be no mercy for anyone like me, that had joined in al-Jihad against the army or Security Forces. Therefore, I didn't have any other choice. The decision was to sneak out at dawn, under the cover of darkness, when the soldiers were exhausted. I said goodbye to my sisters and grandmother, who prayed aloud for me, while my sisters cried. I have only visited them once or twice since, as it wasn't possible to move a lot. Nor did I have time, because the work was day and night, nonstop. We would sleep for some hours in the day and eat our food quickly. For the first time, I skipped a prayer.

At two in the morning we sneaked towards the Al Dabagha neighborhood. We moved from alley to alley and from street to street, through the houses. The fighting was still severe in the area near the castle, in addition to the al-Hader district. Some of the Brothers remained in the al-Dabagha neighborhood, while we kept on walking towards the al-Barodia area. The next day dawned as the bombing and fighting intensified.

We had to cross Saed al-Kas Street, which was occupied by the Regime Forces. We paused a while in a burnt out building, watching the street and the surrounding areas. There was complete silence dominating the place. Some brothers decided to start crossing the street but as soon as they reached the middle, bullets started pouring down from a nearby building.

"Ambush!" Screamed Mulham, as he collapsed on the floor with a bullet in the chest.

Two martyrs fell immediately and a third was injured. Two of the Brothers near me, started shooting towards the fire source, aimlessly, unable to see it clearly. However, the severity of their fire was enough to protect what was left of the Brothers, as they made it across the street. The injured Brother was moaning from pain. Some Brothers ran towards him. The fire blanketed both sides of the street but they were able to drag the injured man with them. Luckily, it seemed a new outbreak of fire started elsewhere and drew the ambush away. So, we were able to cross the street together with no more injuries.

It was only moments until some stationed Brothers appeared, to lead us through the alleys, towards al-Barodia. I was the only one that didn't carry a rifle, so they gave me one. I had received some experience with guns at school but I had never been in a battle. No one asked me how old I was, or if I knew how to fight. There was no time for that.

We slept that night in a basement, for a couple of hours before the bombing intensified and woke us all up. Soon, one of the Brothers came to explain to us the situation of the battle. He told us the happy news about the triumphs of the Brotherhood, over all of the fronts. How we had made the army pay dearly with great losses in both men and equipment. Then some Jihadists joined us, to tell us about their combat actions. What mostly remained in my memory were the first days of the Insurrection, when some informers, Security Men, and Alawites were arrested and killed, in revenge for our brothers. The meeting celebrated the beheading of some dirty informers, in application of the Islamic ruling. This was the news that increased our determination to resist, until the rest of the cities blew up and we became more powerful.

In the evening, everyone got distributed across the fronts, while I was chosen as an assistant to the Liaison Officer, between the fronts. Our mission was very dangerous, since we had to cross the occupied areas to deliver the messages and news to other fronts, from the command center. I was happy to do so, I would be able to visit all the neighborhoods in addition to mine, al-Shajara and I thought to visit my family there. That didn't happen. Instead, we received news that the authorities had entered the al-Suq district and committed massacres. They killed many from my neighborhood and destroyed many of their houses.. Thus, I lost connection with my family. The news would come from here and there that they were still strongly resisting, confident that patience would bring victory and we were patient.

We would proceed in darkness, most of the time, from one neighborhood to another. Through the open windows of the adjacent Arab houses, trying to avoid the streets and the alleys, as much as we could. Abu Osman was a young man in his twenties, he'd memorized the pathways, the entrances and exits like the back of his hand. He knew the locations of the Mujahedeen and the infidels. He was confident of his steps, always smiling, even in the moments when we were surrounded and almost perished. The smile remained on his face, full of life, as if he was living in another world, an eternal dreamlike world. I would feel confident and strong accompanying him. I wouldn't ever hesitate following him, on any mission. We would cross the dangerous neighborhoods, only for the bombing to intensify and the explosions and flames to fire up, all around us.

The bombing became more brutal during the last week. The army began to tighten the siege. They were able to control all the al-Souq neighborhoods. The only thing that remained in al-Hader, was al-Baroudia and a few of the small neighborhoods, isolated under the heavy bombardment. We were in an advanced mission in the Kilanyia neighborhood, trying to reach the Brothers that were stuck there. Then, whilst we were hiding in a house, waiting for a chance to cross the street, a shell fell directly on our refuge. I passed out. When I woke up, I found myself injured in the head and leg, while my forehead bled. The building had been destroyed completely. I was crammed under a cement ceiling. I looked around, trying to see Abu Osman but couldn't find him. I wrapped my head with a piece of my ripped shirt, then inspected my leg. The wound wasn't deep, so I tried to move it, slowly. It was hurting me but I could still move it. However, I wasn't certain I could use it to walk. I crawled with difficulty, trying to extricate my body from the ceiling, in the narrow space that was left. I crossed over a couple of unknown legs, until I saw Abu Osman's leg under the wreckage. I called to him quietly but he didn't answer. He had surrendered his soul to death. I crawled upward to the top of the rubble, while the bombing and gunshots remained deafening. I heard noises outside, so I listened attentively. The military were outside, cussing and yelling, so I froze in my place without moving.

I spent the entire day without movement, until darkness fell and I couldn't hear any nearby noises outside. I began to crawl with great difficulty, as my shirt ripped and my pants became mixed with blood, soil, rocks, and cement. Nevertheless, I slowly kept wriggling my way, until I reached the outside where I could overlook the nearby street. The buildings were destroyed. One of the soldier's shadows loomed behind several tanks, about 100 feet away. I froze in my place, watching the street and nearby areas. An hour passed before I decided to take my chance to escape, before they woke up. I had to cross the street and sneak into the alleys and destroyed buildings.

Immediately I put my head out, I found myself surrounded by vehicles and tanks. I hid my head quickly, slithering back under the rubble as I heard footsteps approaching me. Soon the street roared with soldier's movements, weapons and the rumbling of tanks. Minutes passed before the bombing flares started everywhere. I crawled around trying to explore the area; with difficulty, because the dawn light leaking through the cracks in the rubble, was weak. I could barely see but my eyes started adjusting. I was hungry and thirsty, trying to find anything I could eat or drink. I dug some rocks and dirt with my hands, hoping to escape to another place, or another room where I could find some food and water. After hours of work, I was able to enter the remains of a bedroom. In one of its corners was a child's leg, detached from its body. A cement wall had fallen on top of it. I called and screamed, trying to see if she was still alive behind the wall but the silence of death was filling the place. I studied the leg. It belonged to a girl, because it wore a feminine shoe. I buried the leg in between the rocks and dirt and continued looking for food and water.

In the bedroom, there were only women's clothes and it didn't look like there was any pathway towards the kitchen, or any other water source. I dug a lot, until my eyes got tired and I fell into a deep sleep. When I woke up, the bombing had calmed down a little and darkness had fallen again outside. My thirst was severe, burning my lips. I crawled carefully, to where I could see the street, thinking that maybe they had left. Maybe, now I could find a chance to sneak out but everything was still where it was. I heard some soldiers laughing near the tanks. I stayed in my hole, listening for any noise, watching for any shadow moving in the area. I remained there until the morning dawned and the movement started. Then, I crawled deeper inside, hiding form sight once again. I found refuge in praying and reciting the Quran silently.

That helped me to bear the thirst and hunger and I could even sleep a little.

In the evening, when the darkness fell I began to shiver, so I started looking for something to wear, to protect me from the harsh cold. I found some light women's clothing, so I wore two shirts over each other, while I ripped another shirt to bandage my wounds. My pants were completely ripped, so I started looking for a pair that fit me. All I could find were Jellabiyas and women's dresses. I squeezed myself into one of the Jellabiyas; now I felt warm. I heard sounds outside, emboldened, I crawled to explore what was happening. There were a few corpses thrown atop a destroyed building, near another nearby street. I guessed they had been executed while I was sleeping inside, since I didn't remember hearing nearby gunshots. There were about ten corpses piled upon each other and there was blood splattered over the wall and street. I heard some soldiers cussing and complaining about having to stay near those corpses with their wafting smell, thus they requested moving them, or transferring their deployment.

I spent the night waiting for any chance to sneak out but it was impossible. No doubt I would get killed, just by leaving my hiding place. The thirst became unbearable, the hunger acute and I could barely move. At dawn I struggled to wriggle back inside, where I lay down, half asleep. I'd pray and recite the Quran, in a whisper between my cracked lips. My imagination would wander sometimes, towards my neighborhood and its markets filled with food. I would stop at the delicious candy shops and an intense feeling of thirst would sweep over me. I would stop at a nearby juice shop, to soak up a big glass of orange juice. I remember my grandmother in Ramadan, with her delicious food after a full day of fasting. I could not forget the licorice root juice. I smiled by force as I remembered my sister Mona, how sometimes she hid some pieces of the dessert I loved.

Though sleep came over me suddenly, my thirst was constant, burning my insides and inflaming my lips.

I awoke and explored what was happening outside again. Some soldiers were eating near a tank. My hunger and thirst deepened but the corpses and the bombing noises, brought me back to reality. 'They won't have mercy on me. They will make me an example and torture me to death.' I felt extremely tired and sleep came over me again. I woke up startled, with urine wetting my face. One of the soldiers was peeing on my face, not noticing me but my startled movement warned him of my presence. He pointed his rifle at me as he stopped urinating. There was fear in his eyes and I think he almost shot me. I felt I was dead for sure. He was looking into my eyes, screwed into his place, motionless. I was unable to move, so I shut my eyes waiting for the death blow. Nothing happened. He squatted in front of me, as he studied me, silently. He didn't show any expression. His face had no features. One of his friends' called to him to come and eat. So, he got up hesitantly, turned around and calmly returned to his tank.

I closed my eyes, surrendering to God's will and started reciting Al-Shahada*. I was desperate, hungry and thirsty. Al-Shahada, was something I craved. I watched the guard leave quietly, to join the dining table with his friends. Many thoughts attacked me. 'Is he going to come back with his friends to kill me? Why didn't he kill me then and there? Or, is he waiting for the time to amuse himself with killing me and avenging his friends?' I heard him talking with his clear, coastal, Alawite dialect. 'He will kill me no doubt but he will torture me before that and his friends will share his victory.' I couldn't do anything, so I stayed in my place without moving. I could hear their laughter and their dirty jokes. I guessed they were from the Defense Companies or Special Units, because of their camouflage military outfits. The twilight was upon us when I watched him approach me, his rifle hanging from his shoulder. He stood directly in front of me, pretending to urinate. Then, he bent down carefully, opened up his jacket to drop a small bag and a flask of water by my side. He smiled at me as he looked over my body to check my wounds, then he turned around and left.

I took the bag and the water flask with extreme caution. The water flask was full, so I drank from it quickly and life came back to me. I drank a few more doses before going back inside, pushing the small nylon bag in front of me. Inside it I found a loaf of bread, a couple of pieces of cheese and two tomatoes. I devoured everything in a flash of light. I drank a little more water after that and my fears calmed down. I thanked Allah, prostrating myself.

I slept all night, even the constant bombing and gunfire couldn't wake me. Actually, my ears had gotten used to it, for the only thing that woke me up was when it stopped. I didn't know the exact time but the dim light from outside, told me it was during the day. I was still thirsty but I decided to ration the water, until I figured out what was going to happen. I felt strength returning to my body. I began digging with a big spoon I'd found between the ruins, along with some scrap iron shapes. I looked in each corner, searching for an opening to lead me to a safe exit but it was all blocked with heavy piles of rubble, from the destroyed houses. The day passed quickly and night fell. I climbed to the top of the rubble to explore the place. The tanks had disappeared and the only things that remained in their place were two tents and a couple of military vehicles. It seemed to me that the battle had calmed down a little. I remained there until the morning and then I went back inside the destroyed bedroom. Then, after I spread some clothes I'd found to use as a mattress, I went to sleep.

I woke to al-Takbeer, (The verbal glorification of Allah)

'Allah-o Akbar, Allah-o Akbar!' mixed with the sound of gunfire. I couldn't resist my curiosity, so I crawled from my hidden nest, to explore what was happening outside. There was a group of men, raked with bullets, twisting in their blood while three of the young soldiers were hitting them with iron bars. They writhed in pain as their bones were smashed and blood splattered everywhere. An officer approached one of them angrily and started cussing and kicking him, then he commanded the soldiers to tie him by one foot with an iron chain, to a military truck. The other foot got tied to the electricity pole and the truck moved forward, ripping him into two pieces. His dying scream rose to the sky. Two tanks crushed the other young men's heads. I crawled back inside. These scenes shocked me, while some soldiers laughed as they shot some bullets into the sky. I rolled myself like a ball in my nest, reciting some verses from the Quran. Also, reciting al-Takbeer, every now and then. I drank some water and took a nap.

When I woke up, the night had closed its eyelids. I crawled to the outside with a severe headache. I found a small nylon bag and a big plastic water-bottle that my soldier friend had left for me. I took them carefully to my hiding place and drank a little as I studied the street, empty except for some military vehicles. They had cleared the street of the corpses but traces of blood remained. Soon, movement started in the street. Some tanks, accompanied by soldiers, were approaching from the direction of al-Barudia. It was only moments until the bombing and gunshots started again. I waited patiently in my hidey-hole, watching. My leg wound started hurting me. I couldn't check on it but it looked like it had become swollen and infected. I went back inside, looking for a clean piece of fabric but the darkness was grim and I couldn't see anything. I depended on my senses to feel for a suitable piece of clothing. I located something that seemed to me like underwear. I ripped it into several pieces, then wetted one of them with some water and started cleaning my leg wound, gently.

Suddenly, fumbling sounds came from behind the ruins, I froze. Something made of iron struck the ground. I listened attentively, in the direction of the sounds but I didn't hear anything else. I waited a long while, barely breathing, before I started hearing muted crying. It stopped abruptly. Then I called with a quiet voice:

"Is there anyone there?" Silence, so I called with a louder voice:

"Is there anybody out there?" I called a couple of times but with no answer. I insisted:

"I'm just like you, stuck here. Don't be scared, we are safe. They think everyone here is dead."

The sound of a muffled cry, came from behind the ruins. I started digging, slowly removing the rubble from my side. There was a lot of it and some stones and broken pieces of concrete were too heavy to move. So, I resorted to winding routes, where the ruins were smaller and contained lots of dirt. Yet, I wasn't sure if I was digging in the right direction. I was behind the ruins on the other side. I called and asked them to dig towards me. They didn't answer in the beginning but after I insisted, I started hearing rumbling sounds on the other side. Although I couldn't tell if they were a boy or girl, this helped me to identify the right direction to dig. We worked for hours, until my hand could go through to the other side. Then the dawn started sending its dim shafts of light, into the place.

"Are you alright?" I said, my hand looking for the other person's hand.

"Yes," she replied, with her childish voice as she touched my hand.

"What's your name?"

"Nana," she said, hesitantly.

I had to calm her down in the beginning and get to know her while we rested. Gently, I started talking to her, asking questions.

She was a five-year-old girl. She was in the bathroom when the house exploded. She collapsed in between the ruins. The small bathroom doors had protected her. She was stuck in the bathroom for a while, until she'd been able to sneak to the destroyed kitchen and use the remainders of the food to stay alive. Her two sisters, her older brother and mother had passed away. Her mother's corpse was in the kitchen with her but she couldn't see the rest of her family, since they were in their bedrooms. She was in a state of shock and horror, talking helped calm her down and reassured her.

"'I'm very thirsty,' she said with a shy voice.

I hurried to the water bottle immediately, trying to push it through the small gap to reach her. It didn't fit, the gap was still too narrow. So, I started to dig, to widen it until I could pass the water to her. She drank a lot but I didn't stop her, despite my severe need to save water. When she gave the bottle back, she had drunk about half of it. I went back to widening the gap, in order to reach the girl. The work was hard and I made little progress. We talked for a while, then I decided to sleep and so did she.

I slept for a while, then I went back to working on the gap between us. I estimated that she was a small girl and would be able to escape through a relatively small hole. By the evening, I had accomplished a lot and we were able to see each other. I smiled at her and she smiled back. She was a little girl with short black hair, covered with dust and dirt. I wiped her face, which was caked with dust and traces of tears. At a late hour of the night, I decided to crawl to my hiding space that overlooked the outside. A large military vehicle had stopped in front of the hiding place, making it impossible to see. I just heard some voices mixed with gunshots. I didn't find anything my soldier friend may have left for me so, I crawled back down inside. Nana was still sleeping and I didn't want to wake her. Praying and reciting the Quran was my only amusement. I slept for a while, only to wake up in the morning to Nana's voice. The explosions, happening close by were scaring her. I calmed her down, reassuring her that it was safe where we were, so long as we stayed calm and quiet. Otherwise we may be discovered.

I gave her some water to drink and she brought me three apples, I ate one of them. Then I found some large kitchen tools that helped me to widen the opening between us. In the evening, I tried dragging her to my room but the hole still wasn't wide enough to pull her through. I checked again but nothing new had been delivered, from my soldier friend. That evening I watched the street, so maybe I could hear news, or see him. Perhaps he had been killed in the intense fighting.

There was only a little bit of water left and I was extremely thirsty. I asked Nana to look for a water source but she couldn't find anything. We drank what was left of the water in two doses, that day. The next day she found a half-full soda bottle which had been opened for a long time. It tasted bad but I estimated that we could depend on it to stay alive, until God relieved us. The sugar in it only increased our thirst. A day had passed since the bombing and explosions had calmed down outside. That morning, I was able to get her out through the hole in the wall. She laughed at my clothes:

"Just like girls!" She said, laughing through what remained of her teeth: "This is the Jellabiya that belonged to Nuha."

I was wearing her older sister's Jellabiya. I didn't think about it before. We laughed together and ate a little bit from what we had. I heard voices and chants outside, so I crawled form our hiding place to explore what was happening.

They were shouting their dirty cusses at a group of protesting women, along with humiliating, mocking commands. At the front of the group there were two women with head-scarves. They were being forced to dance, amidst the dirty sexual comments of the soldiers, while one woman started singing to Hafez al-Assad, her tears pouring down her cheeks. The scene was painful and sad. Then, in that moment I saw this was our chance to survive. I crawled back inside quickly to put on a colored head-scarf. I smiled at Nana saying:

"Yes, now I'm a girl, good?"

She smiled as she nodded her head, in agreement.

She followed me towards the gap overlooking the street, where the front of the protest group crossed by us. We were almost in the middle of it. I peered around, exploring the area close by. I didn't find any soldiers nearby. So, holding on to Nana we went out quickly, to join the protest. Some women and children saw us, so they made space for us to enter into the middle, away from eyesight. Then, a woman pulled me near her, to make me join her family in the middle of the crowd. I walked with difficulty, my leg hurt severely but I endured it, chanting the slogans with the women and children.

We crossed the streets and the neighborhood, towards Halab's street. We walked for a long while, amidst the mockery and cusses. Nana held my hand tightly as she repeated the slogans with the group, until a crowd of people welcomed us. They were waiting for us from behind the military border. Most of them were from the surrounding countryside of Hama city. They were trying to find any news about their relatives and friends. Some of them found what they needed, while others found nothing. No one noticed Nana and me, except the woman that hid us between her children.

She took us to where some relatives were waiting for her. We sat down between a group of women and children, in the back of an old truck, which drove to one of the villages.

I stayed there for a couple of days until my leg was almost healed. Then, after the fighting stopped and the military and Security Services controlled the entire city, I sought news of my family. The news came quickly. Massacres were everywhere. Corpses were being transported by truck. In the al-Shajara neighborhood, it was said that they had committed a large massacre of men and boys. There was talk about them raping and killing women sometimes. I was told about the work of informers, who helped the security forces, by telling them about who'd joined the rebellion. The rebels were sought out and either killed immediately, sometimes on their doorsteps, or tortured before killing them.

I didn't dare to go back to my neighborhood. One of the women went to check on her house in one of the nearby neighborhoods. She visited our house, only to find it mostly destroyed. She couldn't find a trace of my family. She was told that they were led away somewhere and none of them had returned yet. Someone suggested visiting Sarehen trench, where thousands were killed and buried.

We went with a group of women and children, to the nearby Sarehen village trench that had been recently covered over. There were a large number of families there, desperately looking for the remains, or any trace of their missing loved ones. We knew one of them, who found a trace of her family. We heard the screaming and wailing that accompanied her, as others gathered to console her. As for us, we inspected whatever we found but with no success. We looked in the dirt, hoping to find something but not deep inside the trench. No one really wanted to find those missing.

Without proof, there remained the huge hope that our families were still alive, somewhere.

After a week or more, someone came to tell us that he saw my grandmother in the city of al-Salamya. I was very happy with the news, so I said goodbye to everybody, thanking all of them for their care. I begged them to take care of Nana, until she found someone from her family. I took a bus going towards the city of al-Salamya. I was full of excitement, hoping soon to see my sisters and grandmother. However, right before entering the city of al-Salamya, we got stopped by the security checkpoint. I got arrested because they suspected my name, then they received information that I had joined the rebellion.

I couldn't survive for long under the severe torture, first in Hama, then in Damascus. There I confessed everything and after, they led me here.

***

---

*__Em Muhamed:__ (mother of Muhamed) Em = mother. Traditional Arabic way to call the mature person.*

*__** Al-Shahada:__ Muslim Declaration of Faith.*

# 10 SAFAR BARLIK *

At a time between the seventeenth and eighteenth centuries, the Syrian coastal mountains were packed with Alawites who had survived the Sultan Saleem massacres. They had a meager existence. Scattered in those mountains and deep valleys, sowing the few cultivatable areas and growing just enough to keep themselves alive. The harsh landscape and dense forests, gave protection from those that stalked them. Those hunters, who in the name of religion, sought human prey. The blood of the Alawite would be wasted wherever he was found, along with the rest of his family, including his children. His repentance would not be accepted, no matter the pleading. No mercy would be shown.

*

My maternal great grandfather, would always start conversations with his peers that were mixed with images of heroism, massacres, fear and lots of injustice. The stories which told of battles, heroism and escaping, were scattered over hundreds of years. Memories passed down from generation to generation, becoming myths mingled with Alawite Doctrine. These stories would be recited at the edge of the small village, where the ruins of the older village began. There, they would recall the stories their predecessors had told them, about the huge battles to kick out the occupying force of Turks and Ottomans. The remains of the old village seemed as if it was abandoned, or destroyed tens of years ago.

The ancestors recited how, when the cold and hunger intensified in the high mountains and there was nothing to stop their children's hunger, they started attacking these Turkish villages, to steal their crops and livestock. Overtaken by hunger, these men had turned into predatory monsters. They would go at night, in huge numbers to the small isolated and defenseless villages, to take what they needed for survival. Once they obtained what they needed, they would escape into their mountains and harsh thickets. Not many of the villagers dared follow, unless they were accompanied by a large military force.

These attacks continued for tens of years and resulted in the destroying and abandoning of most of the Turkish villages. My mother's village was a result of these wars. A group of the Brother's in the mountains emigrated to this village after its family abandoned it. The houses had been destroyed but its lands were still fertile and a big part of it was cultivatable. Those Brothers were ones that had lived in caves. They had ambushed travelers and traders moving on the roads, between the villages, taking what they needed. When there were no more villagers to ambush, they decided to settle down in this abandoned village.

My great, great grandfather and his brothers were feeling powerful and proud of their ancestors. When they recited these tales of the brothers, they amplified their strength and manhood, especially that of their first grandfather. He was one of those brothers who had defeated the Turks and then resided in this village. They were once free, with no one's authority over them but in settling down, they lost their freedom. They were at the mercy of the Ottoman State, which soon started organizing the villages, assigning mayors that did the authorities bidding.

The villagers didn't know what was happening in the outside world. They were living in their small worlds with some neighboring villages; planting, rearing cattle, exchanging their produce and marrying each other, without realizing what was happening beyond that world. Then, one day they were shocked to find Turkish soldiers surrounding the village, while the mayor welcomed their leader. The mayor told the men of the village to gather, whilst the Turkish Captain addressed them. He informed them that the Sultanate was leading a war on the infidels and that they had to help the war, by Pasha order.

When the villagers realized the situation, the soldiers had already confiscated lots of the cattle and seeds, while they led some of the young men of the village, into military service. They had heard of some young men being led into military service, from distant villages but it hadn't happened to them before. The men said their goodbyes to their children with extreme sadness, while the women sobbed, afraid they might never see them again. My great grandfather was working in his field when that happened, so he was able to escape from them with the rest of his brothers. They hid in the nearby forest, until someone came to inform them of the soldiers' departure. They returned to their houses to find them empty of food and the few cattle they owned. They mobilized all their effort to face the disaster, since winter was knocking on the door and now they didn't have what they needed, to prepare for it. They started planting some of the late season greens and picking what fruits they had to dry them, especially figs and grapes. The winter passed harshly. They cooperated to gather the edible wild herbs, whilst they fed their kids what remained of barley bread and goats milk.

The spring had come and the land grew green anew. My great, great grandfather admired his small field happily. He planted it with grains and Chickpeas, with what was left from the seeds he'd saved from last year.

"It is going to be a good season this year."

He thanked god for his grace as he addressed his oldest son, my great grandfather. At noon, while my great grandfather was working to organize one of the new mountain fields he intended to plant, he felt a bug falling on his face. He wiped it away with his hand, carelessly, as he would any other spring bug. Soon, he saw another one falling near him, then another and another. He examined it since its shape was strange and unfamiliar. He called his father to look at it. His father held one of them, examining it while many others fell around them. Immediately his face scowled as he looked to the sky saying:

"Locusts!"

My great grandfather didn't know what to do as he saw swarms of locusts coming from the west. Brown clouds touched with redness, covering the horizon.

My great grandfather had heard the stories of locusts, he knew that it was a huge disaster but he hadn't dealt with it before. He looked at his father, questioning what could be done to face this pandemic but my great, great grandfather's grim face, filled with a gaze of despair, warned him of the greatness of the disaster.

"What do we do?" My great grandfather said mutely.

"Let's hurry up to the house; there is no hope for us here."

He called the rest of his brothers and they hurried to the house, as they watched the locust swarms darkening the horizon. There was nothing they could do. They had to protect their stored supplies in the house and get ready to fight the locusts, with the rest of the village.

They gathered some grass for the cattle, before the locusts came and ate everything green. They stored it in their houses, blocking the windows and doors. In the next few days they fought the locusts by killing their eggs and young ones, before they could reproduce again. It was a daily struggle with the locusts and the entire village cooperated to face this scourge. No one escaped this destruction. It destroyed most of their fields and made them miss their growing season entirely. However, the locusts became food. They became the daily meal that with a little creative cooking, was turned into a delicious one.

No one showed them mercy after the locust disaster. The Ottoman soldiers remained moving through the villages, taking what they found. During these times, the head of the clan didn't get his share of grains but the religious men didn't stop asking for theirs. They would cry angrily and curse to the moon. The mayor was the only one trying to ease their burden, for he was a Turk living amongst them. He knew that there was nothing left to give him, for the summer was harsh that year. Only a few trees survived and there were no fruits left to store. Hunger stung everyone. When the winter came, they didn't find anything to eat but some herbs, some bugs, birds and maybe some wild animals for those who were lucky and strong enough to catch them. For those who were weak, their fate was to die from hunger in the wilderness.

**

My maternal great grandfather was sowing barley, when he heard screams and dogs barking. Alarmed, he looked towards the village. His land was on a plateau, overlooking his nearby village but he couldn't recognize the voices, or see what was happening. He took his scythe and started walking towards the village, carefully. Something dangerous was happening in the village. His father who worked on the other side of the fields, called to him, cautioning him to stay in the field. He ignored him and continued towards the village to explore the situation, while his brothers obeyed their father's order and stayed.

He was a strong young man in the prime of his life, full of potency; he would always beat the village's young men in the arm wrestling games and weight lifting. The weights were made from rocks and a single drum roller from a caterpillar. It looked to him like a fight was happening in the village, so he decided to investigate further. Maybe he could stop the fight and solve the problem. Or, maybe he would join the fight if one of his relatives or friends were in trouble, for he was proud of his strength and no one dared to fight him.

The small village consisted of few clay houses. It was located on a plateau between two valleys that dropped down from it.. As soon as he entered the village on the dirt road that ran between its houses, a group of Turkish soldiers surrounded him and caught him. He tried to pretend he didn't know what was happening but a quick whip from the captain's lash, sitting on his horse, made him fall to the ground from pain. Soon, the mayor came to inform him that they were drafting men into the military. They rounded up a group of the village's young men; the soldiers surrounded them from each side of the mayor's courtyards, while the families gathered outside crying and wailing.

None of those who had left to go to the war had returned. They didn't know what was happening beyond their village, except what they heard in passing. The villagers knew little of the war, only that it was still happening. Sometimes they heard whispers about the horrors faced by some of those who were able to escape and hide in the nearby forests.

In the morning the draftees were lead to Masyaf city. Their families accompanied them on foot for a while. After a couple of hours they cried, saying their final goodbyes, before returning and handing their situation to god. By the time the men arrived at Masyaf, they were very hungry and thirsty. So, they received some food and drinks while they fell asleep in the open. Meanwhile, young men were gathered from all the villages around. Together they were lead, on foot, to Aleppo. They walked for a couple of days with no food or drink, until the thirst and hunger almost killed them. So, the officer demanded they stop in one of the villages. There they confiscated what they could from the villagers' meager stocks. Their circumstances were a little better than the villages they passed through. Hunger kills the weak, so the roads bristled with dead women and children who had no one to bury them. One of the soldiers told of a starving, six year old child he'd met. Haunted by his mother and siblings who had already died from starvation. The officer, preferring the child to die quickly, didn't allow anyone to feed him, so inevitably he joined his family. The death and hunger was spreading everywhere; villagers in their ripped clothes, taut faces with sunken eyes were lying everywhere, awaiting death.

In Aleppo they received a quick basic training for a couple of days, then they continued walking to Turkey. They didn't know where they were being led. Thousands of men, led to a war they that didn't know where it was located and who it was against. They didn't hold any weapons yet, for they were more like prisoners than soldiers in the Turkish Military. They marched along the wild road, through the Turkish mountains and valleys. Hunger and illness fatigued and killed some of them along the way.

Somewhere near a plateau, where the fighting fired up, they gave them weapons and led them towards where the Bulgarians attacked. They killed lots of Bulgarians but couldn't gain any territory. The Bulgarians counterattacked and scored a victory over the Turks. That is how they remained for a couple of months, the battle moving back and forth. In between fighting, running and hiding, they would lose many of their friends. The hunger eroded them, there was not enough food and not enough clothes to protect them from the cold. Everyone was waiting for someone to die, so they could take his clothes, or his shoes. Sometimes they would take the clothes from the injured, before throwing him to death. There was no chance to heal the injured, especially those who weren't Turks.

Until then, Safi hadn't got injured in the battles he'd fought. He was lucky but death was coming, inevitably. Most of those who were with him were dead, imprisoned or injured. He was sure that it was just a matter of time, before a bullet or a cannon missile killed him. Safi was a believer, a man who believed in fate and the intercessions of the saints. He vowed in the beginning, to the Prophet Saleh's shrine on the top of the mountain overlooking his village; promising to slay a sheep for him and distribute it among the poor, if the prophet would save him from this disaster and return him to his family. The prophet didn't hear his pleads and Safi didn't slay the sheep for him. So, instead he turned towards all the other saints he knew, from near or far but to no avail, he remained surrounded by war every day.

In one of the rough battles that the enemy started, his brigade got surrounded on the mountaintop, cut off by shelling from all around. The situation was desperate but the leader of the brigade was stubborn and courageous. He decided not to surrender, ignoring the opinion of his many officers. The dead surrounded them. The injured lay screaming with no savior, it was impossible to rescue them. Safi was in his trench, blocking one attack after another, without sleep or rest. The smell of the rotting corpses became unbearable, while the moaning and screams of the wounded soldiers, weakened the ears and melted the hearts.

He suddenly remembered his family and his village. Wandering in its pathways and fields, remembering his childhood and youth that he spent dreaming of a beautiful future. It was one spring-time when he'd stopped in the valley leading to his field, where he'd found a small graveyard containing some old graves with no tombstones. They were shadowed by an oak forest that no one dared to cross because of its thickets. It was the village's Turkish graveyard, those Turks that his ancestors had killed. There were many legends and stories about these graves, so no one dared to abuse them. Over time, the graveyard gained an eeriness and an aura of holiness, which made everyone passing it appeal for help from Allah; requesting protection from evil or a misfortune when passing by. No one knew the names of those buried there, they were called Ajam, (foreigners) for they were from Turkey. Remembering this, a strange soul crept into him; he started praying and mentioning Allah.

When sleep embraced him, the battle on the plateau had relatively calmed down, or maybe his ears had gotten used to the war's uproar. Either way, he didn't care anymore about the monotonous noise of the artillery. He dreamt. In his dream, a great Sheikh came to him. He called himself Sheikh Muhamed al-Ajami, who told him that his grave was there amongst the graves in the valley. He said he knew him and would save him from the war, returning him to his family, safe. Safi woke abruptly from his nap, terrified as he inspected the plateau in front of him. His friends remained beside him. Soon he vowed in a loud voice, that he will build the Sheikh, Muhamed a shrine in the Turks graveyard, if he returned him to his village and home safely. Then he would turn to praying and pleading to him, secretly.

The siege continued for a couple of weeks, where it seemed that their destiny was death, just like those before them. They expected it every instant and with every artillery shot, or bullet. Miraculously, they escaped after the Ottoman military was able to start an attack on the enemies' position and open a gap, which they sneaked through.

Safi thanked Allah for his survival. Also, he, turned to the Sheikh Muhamed Ajami to pray and plead, certain that he was the one that saved them from inevitable death, thanks to his devotion and closeness to Allah. However, the promise was that he would go back to his village safely but he was still fighting a war. Later they transferred him to other battles, where it seemed as if they were losing the war and retreating. He found himself just like the many others from the Turkish military, escaping into the mountains with some men from Syria, Lebanon, Palestine and Iraq. They didn't know exactly what was happening. They only realized that they had lost the war and that their enemies were pursuing them. So, they turned their backs and fled, in fear of getting captured. They moved towards their villages and cities, inferring the direction from villagers that would instruct them to move south. Hunger and illness were impeding their path. They were eating what they found in nature, from fruits and grass. Sometimes they were able to hunt a wild animal. About two months had passed while they were retreating on foot. Some wore no shoes, so they tied pieces of fabric around their feet, trying to relieve the pain from the mountainous pathways.

When Safi arrived home in his village, no one knew him. His beard was long and dense, his sunken eyes were yellow and had lost their color. People had lost any hope of their return, presuming them dead. When Safi entered his house, his family didn't welcome him quickly. Some of them had to test him, by asking him some personal questions. Once he answered, the trilling in their house's started, announcing their huge joy at the return of their missing son.

The village's men, women and children would gather at night, over the Baydar, (Wheat threshing square) so he would tell them stories of his daily adventures in the First World War. Unfortunately, he couldn't inform them of what happened to his other friends from the village. He hadn't seen any of them die in front of him, for they were distributed amongst various sections and he hadn't see them after that. However, his return resurrected hope in some souls who had a relative in the war. Sadly, no one else returned.

Safi didn't forget his vow to the protector Sheikh, who saved him from death's clutches, who brought him back to his village and family safe and healthy. Only a few months passed, before he was able to gather some money and recover his strength, enough to build the shrine. The shrine was built to be the village's intercessor and protector, in addition to the rest of the other graves that were now also considered shrines. They would light some incense for them, recite prayers and make requests of intercession to heal the sick, or help the oppressed. This Safi was my great grandfather who wrote his name on the tomb's rocks as Allah inspired him to do so.

These shrines became like Makah for the believers. So, they built for them a living room with food in it, for saving the poor and the passersby.

***

---

*The First World War is remembered in Syria as **Safar Barlik,** which is an Ottoman term meaning mobilization in Turkish.*

# 11 THE ARREST

## MAY1980

I boarded a normal taxi from Beirut, where I sat in the front seat, between the driver and a young man in his late twenties. We engaged in conversation which led us, carefully, in the directions of International and Middle Eastern politics. Soon, we were deep into internal politics, cautiously criticizing the regime while ignoring the driver completely. In the back seat there were two women and a middle-aged man, exchanging light conversation. It seemed that the man was attracted to one of the women.

*

The five months I'd spent in Beirut hadn't been easy. I initially took refuge in a house belonging to a group of Lebanese friends. I started to share the apartment they rented but my money soon disappeared, despite help from some friends. Then, one of my friends got me a part-time job with one of the news agencies, to do some quick, simple editing work. To some extent, that job helped me to handle my living costs. However, the Security Services pursued me everywhere. The Syrian Military had complete control of the Western Region, including Beirut and Lebanon in general. Here, the Security Branches played a role that was even more ugly than the role it played in Syria. They made it extremely difficult to cross the Military Security checkpoints, especially the Mobile checkpoints, which surprised you on the road to the University, or on a visit to one of your friends. So, sometimes I had to avoid crossing the Security Square in the area surrounding the Arabic University. Instead, I had to find routes where there were no Syrian Military checkpoints.

Beirut had been split into two sections as a result of a grinding civil war: Eastern Beirut, where the Lebanese forces, led by Maronite Christian parties under the umbrella of the Phalanges Party, had practically displaced all the indigenous Muslims; and Western Beirut which included most of Lebanon and was controlled by the Syrian Military.

The Western Beirut Security Square was the headquarters for most of the military and political leaders of the Militias, Islamic and Leftist powers; alongside the militarily powerful Palestinian organizations. However, as a result of the diversity in these groups, this small region became an oasis for creative thinking and diverse ideologies. It formed a forum for debate, which was singularly lacking in all the Arabic countries. It became the refuge for most of the escapees from oppressive Regimes and Security Services that infested the region, not only in the Arabic countries. As a customer of a local coffee shop, managed by a Jewish lady in her forties, it didn't take long to realize that you lived in a haven from the balance of terror. You would hear whispers here and there, with some nods and winks to this and that person, indicating that he belongs to one of the Security Services. His importance lowered, or rose, depending on the Security Service he belonged to and the degree of his impact on the organizations there. He could either belong to the CIA, or to the Security Service of Mauritania and no doubt, Mauritania was the weakest of them.

The Palestinian Fatah movement was the strongest front and controlled almost everything. Its Security Services were recognized everywhere. Although you did not notice it in everyday life, the horror overwhelmed everyone when, for example, ( Troops 17*) got mentioned. However, no one would intrude on your political opinion. Freedom of speech was preserved. You could criticize whomsoever you liked and maybe, cuss out those you disliked from the leaders. No one held you accountable on that there. Unlike the other Regimes, such as Hafez al-Assad's, which held you accountable on your dreams.

The Eastern Region of Beirut was completely different. The Christian Lebanese Front was practically led by the Lebanese Phalanges Party, who tried to protect the rights of the Christian sect. Historically, the French mandate had separated the country in such a way that Christians were the majority sect. However, that Regime started narrowing one year after another, because the Islamic nature encouraged reproduction in a way that the Maronite sect wouldn't. Eventually, an accumulation of economic and sectarian conflicts built up, until a crazy civil war flared up. Soon after, the Syrian Regime intruded in the civil war with symbolic powers from the other Arabic countries. These other powers soon withdrew, leaving the Syrian powers in control of most of Lebanese political life.

Beirut, at sunset would fall asleep relaxing at the feet of the ocean's waves as they broke on its rocky beach. I would enjoy watching the sunset, meditating the distant horizons that would escape far away. I wouldn't risk entering the depths of the city at night, for the danger was increasing and we had to be careful. However, during the day I was able to wander around on Hamra Street and sit in some of its cafes.

People walking around Hamra Street during the day, were different than those that walked around at night. At night that district changed to a red color; this color that in my mind is associated with pornography and ladies of the night.

*

The taxi had just crossed Sawfar City, climbing the mountainous pathway towards Deher Al Baydar, when the driver said:

"A Security checkpoint, get your identification cards ready and the red cards."

The red card was the six months temporary residency card, which the Lebanese Immigration Department gave to a Syrian, coming to Lebanon. Although no one from the Lebanese Security Services verifies it afterwards, the Syrian Military Security checkpoints wanted to see it to verify your legal entrance to Lebanon.

The taxi entered a narrow winding lane, which forced the cars to slow down and ended at a sandy Security checkpoint. Here, soldiers verified identification cards and other documents, searching for wanted people from all nationalities. The driver greeted the soldiers there, smiling and it was obvious that they knew him very well.

The sergeant looked through the window near me:

"Identification Cards."

And then speaking to the driver as he verified the identification cards quickly:

"There is nothing for us today?"

"I'm sorry; I didn't have time in the morning. Hopefully the next trip from Beirut if God is willing, this afternoon." The driver answered, smiling.

"My shift ends this afternoon."

"Don't worry; I will leave it at Abu Layth."

"Good, god may be with you." The sergeant said, resentfully.

The driver exhaled his irritation, as he crossed the Security checkpoint saying:

"They never get enough, every journey they want a bag of bread and at the Customs, they want two!"

"Poor them, they are hungry!" The Lebanese woman in the backseat said, sarcastically.

"Ha,ha! Poor them, the bread that they're taking is enough for the neighborhood. They opened a shop there!" The man said smiling at the woman, whom he was obviously flirting with.

The Syrian man continued his flirtation with the Lebanese lady, who seemed to like him back, as the anger of the driver increased. So, he sped up the winding road like a snake.

"We will not make any progress as long as this corruption is flourishing!"

"Robbers sharing our children's food," the driver said angrily, then adding consciously:

"I swear if it wasn't for the Great Leader, Syria and Lebanon would have been destroyed."

"Yes, may Allah extend the age of al-Assad." The second Lebanese woman reiterated in the back seat, then a long silence dawned as everyone stared ahead, piously.

"Look how this fear is blinding their heart," the guy beside me commented, whispering.

"Yes, it seems like destiny." I answered, while the radio started warbling with a folk song. I continued whispering as I leaned towards the young man's ear:

"The issue of corruption cannot be solved with just some measures; the root of the problem is the political regime."

The young man smiled, contemplating the road ahead of him. Then he stole a look at the driver that seemed like he wasn't listening to us, enjoying the song:

"Democracy, my friend, is the thing we need the most. Without it we can't establish anything." He said with a self-assured tone. Then he continued with a critical tone:

"It is a necessary condition."

"Yes, it is an important condition but without socialism, we can't solve some of the essential issues." I said, also with a self-assured tone that knows of all the mysteries.

"I used to think so" the young man said.

"And now?" I asked impatiently.

"Democracy comes first and it comes first, unconditionally. Unless you receive some of your humanity as a free human, you won't be able to build a happy, just society. Freedom is the prerequisite for justice." He said concentrating on the road ahead of him.

We had got close to the Lebanese border, where we passed through the Security checkpoint without any inspections. We handed them the red cards and continued on our way towards the Syrian border checkpoint, when the driver piped up, saying:

"There is heavy traffic today, we might spend two hours before finishing the checks and passing through here." He stopped talking for a while then continued:

"Every passenger pays ten Liras and we could be done quickly."

I didn't comment, neither did the young man beside me as the Lebanese woman exclaimed in the back:

"Why? This is their duty. Aren't the bags of bread you bring them enough?!"

The driver:

"I didn't bring any bread today, for that they will bother us a little."

"No worries!" Said the man in the back, speaking to the woman. Smiling, he continued triumphantly:

"No one will pay. When we arrive, I will solve it with them."

"You know them?" The woman asked.

"Of course." He said smiling, then continued speaking to the driver with a demanding tone:

"Continue to the Customs checkpoint directly, don't stop for the stamps."

"As you like," said the driver and continued his way towards Customs building.

The man peered out of the back seat window, smiling at the immigration officer saying:

"They are all with me, is the lieutenant colonel here?"

The immigration officer: "Yes, in his office."

The man: "Tell him Abu Haneen is here."

The officer looked at him carefully, then isolated himself in his guard post to talk on the phone. He returned to talk strictly, with a sense of mockery:

"The Chief is busy but the commands from above, are that everyone has to be inspected."

We went back to where we came from, where we had to wait in a long line for our cards to be stamped. Meanwhile, the woman gave him a depreciating look as he tried to explain that the lieutenant colonel was his relative. It was just our bad luck that he was busy.

After a long wait, my turn came up. One of them took my identification card, inspected my face and then he asked me to wait a little. I don't know why I remained nailed in my place and didn't run. I was sure that my fake identification card was precise enough, since I'd used it a couple of times passing through this checkpoint and nobody suspected anything. The rest of the travelers waited with me, complaining as the driver started reassuring them that he was used to these procedures. It was usually similarity in names and maybe a mistake in a letter; it would be sorted quickly.

"I was arrested and I got released, almost two months ago." The young man whispered in my ear, as he sought to reassure me. Maybe he realized that he would not see me again.

"What's the charge?!" I asked passionately, as I glimpsed the Customs employees accompanied by some Security people, in plain clothes, heading my way.

"The Revolutionary Worker's Party."

His voice mixed with the voice of the employee calling my name. Then, in seconds I was bookended by two Security Men in plain clothes. While my friend, the young man, whispered in my ear:

"It was nice meeting you. I wish you good luck."

One of the Security Men glimpsed him, so he started asking him harshly:

"Do you know him?"

The young man:

"No, he was sitting beside me in the car by coincidence."

The driver accompanied us to the car, where he asked me to take all my belongings. I took a small suitcase, while I ignored another suitcase that had some secret publications.

I walked between them towards the interior building, while the sad smile of the young man accompanied me. They led me into an empty room, except for some chairs, where they inspected my body and my suitcase. Soon, their Boss started an initial interrogation. He asked for assurance that this was my name on this identification card. Then, he confronted me with the knowledge that they knew who I was and that they were waiting for me.

I didn't react, sitting still in my place. I refused to agree, insisting on my fake identification card and the information on it. He smacked me severely, with some punches on my chest and stomach. Then left me, mockingly addressing the Security men:

"Now he doesn't remember but soon he will warble like the nightingale, after we refresh his mushy memory."

They closed the door and left, as I stayed alone, awaiting my deportation to Damascus.

I sat on a chair and lit a cigarette. They'd taken everything, except the packet of cigarettes and the lighter. Two hours passed, I spent them smoking and thinking of what awaited me. I guessed who told them of my arrival. I'd made a mistake when I didn't listen to my friend that warned me about Salem. Regret wasn't going to benefit me now. I'd got caught. Now, I had to revise the plan of questions and answers, which I'd prepared well beforehand. The knowledge of arrest was always in our minds, hanging there like the Sword of Damocles. Following every step we took. It seemed as if it was an inevitable fate. Therefore, there was no other choice but to prepare for It.

*

Rania wasn't reproachful like I thought she would be, for she wasn't late to come to say goodbye. I didn't know why she said goodbye, I had visited Damascus a couple of times before but this time she was saying goodbye with a sad smile. That was our last goodbye and I've never seen her since. Twelve years later, spent in various prisons, I was told that she'd traveled to Sweden with the rest of her family. No one heard from her after that. Did I truly love her? I don't know but she was a source of comfort and happiness in those months of persecution in Beirut. I spent twelve years remembering her and would sometimes dream that she was waiting for me somewhere.

She was a Christian girl, (Maronite) living with her family that had emigrated from Eastern Beirut. Her father belonged to the Lebanese Communist Party, which was in feud with the Lebanese Phalanges Party. The presence of a Maronite family in Eastern Beirut was little weird, especially for some Sectarian Groups. The Maronites, in the eyes of some were nothing but enemies. We would always accompany each other to the nearby College, to talk about many things, including politics. She was influenced a lot by her father. She memorized by heart his words, reciting them to me but she was warm, kind and truthful. We didn't confess anything but our eyes spoke of something deep, blowing in our hearts.

*

The door opened and a Security Man entered. He had a medium height, a neat look and he had a gun on his waist.

"Smoke as you like here, in the Branch they won't let you smoke." He said smiling.

"Are you going to take me to Damascus?" I asked him.

"Of course, we are waiting for the car. The first lieutenant took it and it doesn't seem like he's returning anytime soon, so we're going to take you in a taxi. You look like an educated young man. I don't think you will be difficult."

I nodded my head in agreement while he left.

Two hours passed before the door opened again and the Security Man, accompanied by another, entered to put the handcuffs on my wrists from behind. He led me to where the taxi waited. In the backseat sat a woman and a middle aged man. I sat in the middle between the driver and the Security man, with difficulty, as I tried to adjust my seating to accommodate my tied hands. I felt severe pressure on my bladder. I hadn't urinated for a couple of hours. I had asked him a couple of times to let me go to the bathroom before boarding the car and each time he would promise, then forget. I leaned towards the Security Man saying in pain:

"I can't take it anymore!"

"What?!" He roared angrily.

"I need to go to the restroom. I can't take it anymore."

"Do you see a restroom in these wilds?" He said mockingly, as he looked to the sides of the road that was surrounded by the mountains.

"Let him go to the restroom. The man is uncomfortable. Can't you see his face?" The woman said, frustrated.

"It's none of your business miss. This is what is commanded and I am required to take him to the Security Branch."

"I don't know why he is wanted but there should be mercy in your heart. This is a human, just like you and me!"

"Fine, we will stop soon somewhere appropriate." He said as it seemed he was affected by the lady's speech.

A couple of minutes passed, until a Customs Patrol stopped us, looking for traffickers. When they saw the Security Man it seemed like they knew him. They exchanged greetings, then indicated for us to continue. As soon as the car moved a little, the Security Man asked the driver to stop on the right hand side of the road. He opened the door to get out of the car, asking me to get out as well. One of the Customs Men asked:

"Is there a problem?"

"No." The Security Man answered and then as he indicated to me with contempt: "This young man needs to urinate. We're looking for a toilet that suits him."

"Ha,ha! Is there anything better than this toilet in the open air?" Said the Security Man, laughing as he joined his friends that had stopped one of the cars and started inspecting it.

The taxi had stopped in the pit of the mountain, on a side that overlooked a valley. The Security Man led me to a nearby place, which was somewhat isolated behind one of the rocks. I looked at him inquiringly. It was obvious that I couldn't unbutton my pants, since my hands were tied at the back. He seemed like he was thinking of what he should do. Perhaps, he wanted to unbutton my pants and help me pee but he changed his mind, patted his gun threateningly, as he undid one of my hands. I started urinating severely, while he was behind me looking the other way. The valley was shallow and pervaded by trees. Darkness had started loosening its shadows over this wilderness. I estimated that if I was able to reach the edge of the valley quickly, I would be able to hide behind those rocks, then sneak to the nearby forest. From there I could sneak into Lebanon, since the border was still nearby.

I didn't think much. As soon as I was done urinating, I turned towards him like I was expected to. He indicated to me to turn, so he could cuff me from behind. I turned while he was trying to take out the locks' key from his pocket. Suddenly, I pushed him as hard as I could, towards the valley. The man tumbled down the slope, as I ran as fast as I could towards the other side of the valley. In a quick turn I glimpsed him hold his gun and aim towards me, asking me to stop. I didn't stop. I kept running to the nearby rocks. It was only moments until the Customs Men joined him and started chasing me. I hurried, trying to lose them between the large rocks on the bottom of the valley. Suddenly, as I was trying to pass through two masses of rocks, I found in front of me, a huge man from the Customs I hadn't seen before. He was blocking my way, buttoning up his pants carelessly. I stopped, confused as if I was stuck between the jaws of a pincer. It was only seconds before I was hit on my head from behind. I collapsed to the ground, followed by brutal kicks from the feet of the Security Man, accompanied with nasty insults. The Custom's Men joined him, without hitting me but they helped him tie me up, then lead me back to the car. The traces of his face hitting the rocks were obvious. He started wiping the traces of blood from his face with a paper towel, whilst the blood ran freely from my nose that had received a brutal kick from his shoe.

No one in the car dared talk after that. An almost complete silence fell throughout the rest of the way to Damascus. The car stopped in front the State Security Building in Kafarsouseh, where he led me, pushing me brutally, towards the office of the Officer in Charge. This Officer commanded my transfer to the Investigation Branch, (Al Halbuni).

***

*__Troops 17:__ One of the security troops of Palestinian National liberation Movement (Fatah)*

# 12 KAFARSOUSEH - PALMYRA MASSACRE (THE SIEGE) 1980

A few weeks had passed in Kafarsouseh Prison. Our beards had grown long after we were forbidden from shaving by the orders of the Branch Chief. This was so we could be differentiated from the prison guards, in case we wanted to escape. The lessons of the seventeen prisoners' escape from Kafarsouseh Prison were still recent.

We didn't have much to do besides playing chess. We made its pieces from the interior mushy part of the military bread that we received. We didn't have any other outlets for entertainment, or reading since almost everything was forbidden, or confiscated after the escape mission. Only chess and the semi-daily active movement of prisoners, to and from our dormitory, were our only sources of entertainment.

The wide arrests that were occurring at the time were the only source of our connection to the outside world. With every newcomer there was news and a new story. We would hover over the newcomer and probe him with questions. We didn't want to lose this chance to get information for he may be transferred quickly, sometimes by the dawn of the next day. Most of the prisoners were charged with belonging to the Muslim Brotherhood. Only a few of them had an actual relationship with the organization but despite all that, they were transferred to Palmyra Prison after interrogation.

The investigator didn't need strong reasons to transfer the defendant to the Field Court in Palmyra. If, in any situation, he suspected that a prisoner hid some information, or that he was a relative of a wanted person, or maybe even read something 'seditious' by accident, this would be enough for him to appear before the Field Court, in Palmyra Prison. Most of them had the signs of severe torture, especially those who were investigated in other provinces. Those who were arrested by the private Security Groups like those belonging to the Brigade Companies, (special brigades belonging to Rafaat al-Assad, the brother of the president Hafez al-Assad) their fate was the worst.

I remember the story of a blonde, handsome young man from Hama City, who was serving his mandatory military service in the Brigades Companies. His bad luck led him to an altercation with one of the snitches, in one of the small parties they used to have outside of their tents. He had accused him of being a member of the Muslim Brotherhood, (The Fighting Vanguards) so, the Security Branch in the Brigades Companies arrested him, believing the snitch. In the interrogation he confessed to what they wanted. He said that he'd joined in all the assassinations that had happened lately and his actions were formulated by doctrine.

When he was transferred to the State Security Branch, the

Brigades officer warned him that if he retracted his confessions they would bring him back for further torture. Therefore, he insisted on his words, despite the torture he was exposed to in the State Security, for it was tolerable in comparison to the manic and unbearable torture of the Brigades Companies. He preferred death to that. He insisted on his confessions hoping to escape death. The Branch Chief was impressed with his resistance. He faced him with the knowledge that those who had committed the assassination operations, were in the hands of the Security Services, long ago. The stupid officer in the Brigades Companies didn't know that. Then, the young man didn't have any other choice but to confess that he was lying, so he didn't go back to the Brigades Companies. Only then, the torture stopped and the Security Branch Chief promised him he would not return him to the Brigades Companies. Despite discovering his innocence, which was supposed to lead to his release, he was surprised one day to be transferred to the Field Court in Palmyra. We didn't hear anything about him after that.

Life didn't become totally monotonous. We were still getting to know each other and discovering a different, diverse world. We, the enemies, suddenly found ourselves facing each other, in the same circumstances. I was part of a diverse group of leftists, facing the Muslim Brotherhood and the Islamic Dawa Party, in addition to the Ba'ath Party, which was related to Iraq and allied with the Muslim Brotherhood. For us, they were the summit of backwardness, while for them, we were infidels that they were supposed to kill. There was no time to grow friendships. The transfer operations would happen quickly, yet indeed, some trust and olive branches were offered, charged by the exceptional situations we shared. For me, this was the first time I truly got to know Syria. To realize the nature of the community, injected with intolerance and sectarianism. Old conflicts renewed, injustices and aspirations growing. It hosts the doom machine through a history full of intolerance and wasted blood, in the name of Allah and religion.

We woke up that day, just like every other day, to get ready for breakfast. This was distributed among the small rooms, in small quantities by one of the prisoners; the one chosen by the Prison Management to distribute it fairly, depending on the numbers of the members in each room. Of course he didn't always succeed in doing so, since he might favor his room, or one of the prisoners, so he would pass him an extra piece of this or that from the scarce food.

We waited that morning in vain. For the first time, the food didn't come at its usual time. One of the guards came to inform us that breakfast would be a little late because of a malfunction in the food car. We waited until lunch, when we assumed that they would send us breakfast and lunch together, that didn't happen. The car still hadn't arrived. The car used to go at every meal to the nearby, Mazza Military Prison to receive the ration of food. The place where we were detained wasn't classified as a prison, it was a Detention Center for the purpose of investigation. That night we didn't receive dinner and the group of guards didn't alternate, as usual. Some of us ate some remains of dry bread with water, while others didn't find anything to eat. The prisoner that was cleaning the pathway outside, whispered to his friend in our Dormitory that the Brigades Companies besieged Mazza Prison. That's why the food car hadn't arrived.

"Is there a coup?!"

A hot debate ensued, filled with pregnant thoughts of hope. There was no hope in escaping but in some sort of a change, even if it were a coup from the worst side, which was Rafaat al-Assad. It would weaken the authority, pushing them to offer concessions like releasing prisoners. Almost everyone with the ability to analyze the situation, agreed that freedom was near.

In the morning the food didn't arrive again and hunger was eroding our courage. Meanwhile, tension appeared on the guard's faces, they avoided entering the rooms, or talking to us. Only at noon, when the group of guards didn't alternate for the second day and the food car didn't arrive, did we feel in real danger for our lives, behind those black iron doors. In the evening, one of the guards peered from a door's window of the room beside us, to whisper that:

"The State Security Department, (Mazza Prison) was besieged by the Brigades Companies."

He said they wanted to enter the prison to kill everyone, just like in the other prisons. What had happened in other prisons? No one knew but the news started coming that the Branch Chief refused to allow the Brigades Companies to enter, so they threatened to bomb the building, together with its occupants.

We couldn't sleep that night, hunger wasn't the reason it was our fear and expectations that kept us awake. No one knew what was happening. Only some dormitories had the news. Some prisoners in one of the dormitories who heard the news before us, were in such a state of tension that they ripped down the iron panel shelves, to fashion as weapons to defend themselves. If their dormitories were invaded, then at least they would kill some of them before they died.

Next morning the hunger was severe, along with our concern. Those who were able to sleep were in a better situation than those of us who weren't able to. We found waiting for the arrival of execution bands, extremely exhausting. Breakfast didn't come and none of the guards appeared. A suspicious silence surrounded the prison. It seemed like there was no one there.

Suddenly, at noon, the door opened and one of the guards appeared smiling:

"The issue was solved and the food car went to bring food."

He talked, whispering with one of the prisoners through the small door's window, then left and the sounds of movement outside, started rising. They were the usual daily noises we were used to hearing, before the siege.

As soon as the guard left, the recent news circulated about what was happening outside: The Brigades Companies had left and the siege was lifted, after military leaders and others, intervened. They became convinced that the Branch Chief had no one imprisoned from the Fighting Vanguards of the Muslim Brotherhood. About two hours later, we were filling our empty stomachs with the food that came, doubled this time.

After that, we were informed that a horrendous massacre had occurred in Palmyra Prison. The Brigades Companies had entered the prison, with the assistance of the Branch Chief, to kill the prisoners of the Muslim Brotherhood inside their dormitories with bullets and bombs. No one survived that massacre. They weren't able to enter al-Mazza Military Prison or Kafarsouseh, where we resided.

**

We went back to our usual daily life and the transfer of prisoners. We were a fixed group of nine people, welcoming and saying farewell to the newcomers from other security Branches, from Damascus and other provinces; most of them charged with being part of the Muslim Brotherhood. Kafarsouseh Branch was a center for sorting; adjusting testimonies, transfer and release. The release situations were rare.

A few months had passed, before the Branch Chief was replaced with a different officer, who soon made a number of positive changes for our situation. He cancelled the ban on shaving and the barber would visit us weekly. He also allowed us to go outside for 45mins in the courtyard on a daily basis, so we were able to enjoy looking at the sky and maybe some sunshine. The courtyard's fence was very high, surrounded by high buildings that blocked the sunrays most of the time. He also allowed some of the families to visit their relatives in the prison. I was one of those lucky ones. My family brought me some food and some money, enough to draw a smile on my lips that were hit with fatigue.

The biggest improvement, was allowing us to use the library. He supervised choosing the books himself. He was an officer that held a master's degree in Law. It was a rich library, no doubt, one that made me sail in the pages of its books with extreme passion. My longing for knowledge was compelling and didn't have limits. That was a habit I gained as a child.

The summer was burning that year. We could barely breathe as the numbers of the room's residents increased. They were crowded with a diverse mix of multiple generations, affiliations and nationalities; about forty people in a space that was no bigger than 270 Square Foot. The month of Ramadan was long and harsh for those who fasted, like the devout Muslims. However, not our group of communists, Nasserist (Arab Socialist Union) and Secular Socialists, we didn't fast with them. Many of them were understanding and kind, or that's what it seemed to us, except for a group of the Muslim Brotherhood members. They came from the far country areas, such as Hama, Edlib, Homs and Halab and spoke out with hostility. Some of them went further, assuring us that when they won, they would inevitably chop off our heads and enslave our women. For we were traitors and no mercy would be shown. I don't know why we dealt with these threats like they were jokes, it became clear later that they were serious and maybe even current; those threats didn't wait for their victory over the authority, or the setting up an Islamic State and the application of the law of Allah.

Some of them, who didn't belong to the Muslim Brotherhood, were less angry and malicious. They used to try to guide us towards Islam, believing we had just gone astray. I remember a man in his forties with his little body and long beard. He was healing after he was shot ten times in his stomach. He belonged to the Mufti Republic Groups, (Mohammed Kuftaro.) These groups were in a state of daily clashes with the Security Men that terrified the residents. In a crazy instance, he was took with anger from what the Security Men did to some of his neighbors, who were arrested in the middle of the mosque where he used to pray. Crazed with anger, he took out a gun he had hidden in his house and started a solitary attack on the police center yelling:

"For Jihad! For Jihad! Allah wa akbar, Allah wa akbar!"

As he shot bullets at the windows and doors of the police center, one of them quickly sprayed him with bullets from automatic artillery. He collapsed to the ground, bleeding copiously. He woke up later in a hospital, where he had surgery to remove the bullets from his body. He stayed in the hospital, tied to his bed, where he was interrogated and tortured as well. When he was almost healed, they led him to our prison cell, before transferring him to the Field Court in Palmyra.

He was a simple believer, exaggerating the following of the Prophet Sunnah. He tried convincing everybody of the necessity of adherence to the Prophet Muhamed Sunnah. He thought that those of us that didn't pray, or fast were outside of his friendship. However, as soon as he trusted us, he started spending the bulk of his time trying to convert us to the Straight Path, by praying and fasting. When he wasn't successful in doing so, he started trying to change some things he considered possible. He insisted that we didn't put our food, or feet on top of the Arabic newspapers; for Arabic was the language of the Holy Quran and therefore the language of Allah, which should not be polluted with feet, food or trash. He used to collect all the newspaper scraps and save them in a safe place, so no one could step on them.

One night, while we were sleeping, we woke up to a nasty smell coming from the bathroom. When we explored, we found him burning the bottom of the plastic slippers that we used to use in the toilet, or the bathroom to avoid the dirty water. He was burning the Arabic letters on its bottom! The makers of those cheap plastic slippers were used to writing feminine names on their soles. He didn't stop until he burnt all of them, despite the pleading of some to stop because the smell bothered them. The Sunnah, according to him, was complete and not tinged with interpretation. Some of the Muslim Brotherhood members argued that it exceeded its century and there was no need for it because he was living in the age of the Prophet with all his traditions and dreams.

He would economize with the ablution water, even though water was freely available and not scarce like in the age of the Prophet, in the middle of the desert. Also, no one was able to convince him, that there are tools for eating, like spoons and forks. They weren't available in the time of the Prophet, so he insisted on eating food with his fingers. Of course, he didn't lack in his defense and sometimes he would imagine that it was scientific, to convince us of the benefits of following the biography of the Prophet and valid ancestors.

In the southern corners of the dormitory were two Iraqis. One of them was a lieutenant colonel in the Iraqi Intelligence Agency.

He was arrested while he was communicating with some of the Syrian officers, to start a military coup. One appeared to be a simple man from a rich family in Baghdad, working in the trade of sewing machines. He'd been arrested while he was visiting Syria for tourism and shopping. However, it appeared to me after long years of arrest, that he was really a big officer in the Iraqi Intelligence Agency. Only this could justify the diffidence and fear, sometimes shown towards him by the Iraqi lieutenant colonel, as they were not supposed to know each other.

Beside them, there was one of the Iranian intelligence officers, (SAVAC; Iranian Shah intelligence agencies) who had run away after the fall of the Shah and got arrested in Damascus with a female friend, who was also running away from the new Iranian Regime. Beforehand, he used to be one of those that cooperated with the Syrian Intelligence. He always expressed his fear of getting surrendered to the new Iranian Regime, which would execute him.

In front of him a newcomer lay down, a General. He was an Egyptian that split from the Sadat Regime and collaborated with Yaser Arafat, before collaborating with Hafez al-Assad personally, in extremely important state security operations. I looked at some of the messages he used to send to Hafez al-Assad, begging to get pardoned, reminding him of his exploits in Mauritania, Egypt, Lebanon and a couple of other African countries. Hafez al-Assad had ordered his arrest after he discovered that he provided some of the Islamic powers with weapons and ammunition, without the Assad's knowledge and approval.

The General was a Muslim believer, praying and fasting for Ramadan. He prayed with the Muslim Brotherhood group, did all the obligations and celebratory ceremonies with them, thereby gaining their trust. This, despite the fact he left every day to meet the prison's management. However, for them, it was justified, considering the fact he was a big foreign officer, with connections to the top authorities. Apparently he didn't have anything to do with internal politics and maybe sometimes he would comment, mocking the Ba'ath Party and the men of the Syrian State. However, his identity was always: the Nation, Arabism and Islam.

The group coming from the countryside of Hama, were stricter Muslims than their colleagues that had passed by us before. Their threats were padded and rude sometimes but we would always suppose that they were in a hard situation like ours, especially most of them who had confessed their affiliation with the Muslim Brotherhood. Or, those who had joined in the armed battles and they were sentenced to death, inevitably. We used to try to understand their circumstances and radicalism, despite almost all of those coming from the Muslim Brotherhood members, finished their praying by showing their affiliation to a different century. That group's views flowed with extreme malice. Their prayers were full of deadly promises. Following every sentence the Imam recited, they would confirm them with the word of Amen:

The Imam: "We ask O Allah to defeat polytheism and all the polytheists"

The prayers: "Amen"

The Imam: " O Allah destroy the enemies of religion, the Jews, Nasserists, Communists, Secularists, Infidels, Shiites and all of the irreligious and Atheists."

The prayers: "Amen."

The Imam: "O Allah, ration them in numbers and kill them like waste and don't leave any of them out."

The prayers: "Amen."

The Imam: "O Allah spread amongst them the diseases, sedition, earthquakes and disasters."

The prayers: "Amen."

The Imam: "O Allah disperse their unity, orphan their children and make their women slave-captives for us O most merciful!"

The prayers: "Amen."

In one of the evenings right after they finished their Tarawih prayer, the door opened for the General to be called, like he was called almost every couple of days. The General disappeared for about half an hour as usual, then came back smiling, to sit amongst us and drink tea. After an hour or two, a group of jailers came in to call the names of about ten of them, to lead them somewhere else. We didn't know what was happening but a couple of days later, one of the guards told us that those men were transferred, after a plan was leaked to them about killing all of those they thought were infidels in the breathing courtyard, in the second day of their transfer. They confessed and they were transferred into Palmyra Prison. It was a shock for us when we heard of the news, for we had welcomed them with all we had, food, medicine and clothes. Nevertheless, our fate was to be death with sticks and iron rods. That's when the General told us that he was the one that informed the Branch Chief of the plan, when he accidently overheard the details of it planned for the next day.

***

# 13 THE MILITARY MAZZA HOSPITAL

## 1981

The first year in prison was a heavy one. It was filled with events, due to the brutal war happening outside. The Muslim Brotherhood and their allies formed one side and the Regime, which harnessed all of its powers to face its enemies, on the other side. The Regime regarded all those who didn't support them, as an enemy. Even though we were from the peaceful opposition, we were considered enemies and arrested; we were called 'Opinion Prisoners.'

Also, in prison we heard of what was called the 'precaution detention' for the first time. This meant arresting a former opposition member, as a 'precaution' against their returning to opposing the regime. There were no clear laws in this regard, so you couldn't tell when you broke one. Conveniently for the Regime, this meant you could be arrested for almost anything. Just announcing your opposition could be cause for arrest, thereby they silenced any criticism.

Many times and especially at night, we would hear the sound of gunshots. A few times, there were even the sounds of explosions. We were eager for news of what was happening outside. Our main sources were the new prisoners that flocked in on a daily basis. Most of them were makers and participants of the war, so we would receive the news from its primary sources.

I had surrendered to the idea of spending a long time in prison, of not getting out for years but I never thought that those years would exceed a decade!

I became dedicated to learning the English language. I only knew a few of its principles, because I'd learnt French as a foreign language, at school. Initially, I didn't have anything to depend on to study the language. There was no one proficient in English in the dormitory; consequently I had no one to teach me. Another difficulty was the lack of pens; they were banned. Therefore, if you were lucky enough to find one you had to keep it hidden in a secret spot. Writing paper was also banned but I found that toilet paper could be used instead. Luckily, after a while, I was able to obtain a book of English Language Principles. It was a book that was almost entirely ripped and many of its pages were missing. However, its value was great for translating some of the simple words. Also, I found that scorched sticks were a useful tool for writing on the, all too scarce, toilet paper.

It seemed to me that the second year of prison was less heavy, as I vanished into my books and my study, which lead me into wide beautiful universes. I escaped into them from the depressing prison world. Everything seemed possible and acceptable, except for the pain that started burning in my guts and would sometimes spread to my chest. Amongst the prisoners, there were a number of doctors and medical students in their last year, so I was constantly diagnosed for the pain I suffered. Most of these diagnoses were speculations based on the progression of the pain symptoms. Their diagnosis of the colon pain was dangerous cancer tumors. The doctors spent all their efforts to help me, alongside the prison doctors, through the application of medicines but nothing worked. My friends and doctors in the dormitory, all suspected I had cancer and after their extreme pressure and my insistence, I was sent to hospital. Little by little I'd become convinced that cancer was the most likely cause of my pain, hence I started planning for my death in various ways.

I had to consider my idea of death first. I wasn't a believer in life after death. So, if I died there and then my death would be insignificant, just like the rest of the creatures and bugs. I'd always thought that I had found my purpose in life and I decided I wasn't going to accept to have entered this life and then leave it, without leaving a trace to be remembered. 'What was possible? And how much time do I have?' Questions I attempted to search for answers to, through devious or neutral questions about the cancer and its symptoms. I considered the problem until it became clear to me that the issue of death might take relatively longer.

Eventually I was approved a transfer to the Mazza Military Hospital to have tests, procedures and arthroscopy for my colon. One day, the guard came to inform me to pack my belongings for transfer. I said goodbye to my friends and left to go to the guards' room, where they covered my hands and feet with heavy iron handcuffs. I dragged them along on the asphalt, remembering the historic films about Roman gladiators, as they were leading them into the Coliseum. We boarded the same military car that used to bring us food from the military prison. This was the first time I had left Kafarsouseh prison since incarceration. From the car window it was both beautiful and entertaining, to watch the almost forgotten, natural movement of people in the streets of Damascus. I was admitted to a solitary room in the hospital, whilst extreme inspections and all the paper procedures of delivering and receiving were carried out. Then I passed through some locked metal doors, into a big room with about ten beds for sick prisoners.

One of the patients invited me to sit on a chair beside him. He was lying in his bed across from the door. It seemed to me as if he had prestige amongst the guards and influence over the other patients. He greeted me while some of the patients gathered, inquiring about my charge and my illness. He requested a cup of tea for me, from one of the patients that were able to walk. Later, I came to know that he was an old prisoner and a big officer in the Arabic Front, (Palestinian front belonging to the Iraqi Regime that was led by Saddam Hussein.) He suffered from hemiplegia, due to the severe torture he'd been exposed to. Consequently, they kept him in the hospital because he was unable to take care of himself in the prison. He had two artificial iron legs, which were built to support his paralyzed legs, enabling him to stand up. He used to move short distances, dragging his paralyzed legs carefully, with the help of two crutches. He was fascinating with his highly positive spirit. He would always smile like a father or a friend. He received all the news from Mazza Prison about the recovery of prisoners who had been in hospital with him. He heard of the names of others as well. Everyone obeyed him in the patients' dormitory, even though he didn't force anybody, just because he asked with respect and kindness.

The regulations in the Military Mazza Prison were different from those of other prisons and Security Branches. The military system, with its strict traditions, dominated the daily life. A political prisoner was treated the same way as the arrested military officers. It wasn't acceptable for the arrested military officer to wash his clothes, or make his food. They would allocate a number of soldiers arrested for different charges, to serve both the arrested military officers and the political prisoners; to cook, clean and do the daily service, while they would leave at night to sleep in their private dormitories. The situation was the same in the Military Mazza Hospital. The soldier patients, who were able to move, would serve the politicians and officers. They would do what was asked of them, with no objections. My bed was clean like all the other hospital beds. The patients' dormitory was extremely clean because three patient soldiers would take turn cleaning the place continuously, under the watchful gaze of the military officer that was appointed as a nurse.

I got to know the rest of the dormitory inhabitants. There was a young man that escaped but then got shot in his lower back, which had paralyzed the bottom half of his body. He'd lost his ability to defecate and urinate normally, so he had to wear large sized baby diapers. They used to call him the 'Trash King,' because during his escaped period in Beirut, he lived by collecting the useful things from the dumps and selling them. He was a scrawny guy that dealt with his situation by smiling humorously and we did in return. His situation was strange. One of his legs had been healed and was full of life, while the other one remained paralyzed. He dragged it, supporting himself on his crutches with strange agility.

He was a poor young man from the Turkmen of Aleppo's countryside. He'd escaped mandatory military service because he was married and there was no one to support his small family, which consisted of a wife and three children. Despite his permanent disability, what haunted him the most were the diapers running out. His wife and mother were able to provide most of their cost and he collected the remainder from monies given to him by prisoners, which he worked hard to serve, as they passed through the hospital.

In the bed next to mine, lay an exhausted looking young man with a yellow face and thin body. He was a soldier with the rank of sergeant. He was involved in a conflict with his direct commander, which led to a hand-to-hand fight and the officer was injured. He was sentenced to prison for two years. He'd had a splenectomy to remove areas that were cancerous, which had made him feel better for a while. Then the illness returned to gouge its fangs into his body with a fury. The doctors told him that there was no hope and he would die in a matter of a month, or two. His family tried to get his release, so he could die at home but the routine military judiciary prevaricated. Every day, he awaited his release to spend what time was left for him, amongst his family and loved ones.

On the other side, beside the Palestinian officer's bed, laid one of the arrested officers charged with belonging to the rightist Ba'ath Party, which was associated with the Ba'ath Party in Iraq. About seven years had passed since his arrest. He had recently suffered from tuberculosis and that's why he was in the hospital, to be healed and to avoid infecting the others in the Mazza Prison. His feminine behavior was obvious, as he winked and flirted with the other inhabitants. He was a kind man who was sociable and helped everyone.

The other patients, with no exceptions, used to wink at each other from disgust and even mockery sometimes. He was an educated man trying to avoid their looks by smiling, without hiding who he truly was but without discussing the subject directly, or confessing it. Only the Palestinian officer was able to talk to him with all honesty. He told me that he did not have a problem with him but his friendship with this gay officer, raised suspicion. I noticed the looks of some and their whispers, when he used to touch him, thinking that they are going to be intimate. Though how this would be possible in the middle of a room semi lit day and night, in addition to the fact that the Palestinian man's legs were completely paralyzed, was beyond me.

The Palestinian officer spent most of the five years that he'd spent in prison, in the hospital. He had organized his life very well; it appeared to me that he depended on the help of the patients from the Military Mazza Prison, to recover. He was able to buy his legitimate and illegitimate needs from the guards. It seemed like a good relationship had grown between him and the guards, so they would sometimes welcome him into the guards' room, for quite a long time. He justified that by saying he paid off the guards to prevent them harming the rest of the prisoners, which improved the level of service and recovery of the patients. Some of them were cautious of him and suspected his connection to the guards. They felt he would snitch on them in a case of conflict. The gay man insisted that he was a clean man, who wouldn't tell on anybody and that he had treated all of them very well, throughout the years.

The prison section in the hospital was down a long corridor, with windows fortified by iron bars. The corridor ended in a turn that emptied into a bathroom and a toilet at the same time, while in the middle of the corridor, there was a small foyer leading to the patients' dormitory. On the sides of the foyer there were two rooms that were always closed. On the top of their doors were two windows that overlooked the foyer. I didn't see any lodgers in them for the entire two weeks I spent in the hospital. However, the Palestinian officer informed me that they got used for those prisoners that they wanted to keep secret. They had included some of those imprisoned in private rooms at Mazza Prison. These were prisoners from the previous leadership of the country and Ba'ath Party; one of them was the previous President of the country,

Noor al-Deen al-Attasi and another was Major General Salah Jadid.

Going to the bathroom had a special protocol. We had to knock on the exterior door of the dormitory, then wait to hear the permission to exit. No more than one person was allowed outside of the dormitory at a time. The food was relatively good. At least for those that came from Kafarsouseh Prison, like me. The number of people was small and the guards were able to take what they needed from the food stores provided by the Hospital Management. Therefore, there was no need for them to steal our food and that was a rare and welcome privilege. Smoking was allowed and the business was profitable for the guards, who would sell us cigarettes for a much higher than market price. I had become voraciously addicted to smoking and like many others, slavishly accepted their profiteering.

A couple of days passed before setting up an appointment for my colonoscopy. The night before the appointed date, the nurse gave me a bottle of castor oil, in addition to a container connected to a tube for cleaning the colon. I drank the oil before sleeping. At dawn, I woke up suddenly with stomach pain and an extreme need to defecate. I knocked on the door calmly, trying not to wake the other patients but I didn't get the permission from the guard. I knocked on the door louder, until everyone in the dormitory woke up and I still didn't hear any answer.

One of them helped me to knock loudly enough on the door, to wake the guard. The voice of the angry guard surprised us with an insult. The gay man informed him of my need to enter the bathroom and the reason behind that, so he permitted me after a number of insults directed at both of us. I emptied my bowel until nothing more came out of it but some liquids. Soon, the nurse asked me to use the intestinal cleaning device. I had to fill it with water, then pump it through the anus into my colon. At ten in the morning, I was tied with heavy iron cuffs and led to a distant section of the hospital. I was feeling joy and happiness as I walked among the people in the long hospital corridors, feeling the air of freedom. I was especially delighted when we had to cross the hospitals' garden, which was scented with the smell of earth and trees.

In the clinic they asked the regular visitors to leave, while the officer doctor asked them to un-cuff me. They refused to do so, obeying their commands; subsequently the doctor was forced to do the colonoscopy with me in chains. I was surprised when suddenly a number of medical students entered and surrounded me, as I was completely naked. I lay on my stomach with my hands tied behind me by the iron hand cuffs, which had a large lock that added to their heaviness and pressed against my hands. I was expecting some anesthetics, or anything to ease the colonoscopy's pain but the doctor wanted to give his lesson to the medical students showing the painful body reactions. That, it seemed, was more helpful for them to understand.

No one asked me, or consulted me about anything. Suddenly, I felt a sticky substance greasing my anus and then a thick tube entering up into my gut. Next, they started to inflate me with a primitive inflating tool that reminded me of a blacksmith's bellows. I felt like an inflated drum, while the tube wandered in my guts and I screamed sometimes, from the pain. It didn't seem to me like anyone cared about the screams that came out of me. The doctor was taking his time in explaining and answering the student's questions, while he invited each one of them to watch the point he was talking about. An amount of time that I couldn't estimate passed but it seemed very long, maybe longer than an hour. I almost passed out.

As soon as we were finished, they helped me to put on my

trousers and the doctor smiled at me saying:

"Healthy, there is nothing dangerous. Your colon is cramping and twisted in a strange way and that reason goes back to psychological issues. There is no cure for it but we can treat it with placebos."

He gave me medicine and some directions for the types of food that I should avoid. Then I was led back to the prisoner's ward, almost collapsing from fatigue and pain. There, I had to spend a couple of hours trying to get rid of the painful air they pumped into my guts.

In the coming days the cigarettes started running out, the guard couldn't buy us anything but a small box. We were all smokers, so we all shared it. The Palestinian officer, the gay Syrian officer and I, would share one cigarette every couple of hours. Meanwhile, the agony of the young man suffering from cancer became severe and the pace of his screams, accompanying his pains, increased. The officer guard would give him a dose of Morphine to sleep but as soon as he woke up, he would start screaming once again.

He began losing weight quickly. You could even notice it on a daily basis. His frequency of Morphine doses increased and he seemed to need larger amounts. The nurse officer wasn't able to meet those doses anymore, so he stopped answering the screams and pleading of the young man, until his patience ran out. Often times the guard would scream at him with insults, to try and shut him up but nothing was able to silence his pain. One day, the nurse officer stormed in, angrily telling him to shut up, using harsh and insulting words but this time the young man seemed incapable of stopping pleading and screaming. The nurse officer began hitting him viscously on his face, trying to suppress and silence him. The young man shut up for a while, defeating his pain but as soon as the nurse officer disappeared from eyesight, he returned to screaming and pleading for help.

The young man's pain continued to increase in its severity, along with his loud screaming. It became intolerable for all of us. I knocked on the door asking to see the nurse officer who was a friend of one of my relatives. This nurse officer had already communicated with me as a family friend, as such he had kindly accepted the charge of my care. I asked this nurse to help the young man because we couldn't sleep anymore, while he was in such pain. After thinking he agreed with one condition; I had to give the young man the shot myself. I agreed, after the ill young man screamed, pleading for me to do so. I'd never given anyone a shot before, but the sick young man said that it was simple and he would direct me. Actually, it wasn't hard because the young man had lost so much weight that his veins were clear and prominent. This made it was easy to give him a Morphine shot and he soon fell into a deep sleep.

In the following days the cigarettes were completely cut off, except for some few cigarettes the Palestinian Officer was able to obtain from the guards, which he generously shared with us. In the last day of the cigarette drought, I desperately needed to smoke and my willpower collapsed. I begged the nurse to give me a cigarette. The nurse hesitated a little, then he gave me one with a look that seemed contemptuous, which was maybe a result of self-reflective decadence. The pain was clawing at my guts. All of my glory collapsed in front of a scummy cigarette! All the winds of humiliation blew in me, my soul scattered outside of my body, 'I am nothing but a servile slave!' The forest monsters screamed and the liberty clouds of freedom sintered, 'Who am I!'

After a couple of hours that day, the guard came with all of our requests for cigarettes. My share was a fortune of boxes. I received twenty-five boxes of cigarettes! Happiness was mighty, that day in the dormitory. Tea and coffee pots started alternating on the table of the Iraqi officer, whom we hovered around in his bed, drinking tea and smoking voraciously. For me that day was insane. I smoked about thirty cigarettes over several hours, until I started to feel my throat sore. Then, I crushed what was left of the box of cigarettes to destroy it completely, while I announced that I would quit smoking all together.

It was a surprising decision for everyone. The joy of the return of the cigarettes hadn't calmed down yet but I was ashamed by my slavish addiction. With great determination I decided the punishment: 'You are forbidden from smoking for at least four years!' and I didn't smoke thereafter, until my punishment was over.

Self-punishment is my only effective tool to reconcile with myself, when I commit a wrongdoing that I can't forgive myself for. I started doing this when I was young, no older than ten years, I think. I remember my chagrin after I ate some of my school friend's food, which his mom had sent with me. The punishment I decided upon back then, was to stand on one leg for a relatively long time. Also, when I revealed one of my friend's secrets, which resulted in a scandal, over which he lost his lover and many of his friends. I was mortified by my blunder and had to punish myself. That time I chose an isolated place, to spend hours under the sun at noon, without food or drink, until I collapsed and passed out.

I became the unofficial nurse to the young man, who would call me every time his pain became intolerable. I continued the arrangement with the nurse, who would supply me with the daily shots. In two days the young man's state had become even more severe and the Morphine was no longer enough. There was nothing left to do but double the painkiller but the nurse refused to supply it because, as he said, it was out of his hands. With just the single shot to offer, we had to get used to the constant screams of the young man. In the evening of the day before I was supposed to return to Kafarsouseh Prison, the young man decided that he was going to die soon. He had lost all hope of living, he distributed the simple belongings he owned amongst the other patients and wrote a letter to his family, begging for someone to deliver it.

A few weeks later, one of the prisoners that went back to the Mazza Military Hospital, informed me that he passed away a few days after and his body was delivered to his family.

***

# 14 OMAR'S STORY

## 1984

In 1980, I was in the eighth grade. I was thirteen years old when the Security Men entered our house, looking for me. When my father asked the reason why, they started pushing him ahead of them. They were extremely shocked when they saw my small, thin body.

"Sir, this is a child that hasn't reached puberty yet!" The Security Man exclaimed to the Officer in Charge:

"Tie him and take him to the car!" Yelled the Commanding Officer, ignoring the Security Man's comment.

They led me to a civil car with three seats, in one of them, already tied and sitting, was my friend Salam. My crying mother followed us, asking for the reason why they were taking me, screaming:

"Have mercy, he is still a child! What did he do? Tell me?"

"Step away!" Commanded the Officer threateningly, as he

pushed her away from the car.

I was in the middle seat, surrounded by two Security Men. My friend was in the backseat, while the Officer sat in the front seat, beside the driver. The car drove quickly in the streets of Aleppo, ignoring the red lights and the Police. I tried to steal a look at the street, as if I was saying goodbye for the last time but a strong punch came from behind, making me double up, my forehead touching my knees. I screamed in pain, as they laughed mockingly with some cusses and threats.

At first I didn't know why I got arrested, because I hadn't committed any crime. My family didn't care for politics and my father was an owner of a small shop in the market, struggling to make a living and educate us. He was trying as hard as he could to keep us away from what was happening in Aleppo, even though he was indignant and disgruntled towards the Alawite regime. My father was a faithful man, conservative, just like the rest of Aleppo city. Therefore, he was eager to perform his religious duties.

I was the second male son, after three girls and I was his youngest kid. My father was happy to see that I always attended the religious lessons that were held at the mosque. My Sheikh had disappeared suddenly the week before. Everyone speculated that he had been arrested, since this was the usual reason for any disappearance. Arrests were happening on daily basis, both in secret and in public. I didn't believe that my Sheikh was arrested for political reasons, for he led an ascetic life of prayer, fasting and worship. I would argue frequently with my friends who thought that way but it turned out they were right. As soon as we arrived at the State Security Branch, they started investigating me because of my attendance at the Sheikh's lessons. It became obvious that he was considered a dangerous prisoner, charged with participation in military operations with the Muslim Brotherhood.

The investigator didn't seem convinced that we were not engaging with the Muslim Brotherhood. He wanted information about the Sheikh and who attended his lessons. We weren't tortured a lot. The investigator was from Aleppo and sympathized with us. I stayed with Salam, in a cell for a whole week, waiting for our release. However, with no prior warning, we were called once again, for investigations. At first, we didn't know if it was for an investigation, or a punishment. We were strung up by our hands, on iron doors for hours; with no food or drink, whilst we received periodic whips from a thick lash.

We were completely exhausted when they untied us. Consequently, I fell to the floor collapsing but their kicks were enough to refresh me, to make me crawl across to the room with a new investigator. This investigator had a thick, Alawite dialect. He talked coldly, like death. He seemed like a living corpse with no soul. Under no circumstances could you consider him a human. I wouldn't even give him the character of an animal. A slim ghost, the bones in his face and chest protruded, repugnant alongside his broken yellow teeth.

I was able to see him sometimes, despite my blindfold. He was sitting behind a long, cheap iron table, in a wide room that was empty except for the torture tools, the tire, the chair and some thick lashes. He was sitting silently, staring out through the window while three people took turns in torturing me nonstop, until I passed out. I woke up to a bucket of water wetting my head.

"What's your name?" He said coldly, still looking through the window.

"Omar."

"Do you know how to write?"

"Yes."

"Well then, write what you know about the Sheikh and how you were organized?"

I tried to talk but he didn't leave me any chance:

"If you don't write all that you know, I will have to start convincing you." He said looking into my eyes as the blindfold fell from my face, then continued as he left the room:

"The convincing session hasn't started yet."

One of them gave me a sheaf of papers, then kicked me saying:

"Write you donkey!"

Through long hours of convincing, I confessed that the Sheikh organized me to commit Military Operations in Aleppo and that we were waiting for commands to proceed. I signed all the investigation papers that I was asked to sign, without reading a word on them. I didn't dare to ask, for I'd decided that death was more merciful in my situation. Salam did likewise.

A few days later we were led to Damascus, where we denied the confessions we made in Aleppo Branch. We didn't know what was recorded in the seizure report we'd signed without reading it. A few days after that, we were led at dawn, to Palmyra Prison. We didn't get tortured in Damascus; in fact, we received some sympathetic treatment. At dawn, they called our names in amongst other names. We packed what clothes we had and joined the men that gathered in the jailers' room.

We were searched, tied from behind and then boarded the back of what they called the Meat Wagon. This was a long military wagon, big enough to transport about fifteen prisoners crammed inside it, on its long side benches. A large cuff was put on one of our ankles, then they threaded a long iron chain through each of our ankle cuffs tying us altogether in one big mass. They closed the iron door that separated us from the small compartment at the very back, where two guards sat, armed with automatic Kalashnikov rifles.

The air in our compartment wasn't enough, despite the small windows on the sides and back of the wagon. The iron covers, encrusted with dust, blocked the cold air coming in from outside. We weren't allowed to talk; hence we sat in silence through the long hours we spent on the road. I remember that I glimpsed Damascus for the first time, when we left Kafarsouseh Prison. We traveled the long dark streets, empty of passersby and with only the sound of an occasional car. I hadn't seen the Damascus streets when they led us from Aleppo to Damascus, since our eyes had been covered and our faces had been between our legs.

In the middle of the journey, Salam had urinated on himself; also, Abu Najeb, a middle aged man who suffered from diarrhea, couldn't hold himself and soiled his pants. No one dared to tell the guards in the back, everyone just tolerated the nasty smell, trying to protect him from their wrath. Unluckily for me, he was sitting beside me and we were tied to the bench, so I couldn't move. The guards soon complained about the bad smell. They shot their cusses and threats, thinking that one of them had passed air. Salam smiled as he looked at, me as if he was saying, 'If they knew the situation of Abu Najib, they would go crazy!'

I knew we were getting near the prison when Salam indicated to me to look through the window, where the distant outline of Palmyra loomed up at me; that Palmyra I'd visited on a school trip. Only a few moments passed, until the car stopped at the Military Police Security checkpoint. Presently, the wagon started moving again but only for a couple of moments, before it stopped completely and the two guards opened the back door and got out.

My heartbeat started to race as I heard the voices of the guards outside. As fear and panic stabbed our hearts, it seemed we were at a military barracks and not a prison. We looked at each other as fear blurred our eyes and some foreheads turned white. We'd heard about the welcoming party at Palmyra Military Prison. It was rumored to be especially nasty for the militants who were arrested for crimes, or regular military violations. This was the extreme of what we expected; the harsh welcoming session, tens of whips on our feet, before they put us in the dormitory. We didn't know anything about the special treatment for the political prisoners. We just heard that a massacre had been committed in Palmyra, where thousands of Muslim Brothers were killed.

The back door opened, followed by the door that led to our compartment and one of the guards entered. He opened the lock of the iron chain then unlocked the cuffs from our ankles. We left the wagon, our hands still cuffed from behind. The morning had dawned, so we could see clearly as we approached a small room where they un-cuffed us. Security Men surrounded us and accompanied us into another room. We watched some of the Military Police Men in the courtyard, who were busy with other issues. The situation seemed different from when we were being transferred to Palmyra Prison. None of the Police Officers came near us, or even insulted us. The Security Men finished untying us while one of the Military Police Men came to read the names, then sign the delivery papers. One of the Security Men said farewell sympathetically:

"May God be with you!" Then he left with the others.

It was only seconds until one of the Military Police Men entered, screaming:

"Your face to the wall, you animal!"

We turned immediately, faces stuck to the wall, while I heard the noise of somebody's head hitting the wall. They screamed aloud from the pain. This was followed by whiplashes, accompanied by insults and whimpering from some of those stung by the lash. Luckily, I wasn't one of them; as I awaited my turn for the lash, he was called away. I didn't dare to turn and neither did the rest, for maybe there was still somebody there. In an attempt to save ourselves from the anger of the guard, our faces remained stuck to the wall for fear of the lash behind us. We stayed in the room for about an hour listening to the voices of the guards outside, without hearing anyone enter or leave the room. Slowly, our muscles relaxed a little, until we heard somebody's steps entering the room and the highest rank officer screamed:

"Your eyes closed! Your face to the ground and everyone go outside!"

The sticks and whips assailed us like rain and in the blink of an eye, forced us to the exterior courtyard. There we were made to lie on our stomachs, our faces crushed into the cracked asphalt. Then they started calling for us, one after the other, to record our names in the Reception Office. Suddenly a heavy military boot fell on my head crushing my face onto the cold asphalt as he screamed:

"Your face to the ground, you animal!"

I shut my eyes, trying to hide my face completely in the Asphalt. Soon I heard one of the guards laughing sarcastically:

"Look, this one shat himself Sir!"

The whips started flailing Abu Najib's body as he screamed:

"I swear I couldn't hold myself. I had diarrhea!"

"You had diarrhea you son of a bitch! I was wondering where this nasty smell came from!"

Then, speaking to a 'Service Man': these were militant prisoners, sentenced for various crimes, who spent their service in forced labor in the Political Prison. In return they had some privileges like extra food; freedom of movement within the prison and many of them would help in torturing and executions. Most of them had a huge build with large muscles reminiscent of Roman Gladiators.

"Come here. Take him and wash this animal!"

Abu Najib was led by two giant Service Men, like a sheep towards the water faucet, where he took off all of his clothes to be showered with cold water; he had to clean his body with his hands. This was followed by some whiplashes. The weather was cold in the desert morning, so a now semi naked, wet Abu Najib started shivering as he returned to lie in his place. When my turn came, I ran quickly to enter the room. A strong slap catapulted me forward to face the Service Man who recorded the wanted information, coldly, like any employee in a scrap warehouse. The truth is, I wasn't any better than scrap in this place. Even so, I envied the real scrap for its lifelessness, its inability to feel human pain.

The recording time took about an hour. Then the second section of surrendering and delivery started. We were pushed between two lines of guards and they assaulted us with whips, thick sticks and heavy iron tubes, as they led us down a corridor. We ran as fast as we could, trying to avoid the brutally heavy strikes, which bruised and battered our bodies. A couple of whips lashed me but fortunately, any iron bars, or sticks didn't strike me, thus I survived having my bones broken. This happened to some of the others and their blood splattered widely, especially from those who received strikes to the head. Maybe my young age helped stay their hands. Yet Salam, despite his age, didn't survive a strike that hit his leg. He fell to the ground in agony and thought that his leg was broken but continuous whiplashes made him get up and keep running, indifferent to the pain.

We lined up against the wall to take off all of our clothes, except our underwear. Then we were asked to do the 'safety movement,' although we didn't know how. When Abu Muhammed stood up confused, not knowing what the safety movement was, he received a strike with the lash on his ass, which made him bend in pain, while another pushed him with his hand to fall on his knees. That was enough for us to do the safety movement quickly and with agility. Later, we got to know that they did that to make sure we were not hiding anything in our anus. It was a routine procedure with the criminal militants held in the military prison.

When we were done with inspections, we were welcomed by kicks and whips, which pushed us to the other wall where another group of guards and Service Men stood. We had already crossed 'Hell's Gateway,' the welcome in the reception-courtyard and now, seeing the wheel and braded lashes, I guessed it was time for the 'Pathway to death.' So called because many passed away due to its brutal torture. They would soon begin those promised welcoming procedures and we didn't know who would survive. First though, there was a group of Service Men, (Baladya) who started shaving our heads and beards with blunt, manual shaving machines. The shaving ordeal seemed more like plucking chickens. When the barber's machine was jammed with hair, he would snatch it brutally, ripping out a mass of hair mixed with wails of pain, followed by the guards' insults and whips.

We were still stuck to the wall with our eyes shut but I couldn't stop my eyes from stealing a glimpse, when the first one of us was taken with brutal strikes and kicks. He was put in the tire. This is an empty car tire that you sit in, while your hands are tied and your feet are held, tied to a stick, by a Service Man on each side. Then, three of the guards assailed the soles of his feet nonstop with whips. There is a strange harmony to the torture, a beating rhythm of the lashes as the screams of the person being whipped, fills the universe. I didn't hear them count at the time and I couldn't keep count of the number of strikes. They stopped after he passed out and the screams stopped for a while. It seemed like his soul had gone to God but a big bucket of cold water was enough to bring him back to life and for the whips to pour down on his feet, once again.

My turn came up and I was the last one, after Salam. I received a couple of punches and strikes on my body, before they tightened my cuffs in the tire:

"How old are you?" The assistant asked, looking at my small body.

"Fourteen." I answered terrified.

"You're fourteen years old and in the Brotherhood, you animal!" He yelled angrily as the whips poured their fire on my feet. I started screaming insanely, nonstop from pain, begging for mercy like all the rest but to no avail. No one answered my pleading as they flailed on me, like machines with their whips, until blood exploded from my leg. Then the assistant indicated for them to stop.

They untied me and ordered me to follow my friends to the wall, where I received my share of another cycle of torture, with strikes on the hands. Soon, amongst yet more stick and whiplashes, they led us to another courtyard through a long black door and from there, to another door. In the second courtyard, Abu Najib received a stick strike on his head that made him pass out amidst a pool of blood. So, two of the brothers held him, as the whips coaxed them and they stumbled while carrying him, their clothes becoming contaminated with Abu Najib's blood.

In the third courtyard, I rushed to follow the brothers that raced ahead of me. One of them fell in front of me, just as he was entering the dormitory's iron doorway. My passage blocked, I received a hail of whips while he stumbled to his feet and lurched into the room. I followed him swiftly, only to collapse in the middle of the dormitory with blood dripping from my feet and back.

Abu Jamil, the Dormitory Chief, asked us to stand up quickly, remain still, with our eyes shut and heads bowed. We obeyed quickly, as the sergeant accompanied by the officers began to scream commandingly:

"The new ones go to the corner, you idiots!"

We gathered, terrified in the corners and shut our eyes tight.

"Where is the one that shat himself? Come out!" Said the sergeant.

No one answered, so the sergeant got angrier:

"I said come out!"

"Sir, he passed out," one of the brothers in front of me said, without turning.

"This one, sleeping over here sir."

"Raise him up, let's see."

The branch chief tried to wake him up but with no success, while the sergeant kicked him on his chest and head.

"Sir, it seems like his soul went to God."

"Better for him." He kicks him one last time before leaving, saying indifferently,

"If his soul comes back let me know."

We heard the noise of the door shutting behind us, while the Dormitory Chief gave the military, 'Stand Easy' sign:

"Rest."

We collapsed to the ground like discarded wet rags and blood dripped from our bodies. Some of the older Brothers came to wrap our wounds and give us some of the food they had, while I drank lots of water. There were a large number of men in the dormitory. All of them had their heads shaved completely. They had thin bodies and faces as pale as death. I wrapped myself up into a ball, scared, terrified even, observing the faces and bodies that sat in silence, looking at us. The Dormitory Chief was still busy inspecting Abu Najib, trying to wake him up with the help of another. I came to know later, that he was a dermatologist from Hama. The doctor said that he was still alive but in a coma. So, he began treating his wound while the Dormitory Chief started to teach us the necessary commands in our new prison:

When we hear a movement beside the door, we have to stand up as quick as we can and close our eyes with our heads bowed.

When he addresses the line, "Rest, get ready," we had to stomp the ground with our feet as hard as we could.

Then, when he continues, "The dormitory is ready for inspection Sergeant Sir!" We stay in this formation until the Dormitory Chief announces the resting, by saying, "Rest."

We had to stand in the line according to the order he put us, for visitation, or taking fresh air, or for any other group movement.

We had to stand in groups of five, behind each other. We had to know who is in front of us and who is behind us, according to the order. By doing this we would save ourselves a huge amount of whips.

We were all assigned in the middle. We came to know later that he wanted to protect us in the beginning, where the sides of the line will receive most of the whips, when passing in front of the guards.

Everyone had to wake up at six in the morning, pack his mattress and sit on it silently. You couldn't talk with your neighbor, or with anyone else.

Going to the bathroom was allowed by holding your hand up, until the Dormitory Chief, or his vice permitted you. At night, meaning after 6pm, you went to sleep. So, you had to hold it until the morning and if you couldn't, you had to sneak quietly, without the guard seeing, to the bathroom. If he saw you through the skylight windows on the rooftop he patrolled, then you would receive a whipping punishment in the morning.

We were looking at him, not understanding and maybe not believing. He was smiling, exploring the windows carefully. His vice helped us in organizing our lines, so we wouldn't make a mistake when we had to exit. At noon, the door opened to the rhythm of inspection:

"Rest Get Ready... The dormitory is ready for inspections, sergeant sir!"

Four young men left the dormitory under the whipping, to bring back two plastic containers, in addition to a bag of military bread. The Dormitory Chief started distributing the food, starting with the red sauce with beans swimming in it, mixed with dirt. The food was split equally, based on the number of men in the dormitory. Every group had one small bucket for sauce and another one for rice or groats, while the few fruits got distributed according to their number. The ration of fruit for our group, consisting of nine people, was one apple. We felt like we couldn't eat but the Dormitory Chief insisted, so we ate with difficulty, while Abu Najib woke up from his coma and the doctor started treating him.

We had barely started eating when the door opened again, to go through the same procedures of call to attention. Then, the Brothers take the food buckets out after cleaning them. An hour passed before the door opened again for inspections. We rushed out, holding each other's hands, to line up in the courtyard in fives as fast as we could. Meanwhile, we were surrounded by a number of guards, raining lashes down on us with whips. I didn't get any strikes for I was in the middle, while those on the edges received most of them.

They inspected us and counted the number of prisoners. Then

we went back the way we came, pushed by the lashes like a herd of terrified animals being attacked by predatory wolves. In the evening the Dormitory Chief and his vice, started organizing the sleeping operation. Our number exceeded a hundred and the area was cramped even if we were just sitting, so how were we going to lay down to sleep? We lay top to tail, with one of the men pressing us against each other to make space for everyone. Only the guard appointed by the Dormitory Chief, remained seated according to the assistant's commands. There had to be a guard awake all night, organizing the shifts. I couldn't sleep but I didn't dare to sit up, or leave my place. There was a nasty smell rising to my nose from the dirty feet close to my face, which belonged to a fat man in his fifties. The man came with our group and he hadn't had the chance to clean his feet from the dirt and coagulated blood.

Suddenly, one of the sleepers screamed in terror, quickly the nearby Brothers covered his mouth, trying to shut him up. He woke up terrified, unable to control himself, before realizing that it was just a nightmare, then he held himself together. The guard screamed from the rooftop across:

"What is that noise?"

"He had a nightmare, sir." The Dormitory Chief replied.

"Hah, a nightmare! No big deal. Tomorrow he will know the real nightmare. Mark him for me."

"Yes sir." There was no chance for the Dormitory Chief to object. There was only one response in that instance and it is to obey. Any attempt to object would lead to a worsening of the situation and everyone might get punished, without exceptions. Even the Dormitory Chief might be exposed to a doubled punishment. The Dormitory Chief wasn't a coward and from what I saw of him later, made me realize that he was a faithful, educated man. He was a philosophy professor in one of the Universities. He had become the Dormitory Chief because he had served his military service at the rank of sergeant. He was a wise and brave man, who did his share of protecting everyone like a father. He cared for everyone like they were his own kids and many times he would bear torture and double punishment, to protect an old, or a sick person.

In the morning, whilst receiving breakfast:

"Hand over the one with the nightmare." The guard demanded of the Dormitory Chief.

"Yes, sir."

In seconds, one of the young men was jumping up before the Dormitory Chief called him.

"Having a nightmare huh! Here you can't have nightmares. You only have nightmares in your mother's house, idiot!" The muted noise of the whips started on the feet and body of the young man, who started screaming from the burning pain. Minutes later he was thrown back into the dormitory, unable to walk on his feet and the door was shut behind him. I looked at him, twisting a little, then regaining his natural state, walking towards the bathroom. To my surprise, he wasn't the same person that was screaming yesterday, terrified. For he was a young man in the prime of his life, while the man that had the nightmare was sixty years old, with a weak build was now sitting in the corner mumbling. I came to know later that this young man was one of the volunteers to receive the strikes for the handicapped and old men. They were called volunteers because they would stand on the edges of the line, where they received the strikes of the lashes and sticks and sometimes volunteer to receive punishment, in place of a weaker culprit, if he was in a situation where his features weren't recognized. Often, those circumstances were assessed by the Dormitory Chief. I was young, so they tried to protect me, to try and help me survive. However, after my body grew and got stronger I joined those volunteers. In actuality, I was dreaming of death in their stead, just to get rid of the daily torture. I prayed to God every day to release me and transfer me to His home. I would plead, just like the others, for Allah to accept our repentance and be pleased by our torture, such that he would accept us and save us from Hells' torture.

At the inspection time we all went out, just like the day before and henceforth every day after that; whips, sticks and quick running, during leaving and entering. To line up inside with our eyes closed and head bowed down. Soon the sergeant called the Dormitory Chief:

"You! Dormitory Chief!"

"Yes, sir."

"Where is the one that shat himself? Is he still well?"

"Sir, he was passed out."

"And why didn't you tell me? Didn't I tell you to tell me, you animal?"

"Yes, sir. I was waiting to see you… Sir!"

"Oh? Look at me so I can see you for myself."

The Dormitory Chief went out immediately. Any attempt to disobey would increase the punishment. Outside, mad whips poured down upon him and continued for a while. His voice was cut off after great screaming and wailing. Two of the Service Men held him and threw him back inside. Blood was splattered all over his face and feet. No one dared to help him, even his assistant indicated to someone who was trying to get close to him, to be patient and remain in his place. We heard the sergeant's voice outside:

"Now you saw me very well. The next time you animal, you will memorize what I say, or you won't get rid of me before you are paralyzed!"

"Yes, sir!" The Dormitory Chief swallowed his pains, to answer with a loud voice.

Silence falls for moments, then we hear the sergeant talking with one of the guards, laughing with words unfathomable to us but I guessed that he was mocking the Dormitory Chief.

"Where is the one that shat himself?" The voice of the sergeant came from outside, mockingly.

Abu Najib stood, without answering. His wounds were bandaged with a worn-out piece of white cloth contaminated by coagulated blood. The vice chief spoke quickly with a loud voice:

"Yes, sir... Here, sir."

"Come out, idiot."

The vice chief indicated for Abu Najib to go out. Abu Najib hesitated, scared as he turned right and left, maybe looking for a savior.

"Where is this animal?!" The voice of the sergeant came angrily.

"He's coming sir, he can't walk." The vice Dormitory Chief answered.

"Carry him and throw him outside, idiot!!" He screamed with extreme anger. There was no choice but to push Abu Najib outside of the dormitory. Abu Najib tripped over the doorstep and fell in front of the sergeants' feet.

"Stand up, idiot!"

Abu Najib stood up with difficulty.

"Look at this animal. He says he's sick!" Annoyed, then mockingly, "Did you not shit yourself today?"

"No sir, I swear I had diarrhea yesterday and couldn't hold myself," Abu Najib stuttered.

"Ha,ha... did you have diarrhea, or did you shat yourself from fear? Ha,ha!"

"He's too embarrassed to say he shot himself from fear. He doesn't have diarrhea," commented one of the guards, scornfully.

"That means he's not scared right now. He didn't do it in his pants yet. What do you think Mahmood?" Said the sergeant sarcastically.

The guard laughed loudly, followed by the laughter of the rest of the guards.

"Put him in the tire. When he shits himself, let him go." The sergeant commanded the guards.

"Go in the tire, idiot!" One of the guards shouted, accompanied by whips and kicks, as Abu Najib screamed, appealing for help from Allah. Nothing stopped them; they beat on him with lashes, almost nonstop. They would stop every now and then, to get him out of the tire to check on his behind, mockingly:

"Look, did he do it or not?" The sergeant said amongst the laughter of the guards and Service Men. Then they took him back to the tire again, until his screams stopped. Then, they threw him into the dormitory and closed the door, amongst their laughter and nasty sarcastic comments.

As soon as we made sure the guards had left to go to the courtyard, the doctor started helping Abu Najib, who looked completely exhausted, while the Dormitory Chief regained his wellbeing quickly. Soon after, one of the dormitory's doors opened and the running to the courtyard started, amidst the usual torrents of whiplashes and dirty insults.

"It is the breathing," one of the Brothers whispered near me as he noticed my confusion.

What they called, 'the breathing' was prison slang for the period of time where the prisoners go outside to a closed courtyard, to breath in the air and get exposed to sunrays. It wasn't long before we discovered that it was also a daily period of time for torture, which could go on for as long as thirty minutes. During that time, we received the most extreme kinds of torture and humiliation.

Immediately the door opened, we started running as usual, amongst the stings of the lashes surrounding us from every side. However, as soon as we got to the courtyard and made the lines in fives, a fence of volunteers surrounded us, for protection. We answered to the command of the guard by gathering in the corners of the courtyard. Presently, we were asked to sit in the middle of the courtyard, of course and as always, with our eyes shut and our faces bowed down.

"Where is the one that shat himself?" The sergeant called and he was a different sergeant than the one from the morning. It fell on my head like a heavy hammer; Abu Najib is going to die today. Abu Najib was walking with great difficulty on his bloody feet, almost collapsing.

"Yes, sir." Abu Najib answered.

"Come here, idiot!"

Abu Najib got up and ran in his direction. Instantly, lashes poured down on him, as one of them screamed:

"To the ground, idiot!" Abu Najib tarried for a little bit, confused as to what to do then, he threw himself to the ground, accompanied by a severe whip. Then, he groveled on his stomach because of a violent kick.

"Dormitory Chief! Did you not teach them how to move?" The sergeant said speaking to the Dormitory Chief who answered without raising his head:

"We didn't have time, sir. Today they will learn everything."

"Come out of the line, you animal. Your brain seems closed today, we want to open it."

"Yes, sir." The Dormitory Chief runs, crawling on all fours, while his eyes are shut and face towards the ground.

"Lower your neck, idiot!" The sergeant says as he kicks the Dormitory Chief's head with his heavy military boot, after multiple kicks, the blood poured from his nose. Then he ordered him to go back to his place and he returned in the manner he came.

"Now, let's examine the one that shat himself." The sergeant says, speaking to the other guards, smiling:

"Did you shit yourself today, idiot?"

"No sir." Abu Najib answered, still sprawled.

"Take off your shorts and let me see." The other guard, ordered.

Abu Najib hesitates, only to be stung by a flurry of whips, almost instantly. He twists in pain then, starts taking off his clothes while still sprawled on the ground.

"Quickly, idiot!" The sergeant screams, while some whips hunt meanly on his body. Abu Najib stumbled to his feet and took off his clothes quickly, remaining in his underwear.

"Come here and stand-up."

Abu Najib approached the sergeant with his head bowed down.

"Let me see your ass, to see if you shat yourself?"

Abu Najib hesitated, before pulling down his dirty white underwear.

"Pull it down more, let me see. I want to see well."

He pulled down his underwear, slavishly, while the guards started mocking his behind with dirty words.

"I swear I had diarrhea, sir." Some desperate words emerged from Abu Najib, in a low voice, as if he was talking to himself.

"What are you saying, you idiot?" The guard insists.

"I said I had diarrhea, sir." Abu Najib answered, terrified.

"You had diarrhea and now you don't, right?!" The guard said angrily.

"No problem. Let us teach you how to get diarrhea, once

again. Show me your ass." The sergeant screamed harshly. Abu Najib bent with anxiety, turning his behind to the guard.

The guards started whipping his naked behind, until they drew blood from his thin skin. Abu Najib's screams rose while two of the Service Men, (Baladya) grabbed him. Then, the guard stopped hitting him, responding to the sergeant's signal.

"From now on you are not allowed to go to the bathroom. I want to see shit stuck to your ass every day. Do you understand, idiot?!" The sergeant screamed at Abu Najib.

"Yes, sir." Abu Najib replied, as he fell to the ground after a kick on his behind.

"You, Dormitory Chief! I want to inspect this animal every day in the breathing. If shit isn't stuck to him, both of you will eat it and if I don't feed you shit with my own hands, my name will not be Abu Alleyth!"

"Yes, sir!" The Dormitory Chief says, with a loud voice.

"Alright, start the sports class." The sergeant says.

The sports class consisted of half of the prisoners lying on their backs, while the other half, jumped on their chests. Soon, two of the guards joined in and jumped on the prisoner's chests with their heavy military boots. I received a severe kick to my chest, which made me whimper from pain.

"Look, you idiot!" He said as he kicked me in my waist. I ran towards the sergeant on all fours, with my eyes shut.

Shortly, he called Salam out as well. He copied me, running on all fours to the sergeant. We held firm in front of the sergeant, awaiting the dreadful punishment.

"How old are you, idiot?" The sergeant asked.

"Fourteen." I answered.

"And you, idiot?" Talking to Salam.

"Fourteen." Answered Salam.

"What grade?"

"Eighth grade, sir!" We said together.

The sergeant became silent, like he was shocked, or was thinking of a punishment that suited us. Then, calmly and with simplicity, like he was addressing himself:

"Is this possible? Eighth grade and they brought you here?" Then addressing the rest of the guards:

"Eh, my students are in the eighth grade and they still piss themselves!"

"Those are born terrorists, born with diapers!" Everyone laughs.

"Ok, we will test you and if you pass, then God saves you but you better not fail!" The sergeant said, with the tone of a teacher addressing his students.

He asked us to recite a verse of poetry. I managed that successfully and the sergeant, who was an Arabic teacher, was happy. Salam failed the test, so his penalty was a couple of whips on his hands. Then he asked me to recite a verse of poetry that I didn't know. When I couldn't, he punished me like Salam with some whips on the hands, just like the schools teachers used to do. Then he ordered us to stand facing the wall on one foot.

Our punishment was gentle in respect to what happened to the Brothers there. Maybe, he sympathized with our situation, or for a moment he regained his true identity as a teacher, instead of his current role as chief whip. The sergeant and the guards continued their entertainment, by doing what they pleased with the other Brothers. From whips and insults, to humiliating commands, until the breathing time was over then, they led us running, back to the dormitory.

Everything was organized. In the dormitory there was the Release or Period Administrators. In Palmyra Prison language, the

Release Administrator used to administrate the turns to use the bathroom. The Laundry Administrator organized the washing of clothes and the Food Administrator distributed the scarce food. While the Voice Administrator was responsible for the voices in the dormitory; he had to warn people to lower their voice when it rose louder than whisper, fearing that loud voices would elicit group punishment.

We started to get used to the daily life in the dormitory and soon we became part of it. We shared with its residents, its sorrows and its very occasional joys. The life became monotonous, punctuated by the sudden extreme torture, or death after torture. We would wake up every morning at six and start the bathroom trip. There would be tens of men, often between 70-90 people, all waiting their turn to enter the bathroom. Then, the turn for distributing food and breakfast comes. The breakfast was extremely small; a pot of tea and some bites of Halva, in addition to some olives, or a spoonful of yoghurt, for ten people.

Lunch was nothing but sauce with some vegetables, filled with dirt and dust, a few groats and rice, maybe some pieces of fruits, or one watermelon for everybody. There were a large number of engineers, doctors and graduates of various specialties, amongst the prisoners. They had all memorized the Quran and its Speeches from those who Allah blessed, before they entered the prison. Everyone studied, or listened to what the others had memorized. It was a blessing for me, as that helped me forget the prison and its pains. So, I started memorizing the Quran and listening to its Speeches. I delayed memorizing the Speeches until I finish memorizing the Holy Quran.

Abu Najib's situation was the most painful, as they overpowered him without any way for us to help him. They would call him at every Breathing, to humiliate him and especially on the shift of the mean sergeant, Nasim, who considered Abu Najib his personal plaything. He would stand in the courtyard, talking in his Alawite dialect, as he gave orders to everyone and especially, Abu Najib. Nasim was a tall, handsome, blond man with blue eyes that were common amongst the Alawites, according to my Sheikh in the mosque, who called them 'Germans.' We called them that too. Some of us would call them by the makes of German cars, as a cover and say, "This Mercedes," or "that BMW," or "Volkswagen," or sometimes due to its shape and as a shortcut filled with contempt, "Turtle."

In the dormitory, we weren't scared to whisper their names and characteristics to each other. We knew what the Islamic ruling had in store for them. The Islam Sheikh promised of killing the Alawite men, while they enslaved their women and children, since their repentance would not be accepted. The Sheikh told me that they were called, 'German' because most of them were blond like the Germans. They thought that the Alawaites sect was produced by Muslim's mating with German Crusaders. The Germans cooperated with the Crusaders and helped them to invade the Islamic States. My Sheikh added that most of them were from the Germans who escaped to the mountains, after they broke down in front of the Muslim armies. Most of those who resided in the dormitory acknowledged that, for it was said by Islam and therefore, should not be refuted; the Alawites are infidels and the worst kind of the infidels. They are nothing but Jews disguised in the body of Islam, to lead it from the inside.

Abu Najib accepted that. He would prepare for the daily roasting and humiliation party, with patience and submission, for it was Allah's will and desire. The infidels' humiliation is naught but dust that doesn't stick to the pious. The Dormitory Chief decided to relieve him of the mockery mission, of cleaning the entire dormitory's mess, instead he designated a place for him amongst the ill. Subsequently, he spent his day worshipping, memorizing the Quran like everybody else and choking down his pain from wounds caused by the torture sessions. What pained him most was the shift of the, 'teacher sergeant' whose name I can't remember anymore. He was commanding Salam and me as well. He would play the role of a teacher but in the style of a Palmyra Jailer.

The 'teacher sergeant' overwhelmed Abu Najib, to humiliate him with the dirtiest and worst phrases. He would force him to dance naked, or repeat vulgar words about him, or his children. The teacher's imagination was rich, without limits and the laughter of the guards surrounding him, just encouraged him. A week had passed since we arrived at Palmyra Prison, when the door opened and we were given orders to take off our clothes and stay in our underwear. The Dormitory Chief had informed us about this and we were ready for the ordeal. These were the worst days in Palmyra, for the prisoners. We left in a long line, holding the waist of the one in front of us, our faces to the ground, eyes shut as usual. We started running towards the other courtyard, where the bathroom is, chased by whips from every side. The number of guards was more than usual.

We split in half. The first half entered the bathroom, which consisted of booths with a showerhead and no doors. In each booth there were five or more naked men and extremely hot water poured on them for five minutes. Then, the next group of brothers was ordered to strip completely naked and enter the, now empty, booth. There was no time for shyness because the lashes never stopped hitting us. First, the boiling water stung us but soon it turned cold so, we started dancing under it trying to escape from the freezing water. We stayed there for about five minutes. Then, they ordered us to go back to the courtyard, naked. There we started to put on our underwear, to cover our genitals when the corporal yelled in his nomad, or Dairi dialect; from the city of Deer al Zour, I think:

"You idiot, come here!"

I didn't know if he was talking to me because I was still busy putting on my underwear, I just continued even faster. Then, a lash hit me that made me stop:

"Yes, sir."

"Come here idiot, son of a bitch!"

I had put a leg in one of the openings of the underwear, so I ran towards him trying to hold them up. Standing in front of him, I tried to put my free foot into the other opening but a violent kick knocked me to the ground. I was sprawled on the asphalt, wet, naked and now covered with dirt and garbage.

"Stand up, idiot!" The corporal yelled.

I stood up immediately, with my eyes shut and my face to the ground, while my underwear fell to my ankles and I cupped my genitals with my hands.

"Your hands behind your back, idiot!"

I opened my eyes a little bit, I saw the sergeant walking behind me, while he indicated to another guard, smiling.

"Why is your ass white, you slut?"

I hesitated, not knowing what to answer. Then I said:

"Allah's creation, Sir!"

"Allah's creation, Aaah. Come let us see the creation of a slave ha,ha!" He said as he laughed then, continued addressing the other guards.

"What do you think boys?"

"I'd like it to be red." Answered one of the guards, while some of the rest laughed. The corporal started hitting me on my behind with his lash and I screamed, amongst their laughter. His dirty sexual words followed each strike. The courtyard's gate opened and some guards entered with more prisoners. The corporal ordered us to gather in the corners, while they passed by.

"You animal, are you looking you idiot?!" The guard standing on the bathroom rooftop, yelled.

"You idiot, get out!" The corporal exclaimed.

No one left, so the guard on the rooftop yelled:

"This idiot there," and he threw rocks at one of them, which struck him hard. Blood poured from the prisoners' head and screaming in pain, he fell onto his friend in front of him.

"Get out, you idiot!" The corporal approached the man that fell beside the wall.

"No, not the one that got hit, the one behind him." He was pointing at Abu Fatwa, a man in his late fifties, from the province of Idlib. They took him out of the line to receive a number of kicks and slaps, before they threw him to the ground and battered him with whips, until blood poured from his back. However, that wasn't enough for the corporal, he started stepping on is back. Soon, others jumped on his back with their heavy military boots, until he lost the ability to walk.

We left the courtyard, moving towards the dormitory, carrying two of the wounded who were unable to walk. The one who had been hit with a rock had completely lost consciousness. The doctor bandaged his wounds, trying to stop the blood pouring from him. In the evening, it seemed like he was healing but soon he lost consciousness again, the doctor decided that his situation was dangerous and he needed to be taken to the emergency room. The Dormitory Chief knocked on the door; a voice from the rooftops came back:

"What is it, you animal?"

"We have a dangerous situation, needing urgent care." The

doctor answered.

A half an hour later, one of the sergeants came to ask form outside:

"What do you have?"

"Sir, he has internal bleeding. He is in a dangerous situation." The doctor answered.

"That's why you're knocking, you idiot. When he dies you knock. Understood?"

"Yes, sir!" The Dormitory Chief says, interjecting after the doctor hesitated.

At dawn, the man passed away. So, some of the Brothers washed him and when the breakfast came, the Dormitory Chief informed the sergeant of the death. An hour later, the sergeant returned, accompanied by the guards and Service Men, to order us to take him to the courtyard. The dormitory door got shut as we heard the voice of the sergeant, ordering the Service Men:

"Take him and throw him in the trash."

Everyone in the dormitory says farewell, with sadness and melancholy. After that we got used to saying farewell, to many others. Maybe, we even envied them for they had moved to their lord's neighborhood and were enjoying peace and comfort. For those who had bad luck, Allah will extend their age, afflicting them with whatever severe diseases he desired. The daily and random torture caused some paralysis and wounds that became inflamed and infected. Sometimes even loss of sight and eyeballs were gauged out. Every day there was a chance for death, or paralysis, or receiving an injury that left you with a permanent disability.

The days all pass alike in the dormitory. We would memorize the Quran and the Speeches, while some of us started entertaining ourselves by making rosaries from olive seeds by rolling them on the wall, or the asphalt. Some excelled in making bones into almost all the tools we needed. Others started braiding the strips taken from nylon bags to turn them in to firm threads we used to make into ropes, bags and sometimes even pieces of clothing.

There were different charges amongst the prisoners in the dormitory. Most of them were charged with being members of the Muslim Brotherhood, while there were a number from the Islamic Liberation Party and the Iraq Ba'ath Party. Only a few of them actually belonged to the parties but most of them were charged with concealing information, or guilt by association because of helping their relatives, or people they knew. There was a group of weapons smugglers who caused us lots of problems in the beginning, until they came to their senses and obeyed, for the sake of everyone in the dormitory. Even the Ba'athists, who seemed to be the poor relations of the Ba'ath Party, when tempted by money soon returned to their origin and religion, announcing repentance and asking forgiveness from Allah, surrendering to His will.

About a year had passed in Palmyra, when I felt the eyes of Abu Omar following me wherever I went. He smiled at me when our eyes met. He was a middle-aged man with some gray invading his thick black hair. In every movement he reminded me of my father, even when he embraced me I felt the tenderness of a father. I accepted his actions with good intentions. Soon, Abu Omar exchanged his place with a young man that used to sleep beside me. In the beginning, it seemed to me as a regular thing that happened. I accepted his looks and even his harassments with good intentions, for he was an honest man with intense faith and everyone in the dormitory respected him.

Little by little, I started to feel that something irritated me behind his looks and smiles, which increased when I found him embracing me one day as we slept. I realized that he was, 'attached' to me. That was what we used to call this kind of attraction, which came over some of the Brothers in the prison. Some considered it a natural case and others considered it an evil that we should resist and reject. I asked the Dormitory Chief to change my sleeping place and he found me a place beside my friend. The 'attachment' phenomenon started to increase year after year; a case of love and adoration that took its owner to a state of insanity. Over time, the diligence of trying to heal this phenomenon increased, because of the political, religious and regional currents that wrestled amongst it. The Muslim Brotherhood movement split into two groups. Some supporting Esam al-Atar and others supporting the Sheikh, Abu Ghada. Whilst the Muslim Brotherhood argued this issue amongst themselves, others, like Sufis or Koranic sometimes called them infidels.

The attachment case was often platonic. In it, a man often admires another without attaching sexual desires to it. It was an impeccable kind of love, which was in the rank of friendship and brotherhood. Not a physical, voracious love like the love of Allah, his prophets and His angels, above all desires. However, some of those attachments did evolve into voracious love-making. Some would whisper and accuse this person or that one of exceeding the platonic attachment, which caused many conflicts and sometimes developed into hand fights. This type of sexual arousal was deemed a crime against the law of Allah.

One day I heard one of the very large prisoners submitted to the lust, without guilt. In prison speak it was called, 'thighing' when men touched each other's penises. This was because they covered their thighs with a blanket and practiced it especially in the dormitories that didn't have a skylight. The news of the attachment and the 'thighing,' reached the prison management through one of the smugglers that revealed our secrets. It was the smugglers way of getting revenge for the isolation the Dormitory Chief had imposed upon him, because of his sexual harassment of one of the young boys.

The smuggler told most of our secrets and we became exposed to the attacks and punishments of the guards. They started using the Breathing Period to humiliate, harass and ask dirty sexual questions about our genitals. These remarks crushed our pride. On one of those days while we were being exposed to their nastiness, Abu Ghadi's rage almost exploded, when he witnessed his fifteen years old son, being humiliated. So, he objected saying:

"Sir, I swear my son is noble, he didn't do anything."

"Come out here, you animal. You are all whores coming here, you can't say you're noble now!" The sergeant yelled angrily.

Abu Ghadi, groveled quickly in front of the sergeant that assailed him with smacks, then used the lash, striking his body as he fell to the ground.

"Take off your shorts!" Then as he whipped Ghadi with his lash, he addressed the son, "you too, take off your shorts!"

They took off their clothes and they remained in their underwear. The sergeant thought for a little bit then with wickedness:

"Take off your underwear, idiots!"

They hesitated for a little bit but the whiplashes made them take off their underwear, becoming completely naked. The sergeant ordered the father to have sex with his son, the father objected complaining:

"I swear I couldn't do that Sir, that's my son!"

"You animal! Grovel you idiot!" The sergeant yelled pushing him towards the ground, so he groveled, naked on the asphalt.

"Lie on top of him, idiot! Let us see the brush enter the Kohl jar." The sergeant said sarcastically.

The father hesitated, so the sergeant pushed him to try and

make him fall onto his son. He instinctively jumped back, colliding with the sergeant, who fell to the ground.

The sergeant went crazy, hitting him with the lash on his naked body. Meanwhile, some of the other guards joined in with him, hitting both the father and his son. Their naked backs cracked as they were writhing in pain on the asphalt. The ground beneath them colored ruby red with their blood. It seemed like the sergeant hadn't yet repaid his grudge for this great humiliation. He ordered the guards to raise the father with the 'fan' movement. Four guards grabbed him, each taking one arm, or leg and started to wave him in the air. Then they released him to fly through the air, only to fall on his back. Howling a monstrous scream of pain, he fainted.

We carried Abu Ghadi back to the dormitory, only to discover afterwards that he'd lost the ability to walk. The lower part of his body had become completely paralyzed. The fan movement was common in Palmyra Prison. Many suffered from it and very few of them survived the paraplegic effects.

The weekly bathroom visit was an ordeal for the prisoners in Palmyra. After that came the shaving day, where we would leave as usual, to the rhythm of the lashes and thick sticks, to go to an area where there was a large container, filled with soap foam. We had to wet our chins with it then line up along the wall, with our eyes closed and heads facing upwards. Then, a number of the Service Men started shaving our chins with a blunt blade, covering our faces with wounds and blood. After which, the guards entertainment session would start, which always ended with a number of whips on our bodies. Eventually, when the shaving stopped, we would enter the dormitory to inspect each other's bodies and count our losses.

We had gotten used to these daily rituals. We would laugh sometimes at our tragedies and sometimes, we would cry about one of us dying. A number of us lost their mind suddenly and some of them got it back, after a while. There was no chance for insanity, insanity meant death delivered by the whips and maybe worse. I still remember how we woke up one day, to the voice of the prisoner who initiated the call to attention, with a strict military dialect:

"Ready...Rest...Ready... The dormitory is ready for inspection sergeant."

Some of the brothers tried to silence him but he resisted, yelling:

"You idiot solider, go into the line!"

"What is this voice in there?" The guard yelled outside.

"Nothing Sir, he is having a nightmare." The Dormitory Chief said, while some of the Brothers were able to hold down the man and silence his voice. He'd lost his mind completely, imagining that he was a general in the military and he was communicating with Hafez al-Assad, directly. He believed that there was a conspiracy by other officers, that caused him to go to jail and he wanted to explain it to the Chief. The Brothers in the dormitory tried to calm him down and return him to his natural state. He soon calmed down, came back to his senses and started to memorize the Quran as usual. So, when it appeared he was fine they left him alone. Just then, the door opened to bring the breakfast in and he came up front with confidence, yelling:

"Where is the animal sergeant, start the call to attention, you idiot?!"

Everyone froze in the dormitory; a stunned and horrified silence fell. The sergeant approached the door calmly, curious. The man kept on approaching him with confidence and military arrogance:

"What? You can't hear me, idiot? Start the call to attention quickly!"

The Dormitory Chief tried to intervene, trying to explain to the sergeant but the sergeant indicated for him to stop. The man passed by the sergeant, exiting the dormitory with confidence and looking at the shocked guards surrounding him with their lashes. The sergeant shut the door while the man remained outside, wandering, as if he was in another world.

A few minutes passed with the sergeant asking him sarcastically about his character. Then the wailing of the man started, he was threatening that he would tell the president about this and that he would take the sergeant to trial. Gradually, his voice faded then disappeared forever. He didn't come back to the dormitory that day, or the next. He had breathed out his last breaths and no one dared to ask about him, after that.

The days didn't go by very fast but they went by, regardless. Despite all of these harsh circumstances, I was able to survive the illnesses that afflicted the Brother's bodies in our dormitory. Cholera infected us and the prison management did not intervene, until we lost two of our Brothers. Those who were suspected of showing symptoms got transferred to another dormitory and none of them returned. However, I was able to find out about them after we got transferred to the Juvenile's dormitory. The spread of lice irritated me; lice had infested the dormitory and there was nothing we could do but pick them out of our clothes and kill them between our nails. We spent a lot of effort fighting the lice, which was time consuming and slowed down my memorization of the Holy Quran. That infestation wasn't the worst though. The worst was Scabies, which started infesting our bodies, digging into them without us being able to do anything to stop it. Scabies is a small bug that you can't see with your naked eye. It dug into our skins, creating black blisters that grew and scattered all over our bodies, killing the flesh. Once the severe scratching started, the Dormitory Chief started to isolate the infected ones, who surrendered to their illness. The prison management ignored the illness, which exacerbated the situation, killing a number of prisoners. Eventually, they brought in medicine, in addition to some procedures that helped in reducing the disease cases, until it was partially eradicated.

The sick didn't get transferred to a hospital, only in exceptionally dangerous circumstances. Often, the patient would die without anyone being able to help him. The doctors in the dormitory, strove to heal the prisoners, with the few medicines and natural treatments they had. They employed all the available materials and tools. However, the dental diseases didn't have any treatment. The dentist wasn't any better than the old market barber, who historically removed teeth with primitive tools. This is what happened to me when my toothache became severe and my tooth got infected. The pain stopped me sleeping for an entire night. One of the men tied my tooth with one end of a dormitory made braded plastic string, while he tied the other end to a piece of wood. Two of the strong men held me down, while Abu Ramez ripped my tooth from its socket. It was a severe pain for seconds and a long sleep after it.

Three years had passed since I entered the prison, when the sergeant entered to read out a couple of names and one of them was mine. In the beginning we didn't know the reason but the Dormitory Chief guessed it was for the court. We were gathered in a small courtyard, amongst the usual whips of the lash, each one of us holding the other's waist. We squatted down, our faces to the wall, our eyes shut while the insults of the guards and their whips continued non-stop. When my turn came up, they lead me into the courtroom, which was a small office in the Palmyra Prison rooms. He asked me to open my eyes and to face the three people in civilian clothes sat behind a large table: the person in the middle asked me, as he was reading in the dossier:

"Oh my god, you did all of that and you're only fourteen! What would you have done if we left you outside, to become fifteen?"

"Sir, I swear I don't know anything."

"Get the hell out before I hang you!" He said it with disgust, indicating for the guard to push me roughly outside.

I didn't know what my ruling was but I knew that there was some kind of ruling. At least that is what some of the Brothers in the dormitory who were at the court, informed me.

Death sentences were an indication for the Brothers to stop all activities, except worshipping. Two of them were busy fasting and worshipping as two others joined them, asserting that they too were sentenced to death, because of the similarity in the charge. Despite the effects of fasting, they would race to volunteer to receive punishment to protect others. Some of that was part of their worship; a way of asking for forgiveness and some of it was their eagerness to join the predecessors of martyrs. Our share of executions wasn't large, only about ten were sporadically executed in the first two years. However, that year we said farewell to more than twenty people, most of them were organizers for the Brotherhood.

The executions would occur at daylight. Once the names were read in the first hours of the daylight, we would realize that there were executions that day. We would wait for our dormitory's turn, anticipating in terror whose turn it was. For those who knew their sentence seemed served, they surrendered to God's fate, facing the execution with a steady content heart, near its salvation from the constant torture of the prison. They were confident of Allah's forgiveness, eager for the rewards and for his soul, to shield them in an eternal heaven.

Those whose names were read that morning would enter the bathrooms, to perform ablutions publically. Their traces of fear had faded from the torment that would soon be over. They would pray the Morning Prayer, then change their clothes to worn-out ones, leaving what was left of their few belongings for the remaining Brothers. They said goodbye to everyone, asking forgiveness for any wrong they had committed towards any of the Brothers in the dormitory. Everyone prays for them, in the hope that Allah will be kind to them and make them follow him in heaven.

In the distance, in one of Palmyra courtyards, their voices arrived to us saying Allaho-Akbar after they mentioned their names, before the hangman's noose tightened on their necks.

Tuberculosis started crawling inside our dormitory and we heard that it was spreading quickly in the other dormitories. As usual, the prison management didn't answer our calls for help, until the disease took hold and then they started isolating the prisoners in the tuberculosis dormitories. I was lucky to not have suffered from tuberculosis and I decided to isolate myself, devoting my time completely to prayer and memorizing what was accessible from Speeches others had memorized.

In the fourth year, I was transferred to the Juvenile dormitory in the sixth courtyard. Here, they gathered the young ones between 13-17 years old. We found it difficult to reorganize our life without the Wise Men, which caused us consecutive punishments, sometimes more severe than the regular prisons. Little by little and under the pressure of the punishments, we learned how to organize most of our life, to share what we had with love and justice. Since we were collected from most of the prison dormitories across the prison, we were able to share the news. Many of us were able to hear news of relatives, or friends. Some of them were so happy about that but some cried for the loss of a brother, a father, or a friend. However, Samer was the saddest, as he got informed that his father was receiving a punishment in Al-Sawaleel, (Solitary Confinement) and he was suffering from tuberculosis. The solitaries were frightening for everyone and it was very rare for anyone to comeback physically, or mentally unscathed. Some of them never returned. Samer was a twelve years old child when he got arrested, as a hostage for his father. His father was arrested later but they kept Samer and he was the youngest of all the prisoners. Originally, he got exposed to various types of torture, trying to make him confess the location of his father. However, he didn't know where he was, so they gave up on him and kept him as a hostage. There are many stories of hostages in Palmyra and the other Branches. It was one of the usual charges, (hostage) in addition to other strange charges. Samer joined my food group where I tried helping him to keep himself together. I started making him memorize the Quran that I had memorized and he was my first student.

The dormitory was like every other dormitory in the Sixth Court. Its ceiling had a three square feet skylight; the guard could almost see all of what was happening in the dormitory, which was a surprise for us. We became prone to punishment for any reason and often for no reason at all, simply because the guard got bored, so he started to give us orders that entertained him. He would ask one to sing and dance sometimes and another to imitate the animals. There was nothing stopping him but the borders of his imagination. He would often ask us to mark one of them because he didn't obey the commands, or because he saw him talk to another. The next day he would ask for the one that got marked, to deliver whatever he willed from whips and humiliations.

Only a month had passed, when we watched the first execution case. The crack in our dormitory wall, allowed us to see a section of the execution courtyard and we could hear what was happening there. At dawn of that day, there was a hustle of the regulatory names reading and the openings of the iron doors. About forty men gathered in the room that was called the Workshop. This overlooked the execution court, where they'd installed a number of wooden gallows, from which hung a thick nylon rope that ended with a noose. The names got inspected then, they lead them to where the gallows were installed. The prisoner would squat in front of it, while the Service Men slanted the wooden gallows towards him, for the noose to get tightened on his neck. Seconds later, the muzzled Brother gets raised, swinging in the air. The brother shivers a little bit then soon his body calms down and he has surrendered his soul.

The executions repeat and we would take turns to look through the crack, as if we were watching a movie. Unfortunately it was real life, tens of bodies piled up in the courtyard in minutes. The doctor examined the corpses to make sure they were dead. Soon, a big shipping wagon enters and the Service Men start throwing the corpses inside. We knew the number, from the sloshing noises of the corpses landing inside of the wagon. Before, counting was easier, when we were also able hear their names as they prayed, asking for people to forgive them, saying Allaho-Akbar before they die. Now it was harder as they were forced to put muzzles on their mouths, so we couldn't know who got executed, we only knew their numbers.

Executions became regular and uniform for long while. They took place twice a week on a Monday and a Thursday. The numbers of those executed varied but it never any less than 80 Brothers.

Besides the execution days, everything was normal in the

standards of Palmyra prison. The days passed just like in the past, the torture would ease down sometimes but would soon come back harsher than it was before. Our biggest joy was the canceling of the bathroom and shaving routines.

In the morning of the week before my transfer to Damascus for a visitation, I watched the most horrendous scene. My friend Samer got killed. Samer, with great dignity asked Allah every day, to make him a martyr and avoid humiliation and servility. That evening as we were getting ready to sleep, one of the mean guards who often got bored, so used to enjoy humiliating and torturing us, came into the dormitory.

He started giving us commands, served by his sick fantasies and started making us pronounce words addressing the honor of our mothers and sisters. That was the worst we were forced to do, so we would recite what he asked from us, surrendering slavishly. Inside of us we heard the voices of some of the Brothers, who informed us that they were nothing more than words. Words that get erased, once they are mentioned. But Samer couldn't pronounce these dirty words in the honor of his mother that day. The guard asked him, threatening more than once but Samer was pinned to the ground, silent as a stone. In the morning, the guard came accompanied by the sergeant and asked Samer to go outside as usual, to receive his punishment. The guards gathered around him and the sergeant asked him to recite what the guard had asked him to:

"That is my mother Sir, I cannot." Samer said.

The whips assailed him; he fell to the ground while the guard started kicking his head with his military boot, as he repeated his dirty words against the honor of Samer's mother. Suddenly, Samer pulls the guard from his legs, he fell to the ground and Samer thrust his teeth in the guards' throat. The other guards attacked him, trying to break the guard free from Samer's teeth, as his mouth filled with blood. Finally, they were able to snatch the guard away, who was by now on the verge of death. They started kicking and hitting Samer with sticks, until his head turned into a mass of blood and his strength faded.

The Warrant Officer came and the anger poured from his eyes. He ordered them to whip Samer on his entire body, nonstop. The minute he lost consciousness, they would pour a bucket of cold water on him, then the guards would continue their beating. They soon started to kick him on his smashed face and its features disappeared into a dirty bloody pulp. His strength had completely faded and he was semi-dead, when the warrant officer approached to check on him. Then, he asked the Service Men to hold him down, to press on his throat until he breathed his last breaths and he faded like a static corpse. They kicked him severely after that, to make sure he was dead. Then, they took us out to the courtyard for a violent round of torture, while Samer's dead, bloody body was lying there, in front of us.

\*\*\*

# 15 BEIRUT

# AL GHAWARENA NEIGHBORHOOD

The Ghawarena neighborhood was a gathering place for the poor Shiites coming from the Bekaa villages. They joined some of the poor orthodox Christians who had also come down from their villages, in pursuit of a better livelihood. Later on, the poorer Syrian workers, Maronites and Armenians found it a convenient place for their limited incomes, so they also settled there with their families.

The neighborhood was divided into two obvious regions by a street that separated them; a neighborhood for the Orthodox Christians and another neighborhood for the Shiites (Al-Mutawela.) Most of the Shiites worked by selling kerosene using carts pulled by horses or mules. The Orthodox Christians of the area were workers and craftsmen in different careers. The

Orthodox Shiites were homeowners, while all the Syrians were renting from the Lebanese Orthodox and Shiites. The Christian living region was more refined than the Shiites region, mainly because of the all-pervasive smell of animals the Shiites used in their work.

We were living in the Christian region. Aside from the Palestinians, there were only two families living on the edges of the two regions. One of the families was Christian and the other Muslim Sunnah. The Syrians weren't divided into sects. Their only sect was their Syrian identity. They came from different areas in Syria, united by the Lebanese looking down on them, regardless of the sects, cities or the country regions they came from. The richness of Maronite Antelias Town spread over the sloping plains down towards the sea. It was considered the capital of this region with its stores, restaurants and other urban life. It was similar to most of the towns that spread towards the capital, Beirut. Those towns were called Eastern Beirut during the Lebanese Civil War that broke out in 1975.

The coastal towns that spread towards Beirut would often enchant me. Our house's balcony overlooked the Mediterranean Sea. That beautiful calm lake with the lights of its ships spread out in front of my eyes, igniting my childish dreams and feeding it adventurous Phoenician tales. The sea was only one mile away from our house and it was only about a half mile away, from the school in Antelias. Sometimes, we would spend our free time hanging around on its golden sand. Especially during the summer weekends, when my friends and I would spend most of our time on its beaches, to swim in its safe, calm water. We would make rafts from the wooden pallets that would fall from the huge commercial ships. Our most enjoyable game was swimming to faraway areas in the sea. When we grew tired, we used a stick inserted through a mass of white polystyrene, which had been used to protect electronic tools, as a float so we could rest awhile. We would swim together; a group of boys maybe no more than ten years of age. We usually packed a couple of small sandwiches, together with a bottle of water, in a nylon bag and hung it from our shoulders. Our meeting spot would sometimes be near an anchored ship here, or there. The sailors, would wave at us sometimes, or maybe throw some sodas, or fruits to us. So, we would be really happy and swim afterwards to the beach at sunset.

It was a relatively happy childhood, punctuated by some mistakes and hindrances that didn't gouge deep furrows in my memory. The beautiful moments remained, uncurling its dreamy eyelids on most of my childhood years. My childhood friend, Yasser and his brother, Eyad came from a Palestinian family, committed to its cause. Their older brother had lost his leg in the war with Israel. He remained a prisoner to the bed for a while, before receiving a prosthetic leg, which he took off when he went to sleep. I was assured of that when I visited them one morning, only to find their brother's leg, lying in a corner of the room. They were a poor family displaced from Jaffa. Their father had migrated with some of his family members, to escape the massacres committed by the fanatic Zionist organizations, coming from the West. Their father struggled to work as a waiter in one of the restaurants, dreaming of returning to his home in Jaffa. His family owned a lemon orchard, in addition to a small shop that they had lived off in Jaffa, before being forced to flee one evening, leaving behind all of what they owned. The house key remained with his grandmother, who passed away later, in one of the refugee camps in Lebanon. The dream of going back transferred to their children, who refused this humiliating life they thought of as only temporary. They believed, just like any other Palestinian displaced from his land and livelihood, that they wouldn't get them back without a fight. Yasser and Eyad's family was a small one, in comparison to other Palestinian families; five boys with no girls. The eldest was working as a journalist in a Palestinian News Agency, married with two children. They all lived in a small basement, which consisted of three rooms but they would often use the small yard, shadowed by a lush grape arbor, for sleeping during warm days. Those yards were common in Beirut.

We, the children, sympathized with the Palestinians. We would be sad for their sorrows and happy for their joys, affected by our parents that lived the Palestinian Diaspora and shared it with them. Our imagination was charged with the heroism of the guerillas in their 'dignity battles' and their love of martyrdom. Our games often derived from that. My group of friends decided to create groups of guerillas within our clique. We were a group of Syrians, in addition to the Palestinian brothers, Yasser and Eyad. The thirteen year old, Yasser, was the eldest one amongst us and the most experienced because he had taken a single day youth course with the guerillas. He was the de facto leader of our group, which decided to build its base in the nearby oak forest. A wide oak tree was selected. An entrance was cut into its trunk then, it was emptied of pulp from the inside and the floor of this 'wood cave' flattened. With the help of simple tools, some wood and what we were able to bring from our houses, we built a headquarters to gather at and negotiate our future plans. Yasser took on the role of the trainer, instructing us in a life of abstinence and enduring hardships. In addition, he taught us the training he received on the youth course such as crawling, climbing trees and guard shifts. Soon, this headquarters turned into a small house that contained amenities such as a pan for cooking, food and drinks; we even started planting a couple of tomato and potato plants. I can't remember now if the tomato plant fruited, or not but I do remember that I was responsible for watering it, from the small container of water I would bring with me from home, almost every day.

When the battles started between the Lebanese and Palestinian Army in 1972, our clique disintegrated and our base was deserted; I was only twelve years old. We would hear gunshots in the distance, so my mother forbade us from going afar, she only allowed us to play in front of the house. My father didn't return that day, or the next couple of days and my mother didn't feed our curiosity to know where he was. However, something stirred in our hearts as supporters of the Palestinian side, we had no doubt he had become a hero and was fighting the war defending the Palestinians.

I remember that during one of those days, we were shocked by the invasion of a group of heavily armed Lebanese soldiers, into our playground. They smiled at us as they snuck into another building, searching for a Palestinian weapon cache. I remember my contribution at that time was to deliberately and aggressively throw my soccer ball at the soldiers, which they received with patience and a smile. A couple of days later, my father came back from his disappearance and we restarted the studying that had paused for a while.

In the year 1973, we, the young ones became extremely influenced by the October War between Syria and Egypt, against Israel. The news of victory along all the fronts ignited our enthusiasm. We had the fortune of watching some of the Air War Operations directly over our house, which ended with a Syrian aircraft shooting down an Israeli aircraft. During the war and directly after it, the television shows and some documentaries fed our excitement. We were proud of our Syrian brothers taking revenge over the Lebanese, who treated us like an inferior class, or race sometimes. However, during the war and after that, many things changed and we became a focus of respect by our classmates at school. In secret we would mock the weak Lebanese army and be proud of our brave, Syrian one.

Soon, the war atmosphere faded and life went back to its natural state, or that is what I thought. That beautiful land called Lebanon was igniting under the ash. A political body with class based sectarian privileges, inherited from the French colonialism; mixed uneasily with the conflict of the Middle East, alongside its international and regional alliances. I was only a boy swimming in a mixture of thoughts and events, transfused with demonstrations and paramilitary parades. In the Eastern Christian region of Beirut where I used to live, the most intense mobilization was by the Christian Parties; especially by the two main parties, the Liberal Party and the Lebanese Brigades. Soon, the other Leftist Parties in the Eastern region; the Lebanese Communist Party and the Syrian National Party, started working with remarkable vigor against the regional and sectarian incitement that was focused on the Palestinian presence. This was due to the Palestinian factions being supported by the Islamic sects and the remaining Leftist parties.

I was going back home along the asphalt road, when I met Yasser walking towards Antelias and he looked distressed. I greeted him, so he stopped to tell me that the Brigades had attacked a bus that carried some Palestinian civilians back from a party. They had already killed and wounded tens of Palestinians in the district of Ayn al-Rimmaneh during clashes that broke out there. The bus attack was a dangerous development and would inflame the situation even further. I continued walking home, listening to his advice.

I heard gunshots in the evening but they soon stopped. However, after that it didn't calm down. Mobile Security checkpoints, sporadic clashes and assassinations made life tense. You felt you were in danger with every step you took outside of the house. However, the neighborhood remained safe, the schools didn't shut their doors in the region and we would hang around in the nearby neighborhoods. Gradually some military action began appearing here and there until this delusion of security suddenly collapsed.

We woke up one day to the sounds of a machinegun shooting profusely through the street that our, the children's bedroom window, overlooked. We ran terrified towards the interior rooms, as far away as we could get from that rear street, which the Shiites (al-Mutawala) resided in. Soon, the noise calmed down and we were informed afterwards, that a group of the Brigades men had attacked Yasser's Palestinian house. The eldest son confronted them, so he shot one of them. After some of the armed Shiite men joined him to defend the Palestinian family; two of the attackers ran away, down the street.

Jamal's father was a wise man and had no desire to develop the situation, so he released the Brigade man after he treated his wounds. He wanted to end the agitation that could lead to everybody's death, so he said to the wounded:

"Go, you are free. Act according to your Higher Values."

In the following days, the clashes resumed somewhere far away from the neighborhood. Meanwhile, we started seeing the appearances of protection and military mobilization. In one of the nearby streets, the Armenian Tashnaq Party closed the street where their office was located, to protect their members. What they called the Mobile Inspection checkpoints appeared, which were carried out by the Lebanese Brigades Party and the National Liberal Party. Their presence only served to further fuel the tension and fear amongst the inhabitants. A soon as the summer vacation started, we began to live our lives as if we were in a military camp. Ghawarena neighborhood became a fortress for the Communist Lebanese Party; in addition to some of the members from the Shiite, (Amal) Movement and groups belonging to the Palestinian Liberation Organization. The shifts of overnight guards became something familiar. When they began the kidnappings, many no longer risked going to Antelias town where the Lebanese Brigades had their headquarters.

I was coming back from the mountain in the morning, when the neighborhood ignited with profuse gunshots. I hid down the road, behind the big oak tree, until the gunshots calmed down in the north neighborhood. Then, I ran hunched over, until I arrived at the entrance of one of the houses. Someone opened the door for me, to help protect myself from the gunshots in the street. That was Abu Alyas's house. He was a man in his sixties, kind but with tough features. There was nobody there except him, his son Alyas and his son's wife. The gunshots decreased, so Abu Alyas left to go to his balcony to explore what was happening. Suddenly, we heard a burst of gunshots, followed by a muted scream from Abu Alyas. Then gunshots erupted on all sides. Alyas's young wife screamed, as she pulled back her husband who wanted to go out and help his father. It wasn't safe to go to the balcony as automatic fire was still riddling its walls. I approached the balcony to explore what was happening but I immediately backed away. I was spooked by the vision of Abu Alyas with his stomach exploded and his blood scattered everywhere. I watched his eyes looking at me, as he held the remainders of his guts then, he shut them as if he took one last picture of me, before he died.

I froze for a while in my place, hiding behind a nearby wall. At that moment, one of the men entered to embrace young Alyas, who lost control of himself. He wanted to get out and fight but his wife clung to his arm, hindering his movement. The balcony was exposed to one of the house's yards that belonged to one of the Brigades members. They'd used it as an ambush for themselves.

I looked at Abu Alyas, thinking his soul was with God now but I watched his eyes open, looking at me as if he was pleading for me to save him. I do not know what happened next and how I found myself quickly crawling to the balcony, until I was able to reach him. The gunshots had calmed down but as soon as I rose up a little bit, trying to pull Abu Alyas inside, gunshots burst out again. I felt one penetrate my chest, so I collapsed beside Abu Alyas. I didn't feel any pain; I only felt a sense of anesthesia and my body swimming in a pool of blood. I quickly surrendered to the idea of my death. I wandered with my eyes towards the distant horizon then, I returned to Abu Alyas's eyes, close by and staring at me with no sign of life. 'Soon, I will be a corpse like him. My mother and father as well as all my siblings will cry and maybe some of my friends will grieve as well.' I thought.

Then, a long strip of memories passed before my eyes; my early childhood, my first childhood when I ate my friend's food that I was entrusted with and the day I kissed that young girl, for the first time. We were about the same age and I didn't feel anything, my chest didn't shiver with love like I'd read in one of the adult magazines. Nevertheless, it was an experience we couldn't stop ourselves from having. We wanted to get older and act like the adults. I felt my chest with my hands, to feel for the supposed blood and punctures in my chest. There was nothing but some small gravel, while blood was pouring from my hand. My other hand was still drowning in the blood pool near me. I didn't realize that it wasn't my blood, until some men pulled me quickly inside. One of them studied my chest, looking for traces of bullets but he couldn't find anything, except some traces of the gravel that had hit me. The balcony wall's small barrier had protected me; I was only hit by gravel ricocheting off from the bullets. I was soaked with Abu Alyas's blood, who had passed away and soon we were able to pull his body inside.

Someone covered him with a sheet, which was soon soaked with the blood still pouring from his shredded guts. I cleaned what I could of the blood that stuck to me. The gunshots stopped at noon. When I left, I found a Lebanese Army tank parked near the street, while a number of tanks and other armored vehicles were scattered around. The solider stopped me to make sure I wasn't carrying a weapon then, allowed me to continue on my way home.

I didn't see any armed men in the street, except the Lebanese Army that had intervened to stop the clashes. I entered my house but didn't find anyone. My father had sent my mother and siblings to spend the summer in Syria. I was worried about my father especially, because our house was located on the western edge, where the street was empty of passengers and cars. I waited for a while then, decided that staying in the house exposed to any attack, was too risky. I left the house carefully, heading towards the ground floor where my aunt lived but the door was locked and I didn't have a key. I started trying to open it with a piece of metal, when suddenly the door opened and I found my father in front of me. It was a joyous reunion.

In the evening, a group of men joined us who decided that the Brigade's forces might attack from this side. They thought my aunts' apartment, which overlooked the street and was protected by an asphalt balcony, was a convenient place for guarding. We spent the night with almost no sleep. My father decided that the situation was heading towards a war and that I had to follow my mother and siblings, to Syria.

The next morning, the Lebanese radio was broadcasting the

news of agreements and détente. The army had imposed calm and therefore, there was no more need to fear walking the streets. We boarded a taxi towards Tripoli, where it was decided that my father would return to the house. He gave me a large amount of money to give to my mother, to continue building our house in the village. Then, in his opinion, as the situation was going to get worse, he would return to the house to finish his work and then follow us.

We hadn't crossed through Jounieh city, when the car stopped in a long line. We could see a Lebanese Security checkpoint, inspecting the cars and we could hear gunshots every now and then. The car couldn't go back, because there were a number of armed men on the rooftops of the buildings, surrounding the cars. Any car that risked reversing would undoubtedly receive a barrage of gunshots, killing everyone inside it. We had to wait for our turn and our fate. As we got near the checkpoint we started to realize what was going on. Inspection and killing by identification. All the wanted Palestinians had to be killed directly, in addition to whomever they didn't like from the Islamic sects.

When our car got near the inspection checkpoint, I saw one of the men being led from one of the cars in front of us, towards the nearby bridge. As he disappeared our turn came up.

"Identification cards." Said the armed man on my father's side.

I was sitting in the middle, between my father and the driver. My father gave his identification card to the armed man, while my identification card was given to another armed man on the driver's side.

"Get out of the car." The armed man said to my father, while the other armed man was still inspecting my identification card.

My heart sank suddenly. My world collapsed before me like dust. I couldn't fathom what was happening in front of me but I heard someone saying to the armed man that was inspecting my identification card:

"Syrian! Leave him."

He gave me my identification card while my father got out of the car. I don't know why, I just uttered without thinking:

"He is also Syrian, he is my father." I addressed the guard from my side.

"Syrian, leave him too." I only heard these words as my father re-entered the car and the Inspector in charge, explained something about how Syria had helped them.

The car drove off away from the checkpoint, as a heavy silence fell, which was suddenly interrupted by a burst of gunshots coming from under the bridge.

I don't think anyone in the car talked after that. We lost the ability to converse completely, looking into the distance, fervently hoping to arrive at Tripoli without being faced with another Security checkpoint. In Tripoli, my father's plan failed when I insisted he didn't go back. I threatened I would go back with him if he tried, so he complied and continued the trip with me to our village in Syria. There we were reunited with my mother and siblings who had arrived there before us.

As I recall, a few weeks later, my father and my aunt went back to the house, as they were assured that the crisis had ended and that the situation had returned to normal. Only a few days had passed after their return, when the Lebanese Christian Forces started an attack on most of the areas that had a Palestinian or Islamic presence in the Eastern region. Their intention was to evacuate the area completely of Palestinians, Muslims and other forces that supported them. The Ghawarena neighborhood was one of the districts that faced their attack. They came under siege when the water, electricity and all tools of life were cut off. The small number of armed men resisted. However, they soon ran out of ammunition. They lost some of the wounded, while some of them hid in the nearby mountains and others hid in their houses.

One of them was my childhood friend, Omar, who laid in his bed pretending to be sick but that didn't save him. They cut off his hands before killing him. They burned Eyad alive as he was wounded in his bed. Another young man, who was just working in Lebanon, received the worst fate. He was dragged across the asphalt tied to a car and then, right before passing away completely, they tied him to two cars that drove off in opposite directions, splitting him into two pieces. Later, they found lots of corpses in the nearby bushes, of people who had jumped from the high buildings, trying to escape. That same day, they led all the other men in the district to the Brigade's center in Antelias, as war hostages. Some of them passed away in the torture sessions after that. For the women and children like my aunt, they were led to a church where they were released later, to migrate to areas outside of the Eastern Christian Region.

A few weeks later and in an exchange of hostages from the Lebanese forces, they swapped what was left of the prisoners and deported them to the Western Region; my father was one of them. The houses of those who weren't Christian, were completely destroyed and I saw its remains a year later when I returned after the Syrian Army entered Lebanon. The Shiite neighborhood was completely destroyed, completely demolished and turned into a square filled with dust and wild grass.

***

# 16 PALMYRA PRISON

## 1986

About six years had passed since our arrival at Kafarsouseh. After three years of her arrest, my sister was released due to an illness. Whilst my younger brother was released after six years, just a couple of months before some fellow prisoners and I, were transferred to Palmyra prison. We didn't know for sure that we would be transferred but we suspected it, because a number of prisoners from the Communist Labor Party had been transferred there, two weeks before. At the time, the transfer was explained as being a punishment for some of the new, young prisoners who were still extremely enthusiastic about their cause. Due to their eagerness, they had immediately started a hunger strike, attempting to improve the prison conditions.

For us older prisoners, this was an unwelcome situation as we had gotten used to the current prison regime. Which, after a long while of suffering, conflicts and protests, allowed for some peace and stability. This protest was childish work by young men who hadn't been exposed to the experience of the old prisons; therefore, they didn't realize the relative amount of privileges we now received. There was an acceptable amount of food and periodical visitations. In addition, the family was allowed to bring some books that we requested. These books were a godsend for those of us who found reading the most important way of spending the long prison days.

The punishment of a transfer to another prison, as a consequence of a hunger strike, was not new for the prisoners of Kafarsouseh. They transferred the Engineers and Lawyer Syndicate from the room right beside ours, after they had a hunger strike that extended for more than one year, to protest their long sentences. They were arrested in the beginning of 1980 when a new leadership was imposed. After which, their syndicates got dissolved because of their lively participation in the movement of public protests, active at that time. Although we anticipated punishment continuously, it didn't cross our minds that it would include a transfer to the notorious Palmyra Military Prison.

It was an unlikely occurrence with the presence of the Branch chief, who sympathized with the Left in general but that is what happened. In the first hours of daylight, the guard opened the door holding a white paper and read out our names. He asked us to get ready to be transferred to Palmyra; he uttered it like a person who was just forced to expose an evil secret. Yes, the guards weren't happy about it either. After six years of communal living, regardless of the black iron door that separated us, in a way it was still communal living. They used to spend with us, in the same place, almost half of their lives. Sometimes, they would even share with us their concerns of humanitarian and family issues. It also happened that we shared our secrets with some of them. We had lots in common. We used to share the place, the food and the long hours. We were all jailers and prisoners who hated the Prison Chief (Abu Ahmed). What haunted us the most was when he had an altercation with his wife. This argument, had practically led him to flee his house and reside in his office, above the prison. You can imagine an angry old man supervising prisoners and jailers, while having complete control over their punishment.

The list of names of those to be transferred to Palmyra, included all kinds of Leftist convicts who were held in Kafarsusah Prison; from the members of the Communist Labor Party to members of the Syrian Communist Party (the political office), the Nasserist and us. We gathered our belongings quickly, while we distributed many things amongst those who remained in jail. In the jailer's room we got our hands and feet cuffed, then were lead to the meat wagon. We got tied together with the iron chain inside the car, while two guards armed with automatic rifles sat in the back. A door separated us from them with a window covered with iron grilles.

Anything seemed possible. Many from those who'd experienced the transfer to Palmyra had told us about this wagon. Inside it, movement was difficult and the coldness was severe. It was an old wagon with two side benches, from World War Two. We would bump and swing the whole way to Palmyra. It was a long trip and the sharp, wounding coldness of the desert, crept into our bodies. What we didn't expect was the extreme need to urinate, despite all the precautions we took, from not drinking liquids to going to the restroom a couple of times before leaving. Abu Kareem couldn't take it anymore, so we decided to cover him while Sami helped him take his penis out. He urinated in the corner of the wall separating us from the driver. Soon, that happened a couple of times with others, until there was a small puddle of urine moving in between our feet, whilst we swung with the movement of the truck. When the smell of the urine intensified, the guards' noses caught it and they cussed all their anger on us, threatening us with a special punishment when we arrived at Palmyra.

As soon as we arrived near Palmyra City, we started glimpsing its great ruins from the small windows. I had spent many long months reading the history of this old city, with its great civilization and it had always charmed me. Zenobia was the rebellious queen that faced the Romans and sailed into my imagination as I stole a look at her ruins, waving from afar. I didn't have the chance to visit it when I was still free. Perhaps, I was delaying that to another day but I never imagined entering this city in handcuffs. I didn't know why I was feeling delighted as I watched the palm trees, perhaps because it made me feel as if I was going towards the desert. The desert, that golden land I'd dreamt of visiting. The land that had shaped our history, our culture, our world.

When we arrived, the morning had dawned. We got out of the wagon where Abu Michael was waiting for us. The Palmyra prison guards that lined up on our sides, weren't allowed to do anything to us as he addressed them directly, with kindness in his eyes; whilst avoiding ours, as he felt shame and pain:

"Those are good guys. Take care of them boys."

Abu Michael was in his prime, an enthusiastic Ba'athist; who very quickly ended up being an employee for National Security, believing that he was defending a revolution. However, over the years, he realized that it was nothing but a cheap tool held by some corrupted officers. He complained to us about that more than once, expressing his deep emotional pain and reminiscing over the political struggle; before the series of Ba'athist Coups occurred, which were called a 'Revolution.'

We said goodbye to Abu Michael and some of the patrol members that used to know us, while the two guards who had accompanied us in the back of the wagon, smiled at us. It seemed as if all the Security Men were saying their last goodbyes to us, almost like we were going to be executed. Sad looks accompanied us as we entered the prison gate, led by the Palmyra prison guards, who refrained from hitting us, as if they'd accepted Abu Michael's words. We felt a false sense of security as an astounding shout from behind:

"To the wall, you animals!"

We bumped into each other as we threw ourselves at the wall in front of us. With my face stuck to the wall, I received a kick from a heavy military boot to my back, which made me writhe in pain. Immediately, someone at the rear shouted, commanding them to leave us alone. One of the guards shot an insult, threatening us:

"No problem, you'll see later. Be patient you sons of bitches."

After we arrived, we waited for a severe torture session. It was part of the Palmyra Military Prison tradition. We had been saved from the reception entrance session, where they were supposed to line up on our sides, leading us to the waiting room with the whips, sticks and iron pipes. For this we were grateful to Abu Michael for it was quite possible that some of us would have died during this reception. Almost an hour later, filled with suspense from waiting in the small room, we were ordered to leave to go to the reception courtyard. Once there we were ordered to lie down on the floor, our faces facing the cold asphalt ground. The frost was severe that morning, which dawned with its gleaming desert light.

We were about fifteen men that were called, one after the other, to record our personal information in the reception room. In the room, there were two men wearing the Military Police uniforms, delivering their job with a cold, efficient routine, like we were nothing more than goods entering the warehouse. As soon as they finished recording, we would go back to lie down again, waiting for everyone to finish. Although they hadn't treated us with the evil we were expecting, we were still terrified, our eyes glanced about warily and we winced at the sound, or movement of a guard behind us. Abruptly, a guard's voice rose to call for a giant prisoner with huge muscles, like one of the Roman wrestlers.

The guard cussed him then, asked him to bend in front of him. In an instant, he was thrown in front of me and some of his blood splattered onto my face. He'd received a blow to his face with a wide wooden plank, the type used as construction truss. He looked at me through the profuse blood that covered his face; the ghost of a daring smile drew on his lips, as he got up answering to the guard's orders to continue his job. I came to know later that he was one of the members of the forced labor gang; they were called al-Baladya, (the soldiers convicted with many charges for serious crimes.)

As soon as they finished recording our information, we were transferred to a nearby courtyard where we stripped naked, except for our underwear. We were inspected forcefully during the safety movement, to make sure that we are not hiding anything in our behinds. We lined up to the wall, our faces stuck to the cold cement, trembling from the frosty cold and the threats from the guards, promising us upcoming tortures. Just then, a terrifying loud scream rose from one of us. I turned towards the sound, inadvertently spooked out. I stared as one of the giant Baladya men raised a bright sharp tool above Salah's head, holding his neck from behind. The scene seemed as if it was a slaughter process, with a machete. Salah was trembling, waiting for his fate, while the giant smiled and said:

"What's wrong? We just want to shave your head!"

Salah looked at him, flabbergasted, then his face muscles relaxed and the Service man started shaving his head with a manual razor. We breathed a sigh of relief, despite the insults and some kicks we received because of disobeying orders and looking behind us. The terror had smashed us between its edges and the stories of the horrific Palmyra Prison were stuck in our minds, digging into our imagination. The barber was supposed to shave our heads completely, until there's nothing left on our scalp but a quick look at Salah, after he finished being shaved, made me draw an inadvertent smile. There were furrows of hair wriggling from his scalp, while small locks of hair hung here and there.

We were led through a small gateway to one of the courtyards, then to another where we entered the prison room through a black iron door, accompanied by the usual cusses and yelling of some of the guards. We were pushed inside running, as we stumbled over our luggage that we'd packed in a hurry, only to find ourselves paddling in a pool of water. The room consisted of two small rooms about 13 x 16 feet, connected through a small door. In the corners of the interior room, a small bathroom was constructed with a plastic sink attached to the wall, aligned to it.

The place was basically a section of a public toilet, which had been hurriedly sectioned to accommodate our sudden arrival. The water pipelines had been covered with cement that was still wet and we could peel it off with our fingers. The bigger problem was the accumulated water on the floor that rose to about two inches. We stood up for a while not knowing what to do. We didn't have any tools to take the water to the bathroom. We started using some pieces of our clothes; we would dip it in the water pool and squeeze it in the sink. Everyone contributed to that with spirit, after we lost hope of any help from the guards, or the prison management. We'd been met with mockery and insults, accompanied by threats when we'd asked for tools to clear the water from the room. Soon, a group that was transferred before us to Palmyra joined us. The door opened suddenly, we were ordered to line up with our faces to the wall. Then, we heard the noise of men being pushed into the room, amongst whiplashes and insults. The sergeant entered afterwards, ordering us to line up with our faces towards him, heads bowed and eyes closed.

"Who is a soldier here?" The sergeant asked but no one answered.

"Which of you served military service with the rank of an officer?"

A number of us raised their hands. He asked about their ranks then, chose one that served in the Military Police:

"You are the Room Chief. You will start the call to attention every time the door opens, or anyone calls you from outside."

Sameh nodded his head saying:

"Yes"

"You say: Yes sir, you animal!" The sergeant yelled angrily.

"Yes, Sir!" Sameh repeated.

As soon as the sergeant left Sameh, said loudly:

"Rest."

Some of the newcomers collapsed on each other, resting against the wall, while others dropped into the water pool. Most of them had received a couple of strikes from lashes and sticks. They'd been led from the fifth courtyard, where they'd spent two weeks before our arrival, waiting for the preparation of a new room, which was called the Bathroom room. A number of them were completely exhausted, as they told us the horrors they saw in the fifth courtyard, where the solitaries they called, 'al-Sawaleel' were located. The Sawaleel were small cells, just like ancient solitary graves. They would glance at them when they would receive their meals, when the courtyard would be full of guards. When the sergeant called the number of the cell, the doors would open and a prisoner would dart out holding his plastic container, hunched down to the ground as much as he could, running like a lame duck shuddering under the whips, until he arrived at the big pot. The Service man put some food in his container and he returned as fast as he could, led by the lashes. The punishment for those who dropped their container was severe; therefore, the prisoner would try as hard as he could to maintain the container's balance, despite the whips that shook his body, until he arrived at his cell and they closed the door behind him.

They'd spent about two weeks in the courtyard. Although they weren't exposed to daily whips, that everyday atmosphere of the solitary cells was enough to spread horror in their souls. When they were moved to the Bathroom room, all their dreams of going back to Damascus faded. They had hoped that this was just a temporary punishment and they'd soon to return them to Kafarsouseh, whose regime they were used to. In this situation, more than one person told me they would commit suicide, if we were treated like those Muslim Brothers in their Sawaleel cells. At a time when suicide was forbidden amongst the Muslims, there was nothing stopping those who weren't committed, or who weren't believers, which was most of us, from killing themselves.

By noon we had succeeded in transferring the accumulated water to the drains. Suddenly, the guards stormed into the room, spreading out. The call to attention started in a strange military rhythm, which made us panic and get confused, we started turning to every side not knowing what to do. I still remember how one of us froze in his place, performing the military salute and didn't lower his hand until the Prison Chief asked him to, smiling as he realized the severity of his panic. The Prison Chief's visit comforted us. We were allowed to ask him some questions and converse. He answered some questions and requested some blankets and a pot but the madness occurring outside our door, made us nervous. During the inspection period, we would hear our neighbors from the nearby rooms, running as fast as they could to exit from their iron dormitory door, amongst an insane barrage of lashes. That happened until the counting ended and they would return to their room once again. Hell was flaring outside and it seemed as if we were waiting like fat sheep for our turn to get slaughtered. The next day they brought a group from the Communist Labor Party, who were incarcerated in Palmyra Prison before us, into the Clinic dormitory. The new comers informed us about the circumstances of our new prison, which made us relax a little as they began taking care of dealing with the guards outside, whom they'd gotten used to.

During the next day, the ceiling started shaking from hammer strikes above our heads. We didn't know what was happening, until chunks of cement started falling on our heads. Somebody's head got wounded, so we took refuge in the other room, while one of the older prisoners knocked on the door to protest what was happening. We were informed that it was the Prison Chief's orders. Soon, a hole, 13x13 feet wide opened up to the sky. They left the cements' steel reinforcing grille in place as a barrier between the open sky and us.

The older prisoners reassured us that it wasn't a problem. Rain was scarce in Palmyra and we were able to make a kind of umbrella from nylon sheet. It was connected in the middle to a plastic water hose, descending to the floor where it ended inside a plastic container. In the rainy season we had to empty it every now and then. Those who volunteered to sleep around it during the rainy nights, had to take occasional turns emptying the plastic container, until the morning came and the rain stopped. However, the rain and frosty cold weren't the worst of what we were exposed to from the desert weather. We were surprised one day at noon, when the sky above us turned a red color. Little by little the sun disappeared and darkness fell. We started breathing with difficulty, despite the masks we made hurriedly out of our underwear, after listening to the advice from one of the desert weather experts. It was a desert sand storm called, 'al-Touz' in the local language. It went on for hours but we survived from suffocation, unlike the others in the nearby rooms.

Gradually, life got organized and we spent our time reading, despite the hell that was happening in the room overlooking our courtyard. Gradually, we became inured to the ritual daily torment of whips, continuous whimpering and screams coming from there. As soon as the distribution of the breakfast food ends, the Breathing starts and then, distributing lunch and finally dinner food, began. In every activity the guards would excel in humiliating and torturing the prisoners. I would sit behind the door sometimes to watch what was happening outside, through a small hole. Fear would fill our souls; hence we would escape into a book, or a conversation, trying hard not to hear the continuous pain. No one could guarantee what would happen to us tomorrow. Everything was in the hands of the Prison Chief, who was a friend and a classmate to one of the older prisoners from the Communist Labor Party. He played the role of the middleman between the prison management and us. He delivered our requests and ensured our protection from the guards, who were longing to humiliate and torture us.

More than a year had passed in this place. We were allowed to be visited every two months. Every family would travel to Damascus to get permission from the Military Police, then would go back to their houses to get ready for the upcoming visit, where they would bring some food, clothes and maybe some money. We used to communally share almost everything and manage ourselves through a general authority that decided most of our daily life. Nobody owned what his family brought him. The general authority would take everything, to redistribute it as needed. Later, it was allowed for those who desired it, to keep something personal as a memory of his family, or his wife, like a shirt a mother made for her son, or a wife for her husband. Most of us were smokers; therefore, smoking was the most important daily issue. We had to find ways to buy tobacco from our scarce money, or get it from what the families brought during their visits.

My daily share of smoking was two cigarettes, I accepted that because I had decided to keep a level of smoking that wouldn't harm me, while the regular smoker's share was between six to eight cigarettes. We would often find ourselves with no cigarettes as the purchase of cigarettes stopped suddenly, or the cigarettes got cut off from the market for a period of time. I only felt its absence because of the effect it had on the addicted ones, who were forced to find extremely harmful alternatives, such as smoking the paper bags, or carton coils. Some of them excelled at stuffing them with ta few corn-cobs, or dried grass.

We spent about a year and a half in Palmyra, then we got transferred to Sednaya Military Prison, near Damascus.

We were gathered in a large courtyard, where we got surrounded by a large number of guards, armed with lashes. Whispers spread that we might receive what was called the Palmyra Farewell Session, (al-Tawdeya) where it was customary for the departing prisoner to receive between ten to twenty lashes, to remind him to not return to Palmyra Prison again. We waited anxiously for a while but they didn't hit us. Instead, we got cuffed together to enter the meat wagons as usual, to begin a new, long trip towards Damascus.

\*\*\*

# 17 SEDNAYA MILITARY PRISON
## 1987

The long caravan that took us to Sednaya prison arrived at noon approximately.

Sednaya prison was a modern building. The Prison Chief took great pride in it by calling it the 'Swiss Prison.' He always loved to describe it that way, maybe because it was a Swiss design. It looked like the Mercedes logo. Three wings forming three floors. Each wing consisted of two sections overlooking the hallways of a circular center, amidst which were stairs leading to the upper floors. They were long stairs that wrapped around to connect together at the end of the wing. Each section consisted of ten rooms overlooking the hallways and on the top there were high iron windows. Meanwhile, the two lower floors were for the kitchen, bathrooms and solitary cells, while some spoke of a third lower floor.

We were the first political prisoners to arrive there. Tens of military service men, which were convicted of various crimes, arrived there before us. We got recorded in the prison reception office, calmly and peacefully. They were still confused about how to treat us. One of them thought that they were getting ready for the welcoming sessions. There were a number of whips lying in the courtyard in front of us, in addition to the car tires that were used for torture sessions. However, that didn't happen to us since our protector, the Palmyra Prison Chief was transferred with us, in addition to his crew.

We were lead to one of the right section wings, (A Right) where those from the Communist Labor Party joined us from the Palmyra Clinic Dormitory; to be put into ten closed rooms. Three blankets, one waterproof cover and a mattress were distributed to each one of us. It was the first time we'd received a mattress. The prison dormitory was basically a big room, about a hundred square feet. In one of its interior corners were a bathroom, a toilet and a urinal. The room's exterior door was in the middle of a wall made of thick iron grills and it overlooked the long hallway. It was only a day before the prison was packed with prisoners that were mostly transferred from Palmyra. The section behind us, (A Left) was inhabited by prisoners from the Democratic Arab Socialist Ba'ath Party, (February 23rd Movement) who were transferred from room number 11, in Palmyra.

We were able to communicate with them for the first time, through the skylight windows. Each room was able to communicate with the room facing it, while we were able to communicate with the rest of the rooms by passing on messages through the grilles to the room that was behind, or after us. Therefore, to pass a message from room 3, (A right) to room 6, (A left) for example, it had to pass through the skylight window to room 3, (A left) then in turn, they passed it on to room 4, then 5 and that goes on until it arrives to the recipient. Of course, we had to watch the hallway and make sure there was no one there. That was the role of the person holding the small mirror, which he used to see the hallway through the iron grille.

Truly, it was a fancy prison in comparison to the bad circumstances in other prisons. Some expressed gladly that by comparison, it almost felt like we were released! We didn't hear that daily torment and we enjoyed the relatively wide spaces to sleep, as each one of us owned a cotton mattress about 3 feet wide. That was like a dream come true, to be able to sleep lying on our backs, comfortably. One day, we were informed that hot water was pouring through the pipelines, so some of us were able to take a warm shower. Although that only occurred for a sporadic couple of times, then disappeared completely, it still felt like we'd been transferred from a scummy den to a five-star hotel. The room doors remained shut except for inspections, or receiving food but soon they allowed us to go to the exterior prison courtyard, to sunbathe.

When they let us out together, we had an excellent chance to communicate with the rest of the rooms in our section. All the rooms from our section would open for us to exit to the courtyard simultaneously, where we would spend about an hour. Then, they would return us to our rooms and shut the doors. Some days later, we dared to visit other prison cells in secret. We would exchange prisoners when we would return from the Breathing. Two people would agree from two different rooms, as it was important to maintain the same numbers in each room, so the jailer didn't realize what we were doing.

Only few weeks had passed before one of the members of the

Communist Labor Party, was lead to one of the cells in the lower floors, to serve a punishment. He passed away due to a heart attack because none of the jailers had heard his pleading to get help. It was a huge shock for everyone who knew him, especially those of his friends and the members of his party. The day after his death and while we were in the Breathing courtyard, one of them yelled something I didn't understand in the beginning but immediately most of the prisoners stopped in silence. Then, I came to realize that he'd said:

"A moment of silence."

We, the ones that didn't belong to the Labor Party, were unaware of the plan, yet we joined them, daring the Prison Management and taking the moment of silence. That was considered a rebellion in the Military Prisons. The guards screamed at us angrily, as they commanded us to continue walking but no one moved, until the moment ended. We got led back to our rooms immediately, amidst the infuriated screams of the guards. In the evening, arguments ignited amongst the Communist Labor Party members, regarding a hunger strike they were planning to start. The opinion was divided between the supporters and opposition to the idea; the ones that didn't belong to the party refused to go along. The morning of the next day, they refused to receive the food and altercations started between the guards and the strikers, when they began knocking on the iron doors violently. The Prison Chief arrived immediately; he ordered violent measures to be taken after many attempts to discourage them from the strike. The strikers were led to another section on the upper floors, while we started hearing the sound of whips assailing them. It was a fast strike that faded quickly and life went back to its normal state.

We were allowed to receive books from the prison library and the monthly family visits started. It was only weeks before the

Prison Chief agreed to open the wing doors during the day, only closing them at night. We took great joy in our freedom of movement between the twenty rooms in our wing, thousands right and thousands left prisoners. So, we were able to visit and wander freely in the hallway, building an effective social life inside the prison.

Several months had passed before the new Vanguards from the Labor Party started arriving on our wing. It was quickly filled with new prisoners coming from the Palestine Branch. There were hundreds of them convicted with belonging to the Communist Labor Party. They were arrested in a campaign that targeted eradicating the party. This was ordered after some of the party members kidnapped one of the reporters and tortured him in a very extreme way, in one of Damascus suburbs.

The rooms got filled once again with new prisoners, most of them suffered from scabies and needed treatment, food and clothes. The pressure to share what we had with the new comers, severely taxed our scarce resources. When our wing got filled and there was no more space to absorb any new prisoners, those that remained were transferred to the wing, (A right) on the third floor. This was when the vertical communication network got developed through the skylights. A rope with a basket was extended through the skylight to transfer the messages and small items to most of the wing's floors. In addition, our communication with the outside world was developed though the spread of small radio devices. Almost each one of us had a personal radio, with small earphones that gave him some privacy and allowed him to take an account of and not to annoy, the others.

However, we had a problem, maybe due to the nature of the prison construction but the reception was very bad. I don't know who had this idea first. The Breathing courtyard was covered with a net of wires and someone introduced the idea of using it to receive broadcasting. A reel of copper radio wire, had one end tied to a small rock, thrown out of the window to intertwine with iron wire nets outside. Then, the wire was extended to the side of the room and tied to their small radio. It was a great idea and soon the net of wires spread, hidden under the mattress beside the wall, to connect to most of the radios.

Little by little, the daily activities became routine and we were able to organize, develop and practice various activities, pastimes and hobbies. Musical instruments were made from wood, bread paste and newspapers. There were hundreds of prisoners with all kinds of knowledge, so each one started teaching his specialty, while studying somebody else's expertise. Classes started for languages, philosophy, math, physics and whatever special skills were available and according to the requests from the prisoners. Foreign languages were the most requested classes. I supervised one of the English language classes, in addition to Greek Philosophy; while I was a student in Math, Arabic Language and Music Class. In the remainder of my time, I was prone just like many others, to studying and reading.

My daily program was completely full. I would wake up at 7 in the morning; I would start my daily exercise activities for almost one hour, followed by a morning shower and a quick breakfast. Then, I would start studying and reading, according to a stable program, sometimes paused for supervising a class or two, each one of which lasted for about an hour. I maintained this program for about twelve years. I don't remember stopping it, except for the few days when I was transferred to another prison.

Our life was regular and included medical treatment because we had a good number of doctors, as prisoners. The prison management allowed them to buy medicines and distribute them amongst the patients, as needed. However, the biggest issue was in treating teeth. Despite having a dentist amongst us, his tools were poor and scarce. However, he would spend all his effort trying to treat what remained of our teeth, which had rotted and broken due to a long while of negligence and bad circumstances. In addition, Palmyra Prison, along with other Prisons and Branches' diseases had followed us here. Hence, a large number of prisoners suffering from tuberculosis and scabies joined us. We had to fight it as much as we could under those circumstances, trying not to get infected but I wasn't lucky. I contracted scabies and I had to be treated with burning chemical materials, to kill those bugs that lived in my skin causing itchiness and skin inflammations. That wasn't the first time I suffered from scabies, I'd suffered from it before in Kafasouseh Prison.

There were huge events happening in the outside world and especially in Lebanon, where wide arrests were occurring of members of various political parties, especially of their political leaders. We were a center to welcome most of them: Islamic Unification Movement in Tripoli, Progressive Socialist Party, Palestinian Fatah Movement, Nasserist and the Lebanese Forces, in addition to other numbers of Palestinian Organizations.

In the beginning of 1991, most of the Labor Party members who withdrew from their party were released. The only ones who remained on the wing, were the few leftists. Therefore, we got transferred to Wing (B), on the second floor, where they gathered the members of the Labor Party and Communist Party, (Political Office). The wing was divided into two sections; one for the older prisoners amongst us, while the other section was especially for the members of the Labor Party who got arrested after 1987, 'the new comers.' The sections were separated by a wall at the end of the corridor where they intersected. In the wall there were some windows, big enough to communicate and exchange a few small tools through.

At the end of 1991, (December 15th,1991) the jailer came to read my name among a group of other prisoners; we said goodbye to everyone quickly, in disbelief. Our friends expressed their joy for our release, by carrying us on their shoulders towards the exterior door where they said goodbye. In the Breathing courtyards, we found ourselves amongst a big group of prisoners from all political persuasions, a big pile of clothes and sport shoes. Those who didn't have appropriate clothes were asked to change them. We spent about an hour waiting, until everyone had changed their clothes and had their names inspected, then we were led to Kafarsouseh Branch. We stayed there for two days, where we were asked to sign a pledge to leave political work. We saw that it was a silly paper that had no value for either side. It was like many other inspection papers they forced us to sign with our eyes shut, not knowing what we were signing. Only one person refused to sign. They kept him for two more days, I think, I don't know if he signed it, or not after that.

Two days later, after keeping us in Kafarsouseh Branch, they led us to the Internal Branch, (al-Khatib) where they put us in a big hall. Some of us sat on chairs and others sat on the floor. One of the officers gave a speech and his voice quavered when he reminded us of the motherland and the motherland leader, hailing his great graciousness since he'd pardoned us, after we'd spent a merciful punishment from the Father Leader. The guards clapped for him a couple of times, along with all the prisoners sitting on the floor from the Muslim Brotherhood and Iraq Ba'ath. Their souls were completely stolen by torture, while us, the Leftists, our souls were still willing to persist, we refused to clap. One of the Warrant Officers turned to point out to the officer that we didn't clap but he ignored him and didn't comment. We overheard through the door of the room they lead us to, the officer talking to his soldiers. He told them not to pressure us because there was no way to stop our release; once the Presidential Pardon with our names had been issued.

An hour or two later, the officer came back with a large pack of money in his hand, asking if we had enough money to return to our families. We refused it as we thought we had enough money to do so. Moments later, they called us four who'd been in the one cell together and we were led through the cellars of the branch, to find ourselves on an outside patio, amidst two lines of guards that kept indicating for us to keep walking, while the officer that led us out, disappeared back inside.

***

# 18 FREEDOM

## DECEMBER 1991

Suddenly, we found ourselves in a crowded street with cars. We froze, stuck to the spot as we looked around us in panic and disbelief, suspicious of what was happening to us. We looked behind us; we had crossed through the line of security men. We didn't know what to do. No one had told us that we were being released. Do we keep walking? Are they going to take us to another prison? Is the Meat Wagon parked somewhere? We looked at each other's faces, confused, while the guards indicated for us to go away. We started walking away, tentatively. Soon, we reached al-Khatib Square, which was full of pedestrians and we couldn't see the guards anymore. Abu Khalid said, almost in disbelief:

"They released us guys!"

We looked to the street and the people around us, not knowing what to do. Where do we go?

"Let's take a taxi and go far away." One of us suggested with grandeur.

"Let's leave before they change their mind." I responded, half-jokingly.

We stopped a taxi and loaded our big bags inside its trunk. Then, we boarded the car amidst the wondering looks of the driver.

"Where to guys?" The driver asked.

One of us said:

"Al-Salhya Street."

"What? They released you?"

"Yes, but we want to eat Knafeh* before we go home."

Yesterday, we had planned to go to a Knafeh shop, before we said goodbye. We counted the money we had. Each one of us had about a hundred Liras. We thought, taking into consideration monetary inflation throughout the years, that it was more than enough. The driver delivered us to al-Salhya, in front of one of the Kanafeh shops. He took a hundred Liras from us and later we realized that he took advantage of our situation, he had made us pay double what we were supposed to pay for that short trip. We ate Knafeh as we contemplated the crowded streets ahead of us. It was the most delicious thing we'd eaten for many long years.

We said goodbye to Abu Khalid who traveled onwards to Daraa. My two friends and I took stock; we only had two hundred Liras. It was a big shock for us. How were we going to get around with two hundred Liras, when the taxi had cost us one hundred for such a short distance? My sister had left the prison nine years ago, graduated and worked in Damascus but I didn't have any telephone number, or an address. However, I knew she lived in an apartment in the same building as my aunt. Therefore, I suggested going to my aunt's house in Riken al-Deen.

We took a taxi towards Riken al-Deen. I thought I would know the street once I got there. However, the city had completely changed and I didn't recognize the Damascus streets, so I didn't know where to ask the driver to stop. Then, remembering that she lived beside Abu al-Nafis hospital, I asked the driver to drop us off there. After disembarking the taxi, we only had one hundred Liras. If I couldn't find my aunt's home, then we were in a dilemma. We didn't have any official papers, or money and we didn't know any number to call. It was obvious that we were in a predicament as I stood, confused, in front of the hospital trying to recall the street where my aunt and my sister lived. I exchanged confused looks with my friend but after searching and studying the streets and alleys, it seemed to me as if I was in the right place.

I asked someone if he knew my sister as he was exiting one of the buildings; luckily for me he was one of the residents, so he directed us to her small apartment. However, we didn't find anyone at home. One of the neighbors informed us that she had gone to visit one of her relatives that lived in a nearby building. I asked my friends to wait there whilst I went to find her. After a while I arrived at a house that I seemed to recognize as the same place I'd visited thirteen years ago but I'd forgotten the name of the owner. I knocked on the door, which opened to reveal the inquiring face a young man in his twenties. I didn't know what to say, then quickly gathering my wits, I asked him hesitantly, if I could use his phone. He considered a little and then invited me inside. I told him who I was and he immediately phoned my sister. She couldn't believe it; she broke into tears on the phone and said that she'd be there right away.

It was a warm and emotional reunion between my sister, our aunt and myself. Soon, my sister's small room was filled with the many friends that hurried to meet me. An hour or two later, one of the friends that was released at the beginning of the year, had organized a party in his big house which a number of friends attended, especially those prison friends who were released before us. We stayed up all night laughing and talking. For me, it felt like I was floating like a mass of smoke, not knowing if this was real life, or a hallucination dreamt up by my imprisoned imagination. At noon next day, I took a car with my aunt and sister to the village where my family resided. A group of the villages' men were waiting for me at the end of the street that led to our house. I felt scared as they surrounded the car trying to raise it up, despite the driver's attempt to discourage them. In the square by the house, there was a huge crowd of people waiting to welcome me, in addition to my family, who waited with impatient disbelief. The celebration started in the tradition of the region, with dancing and Dabke, just like the weddings. I had to sit in the middle of a large number of well-wishers, to answer their questions and curiosity about the prison.

Although I had been awake for 48hours, I tried in vain, to sleep that night. What troubled me the most was the comfortable bed that I had to sleep in. Just before dawn I finally began to feel sleepy, so I folded the blankets I had and spread them on the hard ground. Then, at last I fell into a deep sleep.

My mother woke me up the next morning after I'd only slept for three hours, to inform me that there were more visitors wanting to see me. The sitting room was semi full with welcomers that I didn't know. I said hello to everyone and sat down to exchange some words of courtesy. One of them came close to me and with a broad smile, asked to see me in a private room. I felt eeriness but I agreed. I don't know why I felt suspicious, I thought maybe he was one of the opposition who wanted to talk to me about something personal, or maybe ask about a relative that had disappeared, or who was still in prison.

I invited the man to an interior room, excusing myself from the guests. Soon, three other men joined him from the guests, without excusing themselves. He introduced himself as an officer in the Political Security. He started asking me about jail and about my friends that left with me. I felt anxious, especially because he stated that the Branch Chief wasn't pleased with the welcoming home festivities that had happened in the village. Therefore, he'd assigned a Patrol Chief to watch what was happening in our house. I was polite with them; their padded language seemed filled with threats. I felt as if I had returned to prison once again. Or, was this just a temporary reprieve before they returned me to prison through a new gate? I went back to the sitting room while they returned to sitting in a car outside, watching and investigating some of those who visited us. Despite all of that, the congratulators kept on arriving, at least from those who had the courage to come.

On the third day, I was able to wander around our back garden. I was estranged from nature. It seemed to me, like I came from another galaxy. I couldn't identify all the colors. Some of the colors seemed as if I was seeing them for the first time. Green, wasn't what I thought was. It was greener, or maybe another color that looked like green, it was the same with red and yellow. At night, I escaped in the company of my brother, to our faraway field. We left from the back door and I don't believe that the Security Patrol noticed. The rain had stopped and dense clouds had spread across the dark blue skies.

I walked, stumbling on the wet earth, jumping between the large river rocks, attempting to avoid the muddy ground. I didn't succeed most of the time, so my only shoes and pants got dirty with mud. In the field my brother lit some firewood and took me to an orange tree. There were some oranges that he told me that my father had left for me, in the hope that I would get out of prison soon. For the first time, I felt a warm happiness invading my being; it was the joy of love and freedom.

On the fourth day, the patrol chief asked me to allow him to sit inside, since the weather was cold outside and they had to stay there all day. I accepted, not because I wanted to but because of the fear implanted in my heart.

I spent about a week, attending the sitting room, welcoming and saying goodbye, trying to be polite, fighting boredom, mindful of my family that had suffered a lot in my absence. I knew that of those people who were congratulating me today, some were the most extreme enemies when I got arrested about twelve years ago. Then, they had surrounded our house and tried to burn it down, along with its inhabitants. There was an extreme sectarian awareness amongst the villagers that erupted, to denounce anyone who opposed the Regime as an enemy of the motherland. The motherland was really al-Assad, who had tightened his grip, step by step. It was believed by some, that Ali Bin Abi-Taleb had been reincarnated in the body of Hafez al-Assad. Naivety, filled with legends built by a long isolation from civilization; poverty armed with oppression and fueled by bloody events, erased the remainder of their sense and bravery. Fear of the unknown, religion and control by an inferior security figure, replaced what remained of their identity.

I couldn't take it anymore. I left my family's home, apologizing for my need to start a new life and look for a job. My father was still financially afflicted by the burdens of the past, from the effects of the arrest of his three children. Which had exposed him to blackmail and fraudulent offers to affect our release. In addition, he had sent another child to study abroad. Despite this, my father borrowed a small amount of money for me, to start my trip to look for a job and a new life in Damascus. His help was gratefully appreciated.

\*\*\*

---

***Knafeh:*** *is a Levantine cheese pastry, soaked in sweet sugar-based syrup.*

# 19 DAMASCUS

## 1992-1994

I didn't have an identification card. They had replaced the identification cards with new ones and I had yet to get one. I couldn't travel to Damascus by any bus because traveling required a proof of identity. They refused to give me a new identification card and number in the Registration Office, until they received approval from three separate Security Departments. Three letters were delivered from the Registration Office to State Security, Military Security and Political Security departments. In the meantime, until I received the approvals, they gave me a release form which had my picture stapled to it and stamped by the mayor. This Inheritance Certificate guaranteed proof of my identity but was not enough for traveling between provinces. There was a box for my identification number on the travel form I had to fill in. The form had to be completely filled for the Police Officer to give permission. So, each time I wanted to take even a local bus, the officer had to have approval from a higher ranked officer. This meant that every time I wanted to take a bus, I had to go to the Security Patrol that was stationed in the Bus Terminus, to receive a special permission, after long explanations and interrogations.

Damascus had become my city because of my long residency in prison; it was where most of my friends and contacts resided. I lived with my sister in her small room, searching for any possible job. It was very obvious that I couldn't get a State job. Later, I realized that I would have no luck in the private sector either. They avoided employing those who had a previous political history like mine. Soon, my dreams of finding a job evaporated. I began knocking on my friends' doors, searching for an outlet. First, I had to start with obtaining an identification card that allowed me to wander comfortably and safely; that is when the, 'Thousand Mile' trip started.

I decided to start with the State Security Branch in Tartous City. I thought that it was the best place to begin, considering I used to be one of their prisoners; therefore, I would receive a quick approval. I was shocked when I found myself amongst a group of Security Men, blackmailing me to work for them. When I refused, with extreme politeness, they set a second date for me a week later, without giving me approval.

I returned to Damascus disappointed but a temporary job offered to me by one of my friends, who was a businessman, brought my smile and optimism back. It was a company that exported fruits and vegetables. I was assigned to buy amounts of them to transport to one of the European countries. It was a good start but my need to move around, forced me to find a quick solution to obtaining an identification card. I wasn't able to visit all the Intelligence Branches on the same day and I couldn't leave work for a couple of days without risking losing it. I had to go on a morning trip from Damascus to Tartous, to visit one of the Security Agencies where most of the day was spent in waiting and interrogations.

My second trip was to the Military Security Branch in Tartous where, after waiting outside for more than an hour, one of the Security Men led me inside to a reception room. I was extremely shocked to see it was a torture room. There was a naked iron military bed in addition to the torture chair, the car tire and a couple of lashes lying here and there. The room was dark, gloomy and dirty. Its walls were contaminated with dried, congealed blood. After a couple of anxious hours waiting, I met with one of the Warrant Officers who asked me to fill in a long form about fifteen pages long. They were long questions asking about the most thorough details of my life, including my friends, contacts, relatives and my relative's relatives from all areas. It ended with a summary of my resume, especially the political work and arrest. That was followed by long interrogations, then by offers and blackmails to cooperate with them, as a reporter. I didn't leave until their shift was over that evening. Even so, I was unable to receive the desired permission. Instead, they gave me an official paper, ordering me to follow-up with the Branch a week later.

Two days later, I went to my follow-up appointment to with the Security State Branch. Again, just like the last time, they asked me to follow-up with them a week later without giving me the permission. A day later the Military Security Branch appointment arrived. When I attended, they put me in the torture room again. I waited all day without anyone meeting me, then one of them came to tell me, arrogantly, to come back a week later because the vice Branch Chief was busy. Then he gave me the usual follow-up paper.

I felt as if I was going in circles that I couldn't escape. My need for the identification card was extreme. However, even if I hadn't needed one, I still needed to check back with the Security Agencies almost every week. I resided in Damascus and I had to be in front of the Branch gate at eight in the morning. To get there on time I had to travel before daylight from Damascus. It was a long trip that took about three hours by car, in addition to waiting for the bus that was about an hour and time spent at the Garage Center. In total I needed about five hours, therefore, I would wake up about three in the morning. Winter that year was extremely cold, with one snowstorm after another. Most of the time the roads got shut because of the accumulated snow. So, I had to use the train that would leave at one in the morning, to arrive in Tartous at six-thirty in the morning.

The train ride was exhausting; I couldn't get any sleep because the cold was severe in those old carriages. Once there, I had to spend yet another day in interrogations with crude, rough people searching for every detail of my life. Maybe, their sole intention was to paralyze my will to resist their request to cooperate and work with them.

About two months had passed during this satanic dance with the Security Branches, which caused me to lose my job. My dreams to live peacefully and gracefully were shattered. I felt as if I'd fallen under the mercy of a voracious octopus. As usual, for my next dance appointment I took a taxi at midnight that took me to Damascus Station. The snow was falling heavily that night and the ground was covered with a dense white robe. The train was waiting as usual; serpentine, long, colored in white and covered with a thick layer of snow. I booked in the first class, hoping to be able to sleep, if only for a short while, so I could face the next day with a clear mind. I tried to sleep but in vain, anxiety started rising inside me as I was thinking of how I can end this dilemma. I didn't want an identification card anymore and I didn't desire anything but fading and hiding somewhere far away from the human eye. From the eyes of those bugs that fed on terrorizing people and on their fear. The prison years became a nightmare that haunted me every day. I thought; 'what if they returned me to prison?!' It almost seemed to me like a good idea, one that would end most of my pains. It was about 6.30 am when I arrived in Tartous and I still had about an hour and a half, until my supposed appointment. I wandered around the empty city streets, trying to avoid the cold morning winds by passing through those distant from the sea. I felt hungry, so I stopped to buy a sandwich from a kiosk near the Political Security Branch, where I had to follow-up with that day.

At eight, I showed the follow-up paper to the guards in front of the Branch who asked me to wait. About two hours passed before I was ordered to enter, accompanied by one of the guards, who led me to one of the dirty offices filled with torture tools. It was a room containing a naked iron table with an office chair behind it. In one of the room's corners there were some sticks and tubular lashes. I stood in the middle of the room waiting. I couldn't find a chair to sit on and I didn't dare to sit on the office chair. About two hours passed, where I sometimes stood and other times I squatted down. Every now and then, Security Men would enter to check up on me without saying anything. I was smoking my cigarette while squatting, when a Security Man entered accompanied by two guards. He looked at my face angrily, then addressed the guards:

"Who allowed him to smoke?!"

The two guards attacked me; one taking the pack of cigarettes while the other one stole my lit cigarette, threw it to the ground and stamped on it with his boot.

The officer sat behind the table and the two guards bookended me. A torrent of insults started, in addition to questions about things I was interrogated about twelve years ago. Other detailed questions followed about reports from about thirteen years ago. I couldn't answer many of his questions, because it was so long ago and I couldn't remember. He got angry at every word I said, screaming insults at me. My head started throbbing with a severe headache. I almost collapsed from fatigue and disgust. The interrogation continued for an hour, or two. They left after that, to eat their lunch. When he came back I was sat on the floor exhausted, hungry and thirsty. I requested some water but the officer ignored my request, scoffing. Their shift had ended, so they asked me to come back the next day. I told him that I traveled all night to get here on time and I didn't have anywhere to sleep.

"There are lots of hotels in the country, or do you want to spend the night with us today?" He said sarcastically.

I didn't answer. The guards accompanied me outside, without forgetting the follow-up paper for the next day. I took a couple of steps before one of the exterior guards called me, I stopped for him to give me a paper and on it there was an address for a hotel in Tartous. He told me that the Boss wanted me to go to that hotel.

The street was swaying ahead of me, tens of thoughts danced in front of me, 'I can't take it anymore!' I screamed inside. The desire for death immersed me.

Scared, defeated and trembling with anger, I was on the verge of madness. I stopped in front of the requested hotel. I looked in at the reception hall inside it. One employee was sitting behind a wooden table and he was busy writing something as he talked on the phone, his eyes scanning the place like a vacuum cleaner. I backed down to the street as I was overcome by a wave of cold trepidation.

Suddenly, a flame of defiance lit in my face, my fear melted and hot blood roared in my veins. I turned, heading towards the Bus Station and home to Damascus. I took one of the buses and I determined to never follow-up with any of the Branches, ever again. I felt sure that in the end it would only cause me another arrest, torture and imprisonment.

*

That night, after a hysterical crying surge that I wasn't able to control for a while, I fell into a deep untroubled sleep. I realized that the Security Men would need a day or two before they reacted to my absence. I hid for a couple of days, moving from one house to another with the help of some friends. Then, I was able to find a small room in the Mazza neighborhood 86, where a mix of poor Alawites and Kurds lived. I felt as if I was in a small village near Damascus. Most of the housing there was hurriedly built, violating the construction rules without any license from the municipality, just like many of the poor neighborhoods around Damascus.

I organized my room with cheap furniture, which was enough to make me feel comfortable. This place seemed safe and the Security Men wouldn't find it, despite the fact that I practically lived amongst them. Most of those who lived in the neighborhood were Militants and Intelligence Agents from the poor. They were given a small piece of land to build a cement shack, which the whole family cooperated to build.

I was desperate, without hope. It seemed nothing could save me from the anger of the Security Men, who were searching for me. My issue wasn't with just one Security Agency anymore, now it was with the biggest three Agencies! I didn't go to my weekly check-up appointments and for them that meant resistance. I realized their range, when the news started coming from my village that the Security Patrol kept coming to my family's house. They didn't have any address besides the village address, so they started informing my parents of the necessity for me to follow-up with this or that Branch. I continued to resist, regardless of the price I had to pay.

I didn't have a job and my money started to become scarce. I had to find a solution. I resorted to talking with one of the leadership members of the Communist Party, which was allied with the Regime in the National Progressive Front. He suggested sending a letter to the President of the nation, which I forcefully agreed upon. One of the lawyers wrote a letter to Hafez al-Assad, explaining my issue and asking for help. They delivered it to his office. I didn't know what happened but the Security Services stopped disturbing my family, or asking for me. Meanwhile, the issue regarding my identification card remained unsolved, despite the attempts of one of the ministers, in addition to the members of the parliament, to mediate that.

I surrendered to that fate. Instead, my brother, via the villages' Mayor, renewed every six months an extract of the individual civil registry record. However, this extract did not give my identification number. Therefore, it wasn't acceptable in any process, or legal action. I couldn't even receive my registered mail because the postman needed an identification number. Also, I had to put up with the suspicious looks I received, whenever I had to explain the reason why I didn't have an identification card.

It's funny how a public library card with my picture and a random number on it, solved most of the problem. A friend of mine working in the public Assad library, made me a membership card to go in the library and read there. That card looked very similar to the Security Men's cards. It had the picture of Hafez al-

Assad on the top, in addition, it was surrounded with an aura of luxury, the Ba'ath logo and most importantly, it had a number. That magical number was my gateway to civilian life once again. That card accompanied me for more than fourteen years, after that. Actually, many times it helped me to go through some of the official places without inspections. The picture of Hafez-al Assad and the Baath logo were a passport, especially when using it with agility without inspection. Many times I would wave it, not letting the employee, or the Security Man, inspect it just like I'd seen Security Officers do. Everyone feared them and would wave them through, fearing to show disrespect by inquiring or inspecting.

I had to find a job. That was not at all easy without any papers and no identification card. I tried more than once but I couldn't find my old official papers that the Security Men had confiscated on my arrest. I was informed they were lost.

One of the publishing houses was printing my novel, which I'd smuggled out of prison, written on cigarette papers. Then I met a person who introduced me to a lady working in an office for one of the Arabic newspapers, 'Al-Kuwait Voice' that gets issued in London. I visited their office in Damascus and submitted what I had in the form of articles and possible topics. I was asked to step away from politics since they did not want any problems with the authority, especially with my critical situation. I agreed and started working with them as a freelancer. Soon, I became very successful and therefore, my articles started being published on the first pages of that newspaper. The editorial board was impressed by my work, as the requests started to increase rapidly. It was a daily newspaper; therefore, there was a daily need for these pieces. The pay was good, especially since I had a couple of regular weekly articles.

My world became organized and I started feeling that life was smiling on me, once again. My book was published as well and I was ready to print the second book, when someone came to tell me that they were searching for me in the newspaper office.

In the newspaper office, there was an official paper informing me of my need to check in with the vice Interior Minister, on a specific date. Everyone wished me good luck as I left, saying goodbye. While one of them said to me, jokingly, that he would send me Halva. Halva was a symbol for prison food. For me it seemed strange, since I was used to the Security Agents coming for me, not the Interior Ministry, which was part of the police department and didn't scare anyone.

At the set date, I was in front of the Interior Ministry gate, waiting for someone to call for me, having delivered my official paper. I didn't wait for long. Soon, someone came to take me to a big office, where an the officer stood up, welcoming me with a kind smile that brought back what was left of my blood, frozen by anxiety. I sat on a chair in front of his large wooden desk. He greeted me with compliments then, he informed me of the reason behind requesting me to come there. It was an article I'd published regarding a crime that occurred in Damascus. The article was exciting and made the sellers copy it, to sell illegally in the streets. I didn't know about that at the time. He asked me about my source of information and after I insisted that I couldn't disclose my source, he assured me that he didn't care about that. What he cared about was if it was the Director of Criminal Security who leaked this information to me. I didn't know what he was getting at because the article was about a regular crime, which didn't have a political connection. Therefore, I didn't have to worry about it. He gave me a lecture about the love of homeland and that I was publishing the wrongdoings of the homeland, in a foreign newspaper. He felt that made the homeland look bad. At the end of the meeting he informed me that I had to visit him after a couple of days. That wasn't a request but a command. Then, he warned me not to write anything further without receiving the approval of the interior ministry.

I didn't listen to his commands; neither did the publishing management at the newspaper. They kept on the semi-daily publishing of articles without seeking the general's approval.

At the next visit the general was angry, thundering in my face, threatening. I tried to absorb his anger by saying that I didn't have any control over what was published, because it was up to the newspaper. In the following visit, he informed me that I was forbidden from publishing, or I would be arrested. I stopped publishing and said goodbye to my peers, searching for a new job.

The days went back to being pitch black and once again I'd lost my only source of income. In addition, my brother who spent six years in prison was diagnosed with cancer. It was a painful and agonizing time, for a long period thereafter. The doctors informed us that he was in a critical state, especially because the cancer was in an advanced stage. He had surgery to eradicate the tumor and then the chemotherapy began. In addition to its financial burdens, in those harsh conditions, it was a daily fight against death. My brother triumphed over the illness. He surprised everybody with his insistence to resist, with an optimistic spirit that made his illness back down quickly, then to diminish and disappear.

A couple of months passed, suffering with my brothers' illness and heroism. Then, with the help of some of my friends and the investments of some businessmen, I was able to open a publishing house. One of the Parliament Members was able to obtain a license for the publishing house in his name, since it was impossible for me to receive security approval. It was a good start that brought me back to natural daily life. In addition, it gave me the chance to stay in a field that I enjoyed. However, I soon realized that the book world, outside of its content, was nothing but merchandise, in a market of an all-knowing Arabic world that doesn't read. That world seemed to see books as entertainment merchandise for the few readers, or the collectors who liked to decorate their bookshelves with expensive, luxurious books.

*

It was a regular morning and I was busy reviewing a plan for publishing, when a group of Security Men invaded my office, heavily armed with machineguns. The head officer asked for my name, then asked them to tie me up and take me out. Minutes later, I was descending my office, tied up, amidst the terrified looks of my employees. One of them pushed me inside a long Station Wagon; while I glimpsed my wife enter another car. I asked for the reason and the officer answered mockingly:

"You'll see in the branch."

***

# 20 PALESTINE BRANCH

## SOLITARY SIX

## 1994

The door shut behind me and I found myself in a small dark tomblike room. I felt for the walls around me; it was approximately a three by six foot room infused with grilles of iron construction rods. A scarce ray of light, slipped through the rods from a light bulb at the end of the hallway. The iron door in front of me had a small, closed window. I stood around for a while trying to get accustomed to the darkness. I didn't know what to do. I didn't know if I was going to be here for a long while, or for a couple of hours, until the Branch Chief arrived at the Branch. The officer, who had arrested me, informed me that they had discovered a mistake with my arrest. They had come to my offices to arrest someone in hiding who belonged to the Labor Party and was trying to escape. When one of the Security Men informed him of the mistake he commented, in disappointment:

"They are all worse than each other."

As soon as we arrived at the Branch, they started investigating me. Soon, he came back and reassured me that it was only a matter of time before the Branch Chief saw me and released me, immediately.

It was autumn; yet, it was a warm day. I was wearing light summer clothes. A disgusting smell was filling the cell. After a while, I started getting tired and no one had come to see me, slowly I squatted down feeling for the floor under my feet, to find that there was a military blanket.

I felt a plastic container behind me; I touched it with my hands, and then raised it in front of me. It was full. I thought it was a water container but the strong urine smell shocked my nose, carefully I put it somewhere near the door, in disgust. My eyes started adjusting to the darkness and now I could recognize the assets of the place: A couple of plastic bags, another empty plastic water container and some pieces of dry bread.

The night had already fallen when they'd brought me down to the basement where the cells were. I realized, after two hours of squatting down that they would not release me that day and I had to wait for the next day. I could hear the guards' voices at the end of the hallway clearly. Most of them were from the coast, with their unique dialect. My wife was somewhere in here but nothing indicated her presence. I felt for the blanket under my feet, to make sure I could sit on it without touching anything filthy. I was trying to maintain my clean clothes, so I could take a taxi home without having to deal with the taxi-driver's humiliating looks. I eventually surrendered to my fatigue; I sat down, remaining alert to overhear every movement and whisper. Shortly, an intense silence fell and I realized that all the guards were asleep. I took off my shoes and put them under my head, then fell into a sporadic sleep.

I woke up next morning, to the noise of the doors opening and the movement of the guards outside. The door opened and a spoon filled with yoghurt extended from the window. I extended my arm to take it but the jailer outside yelled at me:

"Put your piece of bread here, you animal!"

"I don't have bread, I'm new."

He gave me a loaf of military bread and he put a large spoon of yogurt on it, in addition to a couple of olives. I took it and started eating voraciously. I was hungry, thirsty and my urge to urinate had intensified. After a while, the doors started to open. Each cell was called by its number, for the prisoner to get up and go to the toilets at the end of the bathroom, accompanied by the usual insults from the jailer and sometimes his whip. The prisoner was only allowed to spend about five to seven minutes in the bathroom, where he had to urinate and wash himself afterwards. When my turn came up I ran towards the bathroom, accompanied just by the insults of the jailer. I didn't need a long time. I had prepared myself, to help prevent any punishment for being late.

At noon, they opened the door to throw me an iron container filled with soup, some pieces of zucchini and a loaf of bread. I didn't have a spoon but I didn't dare to ask the jailer for one, so I drank some soup with the loaf of bread. Soon, they opened the doors for us to get out to the bathroom and this time we had to clean the iron containers as well. The same orders were applied at dinnertime. I was able to form a picture of the place during the periods when the doors opened for us to go to the bathroom; two sets of prison cells separated by the main hallway of the prison and at one end, in the middle, was the bathroom which contained firstly the sink-room, which was about three feet wide and then the toilet room, which was of similar size. I was also able to recognize the details of my cell, in the few seconds before they closed the door once again. The wall was filled with drawings and names belonging to men and women who had passed through here. Blood and dirt mixed with the drawings, engraved on the cold cement walls. It was only a short period of time before our spirits intermingled. I breathed with them, sharing their memories and suffering. Everyone who passed through here left a piece of his soul behind and maybe a piece of his body as well. A memory filled with suffering, rot and longing for life. Here, you couldn't utter the word of freedom without the word of life. Freedom was life and life was freedom.

At night, my urge to urinate intensified. I didn't dare to call for the jailer because I'd heard what had happened to the prisoner in the cell opposite me. He received a number of whips with the quadruple cable, some punches and smacks in addition to a plastic bag to defecate in, until the morning came. I looked at the plastic water container half filled with urine and realized that it was the only way. It was cut on its upper part to fit the shape of the penis. I urinated until it was filled to the top and I kept what was left of my urine in my bladder, until the morning.

I had glimpsed one of the prisoners from a cell nearby holding two plastic water containers, one was full and the other was empty. I now realized the reason behind that. The next morning I was running, holding the two containers, towards the bathroom to empty one of urine and fill the other with water.

A couple of days passed and no one had called me. I would wake up in the morning to wait. I would wait from morning until noon, when the morning shift ends. Then, I would wait in the evening, until a really late time at night and then I would sleep. I still thought they were going to release me. A couple of days later, I could hear a woman's voice and I thought it was my wife but I wasn't sure. Two weeks later, one of the guards told me that she was transferred to the doubles, which were the womens' prison cells. I could hear their voices sometimes. I wasn't sure of what was happening but I was informed that they'd investigated her for a while. I was worried about her and I was in pain because she was here. I would have been stronger in prison if they had released her because, unlike her, I was used to prison and felt I could bear many more years.

I believe I'd spent more than a week in prison, before I heard a voice from the cells near me. In the beginning it had seemed as if they were corpses. Then, one day I heard one of them from the cell opposite calling me:

"Six, six." I didn't understand. I listened longer, so he repeated:

"Six, six." I understood he was calling for me, so I didn't answer.

"It's safe, don't worry, what is your charge?" He said with confidence.

"He's still new, leave him alone. What is the news?"

Conversations between the prison cells started through the doors. I found out later that they'd stopped talking through the doors because they feared that I was put there as a snitch by the prison management.

When they were reassured that I wasn't, they went back to talking freely and there were rules and times for that. The conversations would start when the food arrived at the prison and the jailers were busy distributing it amongst the prison cells, before bringing it to the solitaries. Also, in the evenings, when they would turn the television on and the noise would often be too loud. Then, some of them would spend time conversing with their neighbor and transfer the distant cells' messages, from one cell to another. However, when they couldn't talk they would use Morse code, which they started teaching me, until it became the dependable cell language.

Suddenly, those 'graves' became filled with life. Each grave had a story, for each one a life and a name. Their stories started to get colored, some with joy but mostly with pain. Number three, who was fond of smoking, was always complaining about the 'flame,' which was the time when the jailer would come to light the cigarettes for the smokers. Often the jailer would yell after the food time was over:

"Flame!"

Followed by the noise of the small windows in the doors opening and the jailer's arm extending through the window holding a lighter. You had to be ready with your cigarette in your mouth, to light it up, then, he would close the window and move on to the next cell. Number three had spent four years in his cell. He was accused of working with the Israeli Intelligence Agencies. He insisted he was innocent and hadn't done anything. It was a report from one of the spy's, claiming that Israeli Intelligence had recruited him, before he returned to Syria after receiving his doctorate in Physics, in Germany. He was a voracious smoker, so when his urge to smoke intensified he would knock on the door requesting, 'flame.' Most of the jailers would ignore him, sometimes one of the nicer jailers would take pity on him and light his cigarette and maybe, for a couple of the other prisoners as well. However, when the shift of the mean jailer came around, no one could save him from the whipping punishment. Number seven was calm, waiting for his release despite his presence in the cell for more than two years, without anyone telling him his charge. While number four was the loudest prisoner and no one dared to hit him, since he used to be the Co-Branch Chief in Aleppo. There had been a dispute over orders, so the Branch Chief imprisoned him to teach him a lesson. However, number eight was deathly silent, didn't speak or smoke. I never heard his voice at all. They would bring him food calmly, with no insults and many of them would try to talk to him but to no avail. Later on, I found out that he was an old prisoner and it was believed he was an important officer in the military. They'd put him in that cell five years ago and before that he was in another cell in one of the prisons. He hadn't talked, or made any noise since then. The jailers would sometimes open the door, just to ensure he was still alive.

Weeks had passed and I got used to my situation. I lost all hope and wasn't waiting anymore. In the first week, I started passing time by thinking of the future. What was I going to do after I left here? Would I stay in this country? Should I try to travel? I started drawing a life filled with magic and beauty, building worlds of joy in a small shack on a remote distant mountain, far away from humans. I remembered places I'd visited in the past with some friends; semi-virgin mountains and streams. I decided that I could build a distant shack, distant from this insane world. I could live off small crops and some hunting.

I remembered our small gang when I was a child, where we built a shack in a tree and planted some vegetables. I would take many books and papers; I would have lots of time to spend reading, peacefully. That world seemed very true and attainable to me, I dove deeper into its content and became reassured of the future. In the following week, a piece of my summer trousers ripped at the knee area. My anxiety intensified, I took refuge in the past, reassuring myself that I had enough experience and knowledge of how the Agencies worked to survive. Certainly, they would send someone to check up on me. That would most likely be where my family resides and no one knew anything about me there. That would work to my benefit; they would surely release me afterwards. The Branch Chief would have no reason to justify my arrest.

I wandered in my thoughts. The scenario seemed convincing to me, so it calmed my fears. However, with insufficient clothes, or cover the cold in the third week became intense. I had a blanket and under it was what was called, 'the barrier.' This was a piece of fabric similar to the two layered tent fabric. I wrapped myself in the blanket, using 'the barrier' as a mattress.

The fourth week saw the return of the barber, who had been on vacation. He shaved my chin and left my mustache to grow. I couldn't object, I'd never had a mustache but the barber considered it to be essential:

"How could a man not have a mustache?"

I fiddled with my mustache, smiling, 'what would my mother say if she saw me right now!' I also remembered my beautiful girlfriend who forbade me from growing a mustache, because she thought it didn't suit my face.

In the fifth week, I started making chess pieces out of bread dough and settled down in my dark grave. My knees started hurting from the lack of movement and humidity, so I decided to move in my narrow space. One step, two steps, three steps then I turn. One step, two steps, three steps, then I turned back again. I started practicing that a couple of times a day, then I started remembering some yoga and Swedish exercises, that were possible to practice in this place. I felt optimistic. I decided to resist and live. I started to play chess with myself; I had drawn the squares on the asphalt floor with tomato sauce and a piece of bread. I surrendered to the idea of residing here for a long while. All of the other prisoners in these cells had been here a long time. Nobody enters these graves and leaves them quickly. You had to rot; your body and soul had to wither, before you were ready to leave. That was the fate of each comer. It was the law of the dark graves and now I was a part of it.

I had learned beforehand how to spin strings out of nylon bags. I started working on cutting the bags into long strips and tying them together. Then I would tie the end of the strips to a projected part of the iron door and start spinning them between the palms of my hands. I would join two or three strings to make a thicker rope. Soon, my techniques became more advanced, tying the strings to a small wooden block, to help me in the spinning process. I would receive one nylon bag almost every day, when they distributed the food but it wasn't enough, so I searched in detail the trashcan beside the sink-room, looking for anything useful. It was an inexhaustible source of the belongings which the jailers threw away: Nylon bags, newspaper pieces, small iron and wooden pieces, some bones, a lighter and some playing cards. I had a couple of seconds each bathroom visit, to scan the contents of the small trashcan and choose what I could hide in my light clothes.

After some effort I was able to fix the lighter I found in the trashcan. I had a fire source! I also made a needle out of some bones. I started sewing a part of my ripped clothes with it. I was finally able to sew my pants that had ripped in the back. Despite the thick nylon strings that punctuated it tightly, I was still able to cover my genitals. I felt proud of these small victories.

The cold was creeping sharply and the blanket was hindering my movements. I tied its ends to form sleeves, so I could wear it as a coat. A large number of strings had piled up and I started spinning some of them to make my small tools. The most important ones were small bags that I hung high on the sidewalls of the cell to keep the urine container, water bottle and what I found in the trashcan. I remember that I was working on sewing a small sweater to help me with the cold, when the jailers raided the cells to take almost all they could find. I was able to save my lighter, needle and some strings. That happened quickly and with no warning, it made me realize that in the future I had to be cautious and find hiding spots. The room was extremely small and it was very easy to discover almost everything in it but I was able to hide my important tools, by putting them above my cell's ceiling, through a small skylight window.

The lighter was my most important belonging and I made sure to protect it. I was a voracious smoker but I had gotten used to only smoking three cigarettes, based on the prison system. It represented a degree of freedom to be able to choose the time to smoke, not having to submit to the guards' mood. My wife was able to send me some boxes of cigarettes, through one of the guards.

I didn't know how many weeks, or months had passed before they called me at night, for an investigation. I walked behind the guard through a long hallway to the basement, then ascended towards the upper floor, where he asked me to put a dirty rubber blindfold on, made from a tire inner-tube. I grabbed the blindfold from the bucket filled with water, designed to keep it soft. I was tied from behind, then, someone pushed me inside one of the rooms. The blindfold was tight. It seemed to me as if the room was drowning in darkness. The door shut behind me and I stood there waiting. Perhaps one, or more hours had passed before the door opened again, for some people to enter.

Suddenly, with no warning, I received a punch to my face, followed by some slaps. I swayed, not realizing what was happening around me. Soon, a harsh solid lash started hitting my body from all sides. I fell to the ground, while I received many more whips from the lash, mixed with kicks. I screamed from the pain, waiting for the questions to follow. Nobody asked any questions. I was used to torture as a method for investigating and extracting information. Here, I was being hit for no reason and asked to give nothing back to possibly halt proceedings. The whips continued for a period of time, until I heard the door open. Someone entered and the whips paused. A calm voice talked to me with some neutrality and coldness:

"So tell us, what do you know about your wife? What is her organizational situation?"

I swore to God that I didn't know anything about that and that I didn't think she was a part of any political party but they weren't convinced. The lash and torture returned, to eat from my skin. Many questions followed to which I couldn't find an answer. All of it hovering over the connection of my wife with the Communist Labor Party, which I asserted she didn't belong to. Just because of her friendship and social connection with some of the members of the Labor Party in the University, they believed she was linked to the organization.

The investigation and torture continued, until daylight, when I think they were assured that I didn't know anything. The guards then pushed me towards my cell, to collapse into it. I couldn't move my arm and hands, while a burning pain spread across most parts of my body. In the morning I was unable to move, so I couldn't go to the bathroom and didn't feel the desire to eat. My bones were hurting me, especially my hand bones that felt swollen and numb, in addition to some of the dark bruises on my body. My shirt had ripped and most of its buttons were torn off, while a piece of my trousers stuck to the skin of my leg, due to coagulated blood.

At noon, I was able to eat some food and I dragged myself to the bathroom. I was able to see the bruises, swellings and coagulated blood on areas of my body. Luckily there was nothing dangerous, since I was able to move my fingers and wash some wounds. The jailer that day was nice, so he didn't hurry me with insults as usual. A few days later, I regained some of my strength. The bathroom time, which would happen approximately every two weeks, had come around. The bath was in the sink-room and it was a big bucket of cold water, filled from the faucet. We had to run as fast as we could, wearing our underwear, which was the case whenever we had to go to the toilet. There was a bar of military soap, which you would quickly rub over your body, then pour water on it with a small plastic bucket. I washed my body quickly, removing the coagulated blood now mixed with dirt. Then I started washing my ripped trousers, my shirt, as well as my underwear, which I had to wear wet whilst running back to the cell. The water dropped from my body onto the hallway floor the whole way.

Then, I tried to spend some time naked, until my body dried enough to be able to wear my coat-blanket. However, that day was too cold, so I wore it over my wet body. I checked on my small cockroach, which I had put under a plastic cup with holes in it. He was crouching calmly and didn't try to run when I raised the cup. He was living and feeling safe. I stroked him with my finger; he moved lazily then went back to his normal state. He was my partner in sharing the scarce food. He loved the crumbs of bread mixed with jam and I was rich with those materials. Lots of times I would talk to him in kindness and sometimes I would be angry at his laziness. Despite all that, I didn't give him a name. His name remained, Cockroach.

In the first weeks, I would kill every cockroach I would find. As I saw it, these small creatures were competing with me over the scarce space and food. They seemed stupid to me, crawling over my body, unaware of the extreme danger I posed to them. They feared the light greatly, so when the door opened and some scarce light would enter, they would run quickly to disappear into the dark cracks. When the door shut again, they would start to wander,

277

indifferent to my big body. I didn't allow any cockroach to crowd my lazy cockroach. I would kill those who would dare to get near his food but I would leave some of them, to entertain myself with. I would watch them sometimes, as they snuck around the corners of the wall. So, I would put up barriers and traps, just to watch their reaction. They seemed smart sometimes and stupid most of the time. Regardless, they were a source of entertainment. I didn't know if I developed any emotions for my favorite cockroach but I was surely sad when I found him dead one day. I realized afterwards the cycle of life and I accepted it, with surrender and willingness for a new life cycle to begin, with another lazy cockroach.

My torture wounds were almost completely healed and I went back to my daily exercise activities. I found I started to lose the sense of time. For me, time became three periods of the day and nothing else; breakfast, lunch and dinner. The day lost its meaning and I didn't care for it anymore. In the first months, I would count the days of the week, seeing a possibility for my release. Later on, a possibility to be called for an investigation but now I had lost even the possibility of time. All the days were equal and there was no weekend. Each day passed just like the other. In the beginning, I spent a long time trying to overhear the conversations of the guards, or more likely the screams they elicited. It wasn't possible to hear their normal conversations easily. Many times I would, while the food distribution was happening, try to listen for any news about my wife. I would listen carefully every time I would hear a feminine voice. I would glue my ear as hard as I could to the closed door's window, for maybe I could recognize her voice? That proved impossible.

Desperation would take me over sometimes, so I would spend my time drawing revenge plans. Many times, I would imagine myself as a legendary hero, holding my arrows to take revenge on this Security Man, or that. I would draw up the plans, dazzled by moments of insane revenge. It seemed that many times I lost the desire to live but the imagining of revenge, delayed my suicide. I had to live and leave, to revenge. To make those devils suffer what I suffered, their families to suffer what my family suffered.

I woke up one day to insane hallucinations. I suffered from a fever that made me practice exercises for two continuous hours. I would imagine men and I fought them. Some of them would fall with one punch from my fist and others from a kick with my feet. I fell to the floor and the fever overwhelmed me. I woke up to the noise of the door opening and the bowl of dinner in front of me. I dragged it inside and didn't stop drinking the soup, until I was entirely done. I wiped my face with my hand and felt the greasiness of the fat on my face. When I came back from the last bathroom break that day and the prison had calmed down, I wrapped myself in the corner of the cell, hiding under my coat- blanket. I felt as if I had started losing my mind. I began walking inside the cell, turning, drowning in deep thoughts. 'Should I surrender? Am I going to die here?' A memory from all those long years I spent in the different jails came back to me; childhood memories, the first stages of youth, the memory of the first girl I loved. I screamed inside, 'I want to live!'

The will to live and challenge, started growing within me. Soon, a kernel of a daily program began to grow in front of me. By the next day, I had put together a program that filled my day completely. I would start with morning exercise, followed with a break where I enjoyed drinking water and pretending it was tea. I have to confess, I always actually wished to drink it as if it was wine. As soon as I was done with drinking, I would start the English language classes. I started remembering a section of a book that I had learned the principles of the English language from. I started trying to remember its pages and lessons, recalling its most important information. It was difficult in the beginning but with time, I started to envisage its pages and thus remembering it, I started reciting it with a low voice. After the English language I decided to review my knowledge of Geography, so I started recalling the maps of Syria, Lebanon, the Arabic Nation and the world. I would draw a map in the air and put the most important landmarks that I remembered on it, such as the rivers, main cities and the capitals. Afterwards, would be the History class, with the help of the Story of Civilization book that I'd read previously in Kafarsouseh. I started to remember it, partially in the form of a movie filled with pictures. The evening was the time for abstract thinking, of philosophical views, mostly about the meaning of existence. Before sleeping was movie time: I would choose a movie for each day. I would remember it and start telling it to myself, with the help of my imagination, which would reproduce the film with a new garment.

My days became organized and I felt safety and reassurance. The cell became a home that embraced me like a tender mother. The time would pass, organized, without slowing down. The night would come quickly, to sleep at a specific time that didn't change. Nothing hindered that, besides the arrival of the barber approximately every two weeks, to cut the hair on my chin and head with his manual tool. Leaving my manly mustache, as it grew long over my mouth in every direction. The feeling of my long mustache was strange; my fingers would always find their way to play with its long hair. After long months that I didn't bother to count, a daily itching started to invade my body, especially around the neck. At first, I thought it was an allergic reaction from the dirty blankets. Later on, I thought that perhaps it was scabies but no, it couldn't be scabies, since I had it a couple of times in my last prison. There were no skin ulcers after weeks of itching; therefore, it seemed to me that it had to be an allergic reaction due to the dirt. There was no way to wash the blankets, so I surrendered to my fate trying to get used to the semi-constant itching.

One of those days and suddenly, without any warning, the door opened and the jailer brought in a mid-aged man with white hair pervading his head, then locked the door. He sat in front of me in the small cell, without saying anything. It wasn't easy to see his features after the door was shut. Some few minutes later I felt this situation quite strange. I raised my hand, trying to greet him but he put his hand gently over my mouth, indicating for me to be silent. He was listening for any movement outside. Then he stood up, trying to look through the door's window. I remained silent, watching him until I heard knocks through the wall, which he answered with other knocks. He smiled at me afterwards, whispering:

"Safe! I am number ten. They transferred me to you. I don't know why."

I felt cautious and afraid, so I smiled at him.

He was kind and whispered his charge. He was Lebanese, holding a Canadian citizenship. He'd come back to Lebanon to visit his family and got arrested at one of the security checks, due to a report stating his connection to the Lebanese Forces and Israeli intelligences. He assured me many times that he was innocent of these accusations, for he was nothing but a merchant living in Canada. For his bad luck, he'd had a conflict with his ex-wife about raising the children, so her brother accused him of this charge. He'd since spent two years inside these cells. Nevertheless, I felt suspicious of his presence; hence I remained cautious and discreet. However, he loved to talk and that was good after this long isolation. The itching was inflaming my body, he offered to take a look to try and explain to me the reason behind it. He inspected the top of my shirt before he smiled, saying:

"It is bedbugs."

I had never seen lice before and didn't know what they looked like but the man seemed like an expert. He started directing me to how to fight the lice and recognize the small from the big.

The process was strenuous; I had to inspect in detail the sides of my clothes, my shirt, my ripped trousers and my underwear that seemed worn-out, as its sides had frayed. The rays of light, sneaking from the small window in the cell's ceiling, weren't enough to see these extremely small creatures but there was no other solution. I had to find these creatures brimmed with the blood they sucked from my body, to squish them between the nails of my thumbs. There were thousands of them and they reproduced every day.

In the morning of the next day, they called for 'Number 10' and he never returned because he'd been promised his release. I kept on fighting the daily battle with the lice. The mission was to kill as many as I could on daily basis, to reduce what lived on my clothes, so I could sleep. However, by the next morning, a countless number of lice were again on the blanket that I wore, sadly I had to begin all over again. My daily studying program was paused. The daily battle with the lice was killing most of my time so, one day I dared to talk with the jailer about it. A few weeks after complaining to most of the nicer jailers, someone who was called the nurse, came to see me. He was a man that made his living by supervising the purchasing of medication for the patients. He asked me if I had any money in the property room, I answered that I'd had lots of money when I was arrested. A few days later, he came back with two boxes of powder and instructions about how to use them. He also asked the jailers to allow me to wash my clothes and take a shower, twice. His smile was wide and his face was cheerful. I felt as if I was in front of a kind human who respected me but later on I realized the secret behind his smile; he'd stolen all of my money in the property room and charged me ten times more than the actual price of the medicine!

I finally beat the lice and the itching stopped. I returned to my tranquil tender cell to live my days organized with my daily program.

***

# 21 THE DORMITORY
## 1995

I had spent three or four months in this dormitory, after I was released from the solitary confinement in Cell Six. In this release, my name was returned to me and I forgot my other name, 'Six.' The beginning was hard. I had to sleep in the middle, where we were crammed and pressed against each other with what was called, 'al-Tasyeef' for an eight-hour period. The next eight hours I had to join the sitting group, before a further eight hours in the standing group. However, I soon enjoyed special sleeping privileges, after a group from the Kurdistan Worker's Party, (PKK) joined me to their group, which was the only political group in the dormitory.

The dormitory was full of all kinds of criminals. It was obvious that the Security Branches at the time didn't have enough political customers anymore, so they'd branched out to work in all kind of fields. The prisoners from the PKK, received good treatment from the prison management; therefore, the dormitory Chief didn't dare to invade their rights, he avoided them, especially since they were a solitary group who took a section for themselves, in one of the corners. They were a group of poor Syrian and Kurdish young men, who'd found national and social liberation in the ideas of the PKK. When they became aware of my presence in the dormitory, they assigned me a space in the corner where they resided. Whilst one of them, who was a kind, tall, muscular young man, would sleep beside me to form a barrier between me and the rest of the prisoners. This way he reserved for me a space good enough to sleep in. I reciprocated by advising and educating. Most of them hadn't finish Junior-High and some of them couldn't read the Arabic language. So, I decided to teach them what I could from the Arabic and English language, in addition to answering many of their questions about all kinds of science and especially political science.

I gained their respect and protection particularly because I tried to learn more of the Kurdish language, which I had started learning years ago in Sednaya Military Prison. I still believed in people's rights to decide their fate. The Kurds were a poor oppressed people, who were denied by the Nationalists, Arabs and other nationalities, their rights, culture and the right to decide their fate.

I got rid of my thick mustache after being able to see my face on the cover of a milk container, under the light of a big carbonated light bulb. One of the Kurdish men, volunteered to shave it with a razor that the dormitory Chief kept. Soon, my health improved and I gained a little bit of weight, since I occasionally enjoyed some of the foods the Kurdish prisoners received, or bought for double the price.

Weeks before we were released, my wife was allowed to visit

me. We spent about half an hour in one of the investigation rooms, with the company of one of the guards. It was obvious that they were going to release us and it was just a matter of time and routine procedures. My wife had lost lots of weight. Also, her face was pallid due to not being exposed to the sun for a long period of time. Despite all of that, she was in a good psychological standing and that is what helped me to pull myself together, regain my balance and return to the human life that I had lost, in my long absence in a solitary cell.

\*\*\*

# 22 THE RELEASE

## AUTUMN 1995

That morning, I was led to the Justice Palace, handcuffed with chains. I was kept in a dirty room, accompanied by criminals coming from the civil prisons to attend one of their trial sessions, while I was waiting to meet the investigation officer. This year, the Military Security agencies started to transfer some of the cases to jurisdiction, according to directions from Hafez al-Assad. The Security agencies seemed confused by these directions, not knowing quite what to do. They decided to release the prisoners through jurisdictions. After the investigation and serving their sentence, it was appropriate to transfer them to jurisdiction, which will release them for the lack of a charge the law could judge upon.

It was guaranteed that they would release me. At least that is what the officer who handed me over to the Civil Police, informed me of. I waited in the Justice Palace jail room, until they called for me. Then, two Civil Police Officers led me to one of the upper floors that were packed with reviewers and lawyers. I sat, handcuffed, on a wooden bench watching the people busy with their various cases. I was ignored and maybe some of them felt contempt towards me, like a criminal waiting for his sentence. It was only moments until the door opened and my wife came out, smiling, with no handcuffs while I was called. The judge asked the police to untie me, then, I was left alone standing in front of the judge and the court recorder, who started routinely writing what the judge was saying. After studying my file that came with me from the military intelligence department he said:

"You are accused of thinking of traveling outside of the country."

Then with an overrated seriousness:

"Did you think of traveling outside of the country?"

"No. No sir I didn't think at all!" I said quickly and I was filled with a feeling of purity, for I was not guilty, I had never thought of that at all.

In truth I had thought, when I was desperate, more than once I thought but I thought it to myself, I'd never told anyone. There was a report from someone who said I had and the judge had asked my wife about it. My wife assured him a couple of times that she had never asked me about that and maybe didn't even think of it. In truth, perhaps she did think, because in her weaker moments she would sometimes fall into the water of brackish dreams.

I repeated a couple of times desperately: "I vouch and swear that I did not think. I didn't think my sir ever, ever."

Yes, yes! I was innocent of thinking, innocent of dreaming.

\*

One of the autumn mornings in the year 1995, we found ourselves in one of the overcrowded Damascus streets and we were released. I grabbed her hand without looking into her eyes and we started walking down the street, moving away. We exchanged looks sometimes, smiles at others but we never stopped walking in one direction, far, far away. In a place at the end of the street I stood in front of a flower shop. I admired a small ruby red rose that was left alone at the front of the glass display.

We held our flower and walked, not looking back and another story began.

***